I am fifteen
and I do not
want to die

I am fifteen and I do not want to die

The true story of a young woman's wartime survival

CHRISTINE ARNOTHY

Translated from the French by Antonia White

Collins

Collins
A division of HarperCollins*Publishers*
77-85 Fulham Palace Road
London
W6 8JB
www.collins.co.uk

First published by Collins as *I am fifteen and I do not want to die* (1956)
and *It is not so easy to live* (1958)

This edition 2010

Translated by Antonia White
Additional translation by Catherine Castledine (2009)

1 3 5 7 9 10 8 6 4 2

A catalogue record for this book is available from the British Library

ISBN: 978-0-00-732867-3

Set in Garamond by M.A.T.S. Southend-on-Sea, Essex

Printed and bound in Great Britain by Clays Ltd, St Ives plc

Find out more about HarperCollins and the environment at
www.harpercollins.co.uk/green

In memory of the 17th of December 1957 in Paris, where the
founder of the *Parisien Libéré*, Claude Bellanger, bestowed
upon me the 'Grand Prix Vérité'.
It was love at first sight, and this great journalist, whom
I still love as if he were still amongst us, took ten years
to divorce so that we could at last be married.

I also dedicate this book to the lawyer François Bellanger, our
son, who is the physical and moral fruit of our passion.

With fathomless love for both, Christine Arnothy

I am fifteen
and I do not
want to die

Preface

I WAS NO more important than a sheet of white paper in a paper press. The paper press was the town of Budapest that had been condemned to death and I was a fifteen-year-old girl who wanted to describe its death. I needed more paper, pencils and, most importantly, a pencil sharpener.

The only light came from a candle of string soaked in lard, which was not very good for my eyes, but in spite of everything I managed to write my diary. My parents had always been determined that I was to be a pianist. But I hated the piano. I had been forced to play for four to five hours a day. Now a bomb had gone right through our piano. Down in the cellar, I was allowed to write; a little bit of pencil came to mean happiness and freedom for me. I wrote on an overturned box which became my desk. I would write by candlelight, at times sitting on the floor, at times on my knees. The only things of importance to me were the still-virgin pages of my school notebooks, my pencils and a miraculous pencil sharpener.

At the age of ten, I understood that I had been born amongst some of the most devastating events capable of being produced by a History full of horror. We were squeezed with a vice consisting of the Russians and the Germans. The victory of one side would have crushed my aristocratic father, and that of the other would have resulted in our deportation to one of the death camps. My mother was a Jew, although one who had always hidden, camouflaged and renounced her origins. It was without doubt a kind of intellectual unconsciousness that was to save us. The glory of ancestors was the subject of daily conversations, as well as the love for France. The first language learnt by my mother was French, then German as the language of everyday life. I learnt Hungarian from the domestic help, and after that at school; our mealtime conversations revolved around politics. I understood the atmosphere within which I was to live in the future. At times I imagined being elsewhere as in some magical fairy tale. I did not foresee the time when I would have to descend into the basement of our building and witness the agony of Budapest during the siege. Having only loved the invention of characters in the past, I was suddenly presented with such a spectacle of change in those persons surrounding us, and the town streets littered with corpses, that I decided to write down that which I saw.

We lived in an old, elegant building by the side of the quay that skirted a residential area on one side of Buda. The Germans had entered the town and wanted to win their last battle there. The Russians were approaching and had already claimed the east side of the town as a stronghold. As soon as the first Russian shells fell on Budapest's eastern suburb, my father ordered us, although this word was at odds with his elegant Austro-Hungarian vocabulary, to move into the cellars for a few days. The bombings came about at three-hourly intervals, except at night, under a violently lit sky. This was a Russian war tactic that allowed them to work out precisely the neighbourhoods they wished to destroy.

From the 18th of December 1944 until the Germans exploded the magnificent bridges that crossed the Danube we stayed in the cellars. The air pressure from the explosions made the house's inhabitants deaf; we didn't even hear the clicks of the Russians' shoes as they entered the city. Their boots were spotless, as were their white gloves – doubtless a tactic meant to upset the inhabitants of Buda only a few hours later. We packed into the doorway and watched; it was like silent film – no noise, just the soldiers advancing and us watching on. We had become a powerless human mass. Even days after that, although we were no longer deaf, we remained hard of hearing.

After the war, during the three years we were living in the

country, before our escape to the West, I wrote stories. In order to live we had to barter things with the peasants, even a part of our bedding, for food. It was always I who undertook negotiations and the people I contacted provided me with rich material.

One story I sent to the Budapest Radio; it was accepted and a month later I heard it broadcast. I had submitted it under a false name and never dared go to Budapest to collect the money. The Communists were in control and I would have had to show my identity card. However, I was thrilled by my first success.

In 1947 I went back to Budapest to complete my studies. I lived in a home for young girls. One day I heard that the National Theatre was looking for someone to play Juliet. After studying the part for a week I applied, along with fifty other girls. At the audition I was given the part. Next day I was to have gone to the theatre taking my papers. I did not go. One cannot play with communists.

After our escape I continued to write. I had a novel published in Munich in Hungarian. The publisher gave me a hundred marks for it; it went into several editions. In Paris I worked in a bookshop from eight in the morning until seven at night. When I reached home, I had a baby and the house to look after. I got up at three each morning to write a few more pages of my book before going to work. When I learned that this book had won the Prix Vérité it seemed like a miracle. The happiest part of my life is being free to write.

Part One

Chapter One

PISTA'S ARRIVAL THAT evening seemed to us like a deliverance. Night had almost fallen but we did not know night from day, buried as we were in this mildewed cellar of a house on the edge of the Danube.

Nevertheless, our watches went on serenely registering the time; the hands moved untiringly round the dials. Was it for two weeks or for two years that we had been living like moles?

Would there be a 'today', a 'tomorrow', or just an eternity of dark, smoky cellars?

The first three days passed fairly quickly. At each creak of the stairs, we thought: 'Here come the Russians; the fighting in this district is over; we go up to our rooms again and pick up the thread of our life just where it was suddenly snapped off. We can finish reading the half-read book, go on playing the sonata that still lies open on the piano, find the right page in the exercise book with the blue paper cover and complete that "Hungarian Composition".'

On the fifth day of our exile underground, it became evident that the Germans had decided to defend the town. It was then that we lost all notion of time. The deadly, anguished days followed each other with oppressive slowness. The mobile A.A. battery that barked incessantly in front of the house attracted danger right over our heads. That little gun mounted on a lorry could not do much harm to the enemy planes: the most it could do was irritate them. It would fire a salvo or two, then escape and begin its little game a street or two farther away, only to return again. The heavy Russian bombers passed over the houses in a roar of thunder and dropped their missiles at random, searching for the enemy that played hide-and-seek with them. In this

3

sinister game of blindman's-buff it was we who were blindfolded! With our eyes shut and our faces buried in our hands, we listened tensely to the passing of the planes and our trembling fingers groped anxiously over the sweating walls. Could those stones resist such violent jolts indefinitely?

The house over our heads was divided into flats. The tenants of these who, up to now, had lived as complete strangers to one another, now found themselves crammed together in the same cellar. Here they slept, ate, washed and squabbled in a promiscuity that could not have been more absolute. The majority of them had staked their claim in the main cellar which had been transformed into an air-raid shelter and was shored up with stout props. But, in the infernal din of the fighting that raged about us and above us, these beams seemed to offer no more protection than a row of toothpicks.

We had chosen a small cellar situated a little farther away and where, in peacetime, we used to store our coal. In this cellar, impregnated with dust and saltpetre rot, there now stood two beds, a divan and a table. In the early days we had also had a little stove whose chimney let out the smoke through a ventilator giving on to the courtyard. But we very soon had to renounce this heating system for, at night, the sparks flying out from the iron stove-pipe might have given the enemy a point to aim at. The town was burning all around us while we shivered on our heap of coal. We used to go and fetch water from a street called Duck Street; by some strange chance there was a tap there that had not run dry. After the first day, we had no more electricity. We put some cooking fat in a shoe-polish tin with a shoe-lace to serve as a wick. This candle, whose smell was sickening, gave out a wan, yellowish light.

The caretakers of the house have installed themselves in the small cellar next to ours. She is a tall, stout woman accustomed to big tips; he is a puny little man with a dead-white face and shifty eyes. Their son lives in the neighbourhood of the Citadel and has just got married. He has a job in the firm where his father worked as doorkeeper for twenty years. This Jancsi, whom his parents have succeeded in making into an 'intellectual' is their one and only pride This family has plenty of provisions. They have no lack of water – and they drink wine.

The little cell which is next to ours on the other side shelters Ilus and her baby. She must be about thirty-six. Lovely fair hair frames her tiny, faded doll's face. As her eyebrows are colourless, she emphasises them with a piece of coal. She never omits to do this, even at the very height of a bombardment. Her husband deserted her a few weeks ago. Ilus was left alone with a baby six months old. Her parents live in the town but she had not the courage to make her way through the torrents of bullets and shrapnel to join them on the other bank of the Danube.

There is also a medical student whom everyone calls 'Doctor'. As he is only in his second year of studies, this began by being merely a joke, but the title has stuck to him for good. It reassured people to tell each other that, if anything happened, they had a doctor on the spot. This undersized youth, whose boyish face is covered with freckles, looks more like a pupil in the top form of a preparatory school but, now that he realises that his presence has a calming effect, he gives himself 'airs'.

The student's aunt is the widow of a banker. She is a plump little woman, as spick and span and shining as a new coin. She spends her time lamenting her fate and wondering whether all her securities will remain safe in her strong-box at the bank. She wears her jewels in a little bag hung round her neck. The banker, her husband, died of the after-effects of some quite everyday illness when it was still peacetime. But his worthy spouse so emphatically stresses the heroic part he would have played, were he still alive, that soon he will become one of the heroes who fell on the field of honour. This dear lady pokes her nose into everything, inspects and tastes everybody's cooking, demands and distributes advice and is constantly talking about herself. When the men hesitate to brave the showers of melted snow and shrapnel to go and fetch the water, she exclaims:

'If my dear Albert were still alive, he'd go at once, *he* would! There was nothing he was afraid of!'

'The Colonel's Lady' is a burly woman. At the time of the bombings that preceded the siege of Budapest, chance constituted her an Air-raid Warden. Her loud, dictatorial voice is the basis of her authority: she wants to give everyone orders. She often makes the round of the cellar for no apparent reason, just to control something or other. Her political opinions are ill-defined since she does not know whether her husband, the Colonel, is still fighting or whether he has joined the dissidents. Sometimes the Colonel is represented in the character of the legendary hero defending the city to his last drop of blood. At other moments, he appears as the liberator of Budapest. In actual fact, he is probably a prisoner of one or the other side, but this possibility is, of course, never even mentioned.

The retired Public Prosecutor and his wife have withdrawn themselves into a corner of the big cellar. The old gentleman was the last to abandon his home. We had already spent five days in the cellar when, in the midst of one infernal night, he made his appearance in a long nightshirt, with a nightcap on his head and his electric torch in his hand. His wife followed him, wearing slippers and muffled up in a thick coat. The lawyer broke into a diatribe against the insolence of the present day. The Russian firing had penetrated right into his bedroom, taking not the least account of his wife's Swiss nationality! The next day, the couple definitely installed themselves among us. The old man had caught cold and took to his bed with influenza. His wife, with her odd accent and her greying fringe, wandered about like a ghost. Citizen of a neutral State, she wore a little Swiss badge, but the combatants did not even respect her person! The Public Prosecutor and his wife were certainly the most wretched of all of us.

During the first days, we made each other's acquaintance. We told each other the story of our lives, almost blessing this catastrophe which had brought us together and allowed us to exchange confidences. Mr. Radnai made an exception to this rule. Being a Jew, he lived under cover of false papers. The entire house had taken him under its wing to hide him. He was a

6

peaceable man who spent his time reading Heine by the light of his candle.

After a week, people suddenly took to hating each other. The banker's widow uttered cries of irritation every time she caught sight of the Colonel's wife and Ilus became hysterical at each coarse remark dropped by the female caretaker. Faces reflected the inner turmoil. The women would have much preferred to be able to hide their spirit-stoves under their pillows rather than disclose to their neighbours what was cooking on them; the men kept ordering each other off to do the job of getting the water. People stalked round one another like furious dogs, watching for the favourable moment to tear each other to pieces.

It was during one of those deadly evenings that Pista made his appearance. He came down the steps, whistling, and, pushing open the entrance to the main shelter, he announced simply, with a broad smile: 'Good evening! . . . I wish you good evening . . .'

He was wearing the uniform of the Hungarian Infantry; a knapsack hung from his shoulder and his smile was as radiant as if the sun had suddenly begun to shine in our gloomy darkness. We made a circle round him. We stared at him as if he had descended from another planet. We wanted to touch him so as to assure ourselves that this was really a living being and not a figment of our tortured imagination.

He threw his tommy-gun on the floor and declared: 'Tonight, I shall sleep here. Do you accept me?'

'Who are you?' asked a voice.

'Istvan Nagy. From Pusztabereny, in the county of Somogy.'

This introduction sealed our friendship. From that moment, Pista was one of us. We besieged him with questions. Where were the Russians? How much longer should we have to stay in the cellar? He was no better informed than we were. We asked him to which Army Corps he belonged.

'To none that I know of,' he replied tranquilly. 'I go here and there. Now I shall stay here for a time.'

Then he sat down on a stool, took some bread and bacon out

of his knapsack and inquired how many of us there were.

'Twelve,' answered the banker's widow.

Pista divided his bread and bacon into twelve equal parts. Each one had a mouthful of it. We observed him with amazed gratitude. The food melted in the hollow of our mouths like a piously whispered prayer of thanksgiving. Pista had miraculously relaxed the quarrelsome tension of the atmosphere. But suddenly the Prosecutor's voice arose from a corner of the cellar:

'Deserter,' he gasped from lungs burning with fever. 'Can't you see he's a deserter? At this instant, he ought to be fighting somewhere and, if necessary, shedding his blood. . . .'

'What's the matter with the old chap?' inquired Pista.

'Pneumonia,' replied the Doctor laconically, as if this were a consultation.

'I'll go and try to scrounge a bit of ultraseptin for him tomorrow,' promised Pista. 'There's still some in a chemist's in the Boulevard Margit. I've got some of it already for several sick people. But now, I'd like to sleep. I'm tired.'

'Are you really going to bring him some medicine?' asked the lawyer's wife, clutching his arm. 'Ultraseptin, that might still save him. . . . Then I'm going to let you have my mattress to lie on.'

Pista shook his head.

'It's not necessary. The floor's enough for me. Tomorrow I'll bring the medicine and some flour. There's still lots of flour in a store in Express Street. You'll have plenty of food.'

That night, towards eleven o'clock, a huge bomber went all out for us. The ground, violently shaken, rang and echoed under our feet. I buried my head under my pillow. But, suddenly, a strange calm came over me. 'My God,' I whispered, 'Your will be done. . . .'

Chapter Two

PISTA WENT OFF at dawn. During his absence we talked of nothing else. The lawyer's wife anxiously awaited his return on account of the medicine and the others were excited at the thought of the flour. Of the entire house, we were the worst off in the matter of provisions – just because we had shown excessive foresight. By a lucky concatenation of circumstances, my parents had succeeded in renting three rooms in a villa situated over in the Hüvösvölgy and protected by the Swedish flag. Since the beginning of December we had been transporting all our valuable possessions there as well as quantities of foodstuffs. Whole sacks of flour; pots of cooking fat; meat; sugar; coffee; and other beverages.

We had counted on awaiting the arrival of the Russians there. But the Russians had already infiltrated as far as the district and we had had to give up all hope of reaching our refuge. Ever since the autumn, my father had installed some friends from Transylvania – a numerous family – in the villa. He had told himself that a small space would be sufficient to house a large number of people of goodwill. The upshot was that they had all the room they needed while we were fasting in our cellar. But nothing could be done about it and, if Pista were ever to bring us some flour, our worries would be over. For it was bread that we needed above all things.

Now, in the joyful expectation of flour, even the couple who keep a restaurant on the ground floor of the building have joined us. Up to now, these two people have kept apart, fearing that the tenants might demand provisions from them. They are unwilling to part with them at any price and do not yet dare to

9

ask for gold in exchange. But now the restaurant proprietor's wife is all honey and has offered to cook a goulash for luncheon. She is ready to sacrifice a few tins of meat still in her possession. Everyone is to have some of the stew but on the strict condition that she is to have one-third of the flour Pista brings back. We have all accepted enthusiastically and she has returned to her stove. Now the hours creep by with exasperating slowness, to the jerky rhythm of the bombs. Ilus is terrified to see that her stores of powdered milk are fast diminishing.

Towards midday, the cellar assumed a positively festive atmosphere. Hearts swelled with joy at the prospect of a good meal. We put a few tables together; we even covered them with a white cloth; everyone laid his or her plate on it. We waited. Even the Public Prosecutor felt better and demanded his share of the goulash. His wife gave the Doctor a questioning glance: the young man shrugged his shoulders. Nothing could make the invalid worse than he was already . . . so let him eat.

We were all there, sitting round the table as if for a banquet. At last the two restaurant keepers appeared, actually carrying a saucepan of handsome dimensions. They went all round the table, depositing the contents of a thick ladle of stewed meat in each plate. Everyone clucked with pleasure. Our revered Doctor bedaubed his face with grease right up to the ears and the banker's widow buried her face in her plate as if she meant to lap up her goulash instead of eating it. Which of us had any thought to spare now for death and for the martyred town crumbling to dust over our heads?

Like so many unchained beasts, we flung ourselves on the pieces of meat; then each one leant back comfortably, staring into space, silently savouring the delight of being replete at last. This meal remained a memorable event for every single one of us. The tenants made an agreement with the restaurant keeper that, from now on, they would make their bread in turn in his baker's oven.

Towards four o'clock in the afternoon, the house was hit by two bombs. Tiles and pieces of the roof were flung down into the courtyard. Our flat must have been hit, or else the lawyer's. It was

10

the front that overlooked the Danube that had been damaged.

On the 24th of December, we had left our home in such a violent hurry to make a vain attempt to get as far as the Hüvösvölgy that my half-read book had remained upstairs. It was Balzac's *Peau de Chagrin*. In my mind, I often re-lived the story I had begun and which I should have liked to go on reading, but I had not the courage to go up to the flat again. The idea of climbing the staircase as far as the second storey filled me with as much terror as the sight of builders moving about on a narrow plank five floors above street level. In the interval between the two direct hits on the house, I thought of my book, telling myself that, even if it were still intact, I should never know how the novel ended because we were – all of us – going to die here in this cellar.

Sitting on the edge of my bed, I felt my eyes fill with tears at the thought of death. It was not sadness, but a dismay that I could not explain. Queer dreams often tormented me at night and strange adventures, projected on to the darkness as on to a cinema screen, reeled off before my eyes. I would see myself walking under palm-trees on the arm of a young man who never once turned his face towards me. I would be travelling in an express train and hear the little bell rung by the waiter in the dining-car. I would be at the theatre and see the actors moving their lips to articulate words whose sound never reached me. And then there would always come the torture of waking-up – waking-up to reality, to the horrible cellar, the stinking candle and the hollow-eyed shapes wandering about in the dimness. How I longed every single time to take refuge again in the land of dreams! But today's good meal had put me in a better mood, as if the blood flowed faster and warmer in my veins because I felt my hunger really satisfied. And, from now on, there would be bread, lots of good bread!

When he returned towards evening, covered with snow, Pista was the living image of Father Christmas. Instead of his knapsack, he was carrying a very heavy sack which he pushed along in front of him, panting with the effort.

11

'Weren't you frightened to come as far as here, loaded up like that?' asked Ilus.

Pista smiled.

'I thought that, if a bomb did hit me, my back'd be protected by the flour.'

The banker's widow heaved a sigh.

'At last a really fearless man! Just as if I were seeing my poor Albert again! . . . Is it pastry flour, my friend, or just ordinary bread flour?'

'One third of it belongs to me,' broke in the restaurant keeper's wife. 'To have the right to it, I've fed everybody here and filled all their bellies.'

Pista gave her a searching look. Then he took a little oblong box out of his pocket and held it out to the lawyer's wife.

'Here's the ultraseptin.'

The woman began to cry as she thanked him.

We surrounded Pista and we all stared, as if hypnotised, at the sack of flour. A sack of life! Pista ordered us each to bring some receptacle so that he could proceed to share it out fairly.

'The one who's got the least food is to bring along the biggest container,' he called out to us.

'You see how just he is?' I whispered to my mother.

In my eyes, Pista had become transformed into a dazzling hero. He was like the Count of Monte Cristo, wasn't he?

The great moment came at last. Pista untied the sack and filled our saucepan along with the other people's. A light film of white dust covered the black cement floor. My mother took the saucepan, and, taking out a pinch of flour, tasted it. Her face took on a different expression.

'It's only plaster,' she whispered, 'it's only plaster, not flour at all.'

She had uttered these words under her breath but everybody had heard. The cellar was transformed into an overturned wasps' nest. Using their elbows, everyone shoved and jostled to have a taste and the restaurant keeper's wife began to yell:

'You gang of cheats! I fed you because I was expecting flour and now he's gone and brought plaster and I've fed the lot of you. . . .'

Her fat face turned deeper and deeper red. Her husband tried in vain to calm her. The woman went towards the exit; when she turned round to face us again, one hand on the door, I was afraid she had had a stroke, her features were so distorted. But it was the vileness of her soul that was making her decompose before our eyes, while bitter, galling words spurted from her lips.

'The goulash you ate, that was horse meat, not beef. . . . In Duck Street, there's a dead horse – it was its haunch we cut up for your meal. Enjoy yourselves now with all that putrid filth in your bellies. . . .'

She slammed the sheet-iron door behind her. Seized with nausea, Ilus leant back against the wall. . . . For a few minutes, there was nothing to be heard but the efforts she was making not to vomit. In my own stomach, the meal turned as heavy as a stone. It seemed to us, at that moment, that nothing worse could ever happen to us.

'I implore you – all this is simply a question of prejudice against a particular animal,' suddenly exclaimed Mr. Radnai from the dark corner that sheltered him. 'The horse is no nastier than the pig or the ox – it's only that people aren't used to eating it. But there's really no need to get in such a frenzy about it.'

My father took up the argument, developing it as if he was at his lecture desk, giving a dissertation on Horace.

'Was it not also an erroneous idea to believe that there would be no fighting in the towns and that, therefore, the war would spare all civilians? Now that the war has invaded our streets, every single person is a soldier, even sick people, babies, women and old men. Therefore, let us not become frenzied on the subject of the goulash . . . we may well find ourselves faced with other ordeals which will demand every ounce of our strength.'

'The restaurant keeper's wife is a filthy slut all the same. . . .' affirmed the Doctor to wind up the debate.

No one contradicted him.

Our saucepan returned its disappointing contents to the big

13

sack. Suddenly I was seized with such a violent desire to crunch a loaf of good white bread, all hot from the oven, that it made me giddy. I went back to our own retreat, and lying down on the bed, I waited for sleep to come. The ground vibrated under our feet; machine-gun bullets hammered the walls with a hard, dry rattle like a shower of hail. My imagination had almost floated me away to the promenade under the palm-trees when a sentence reached me through the mists of dozing off. It was the voice of my father saying to my mother – 'Pista says that they've brought a munitions train up on to the bank of the Danube, by using the rails of the number nine tram. The last truck of the string is just on a level with our house. We may be blown up at any moment. . . .'

Chapter Three

THE NEARNESS OF the munitions train filled us with terror. Men condemned to death must have the same kind of feelings when they hear footsteps coming towards their cell and think they are going to be fetched. . . .

'It only needs a stray bullet for everything to blow up in smithereens,' Pista had said. And the projectiles did not go off one at a time but in batches of five or six. . . .

This morning, the Germans deposited three cases of munitions in the restaurant and brought the horses into the well of the staircase. We spied on them from the entrance to the cellar, where, for lack of anything better, we were using the dirty snow for our ablutions. What would become of us without Pista? Knowing that we are on the brink of a powder magazine is driving us crazy! But the presence of the soldier reassures us; nothing links his lot to ours; after all, we tell each other, he could go somewhere else if he felt himself in danger here.

But the real facts of the case are different: Pista stays in order to keep up our morale. He began by going round to all the tenants and asking each one what he would like to have from his flat. He was overwhelmed with requests. I had a newborn hope of being able to finish reading my book. During the most violent air raid, Pista ranged through every floor of the building and reported to us the state of them all. He also brought me back my Balzac. The blast of the explosions, he told us, had destroyed all the doors in our flat and in the Public Prosecutor's. An unexploded bomb had smashed our grand piano by hurtling through it from end to end and had embedded itself in the parquet floor. This story was, I think, the only pleasure of my entire sojourn in the cellar! To know that that piano, which had cost me so many hours of forced labour, no longer existed, gave me immense satisfaction. But I did not let my delight be seen, for my mother was crying.

That musical instrument, for her, had been a real friend. She sang admirably, accompanying herself. She used to trill out, each note clear as a bird's, charming little French songs whose words I did not understand but which awakened in me a nostalgic unrest. I used to think, with a mixture of tenderness and desire, of the unknown lover to whom I could one day confide all my troubles and who would take me in his arms and protect me.

The destruction of the piano put an end to one chapter of my adolescent life. Perhaps it was at that moment that I realised that my childhood had abruptly ended. A fierce pride came over me at the thought that, at fifteen, I was going to die the death of a grown-up person. I took up my book and avidly resumed my interrupted reading. But I had not read five lines before the effort this demanded blurred my vision. Nevertheless I would not admit that I could hardly see and continued to struggle to make out each word. At that moment, a terrifying force lifted me from the divan and flung me against the wall. As I collapsed, half fainting, I realised that the skylight, through which there normally filtered a pale glimmer of light, had been suddenly blacked out. My mouth and eyes filled with dust and, for lack of air, I began to cough. It would have been preferable to lose consciousness altogether. I crawled on all fours in the darkness to try and find my parents. My mother, lying in the narrow passage that linked our shelter to the main cellar, was conscious. As I gently laid my head on her lap, I saw the Colonel's wife coming down the cellar steps and tottering as she came. She was pressing her hand against her mouth: between her clenched fingers blood was gushing out and running all over her arms and her dress. My mother sat up and said we must help this seriously injured woman but we were trembling so much with nervous agitation that we could not manage to get on our feet.

The victim staggered along to the main cellar: we followed

16

her. In there, too, it was as black as night and dust was so thick you could cut it with a knife. Pista stepped forwards and asked for bandages. The badly hurt woman had been in the courtyard at the very moment the munitions train had blown up. The blast had hurled her against a wall and she had fractured her jaw. We lavished every possible care on her but the blood went on spurting out through the layers of absorbent gauze.

In the well of the staircase, the panic-stricken horses had set up a frantic whinnying that sounded like screams of mortal anguish. Mr. Radnai, my father and the Doctor went up into the courtyard. Falling fragments of the third storey had killed one of the German soldiers. The courtyard was strewn with rubble and pieces of masonry. Above our heads, the storeys were visibly collapsing but we were alive and that was all that mattered.

Pista had gone off to try and find a doctor. At first, this had offended our 'Doctor' but when he saw that he was incapable of stopping the injured woman's hæmorrhage, he had become very taciturn, and removed himself to a distant cellar. The lawyer was better now that the ultraseptin had brought his temperature down; he was complaining bitterly about the unheard-of insolence of those responsible for smashing his home.

'The Swiss flag is hoisted over my door,' he cried out in his hoarse voice. 'It's an extra-territorial domicile, protected by a Neutral Power! . . .'

No one paid any attention to his protests. The banker's wife, kneeling beside her bed, was praying, with her jewels clutched between her clasped hands. Ilus's golden locks were covered with soot and her unfortunate baby was howling with terror. Even the restaurant keepers made a nervous appearance, trembling for fear of reprisals for the horse-meat stew, but we merely ignored them. Death had brushed us too close not to wipe out human passions. In silence, we noted the fact that these people had once more taken up their quarters with us. The ground floor no longer seemed to offer them enough protection since the disappearance of an entire storey over their heads. Had the explosion burst their eardrums? They no longer seemed to hear

17

anything. The Colonel's wife was stretched out on her bed; her blood was still flowing. That bulky, energetic woman watched us with incredulous eyes, as if it were hard for her to understand why fate had struck her down.

At last Pista brought back a doctor. He told us with horror that the big block of flats in the Vitez-utca was reduced to a heap of rubble. The tenants would all be asphyxiated if the safety exit could not be cleared before it was too late. Men were coming out of the cellars under all the houses in the neighbourhood to lend their aid. Our men went off too under Pista's escort.

A strange calm flooded our hearts. The munitions train had blown up and we were still alive. . . . But I had to bite my fingers to keep back the cry of terror that rose to my lips at the thought that we, we too might suffer the fate of the people buried alive in the Vitez-utca.

All the afternoon I struggled against the vision of faces convulsed by suffocation. I kept imagining that we were trapped under the débris and that every breath we took was consuming a little of what life remained to us. These hallucinations did not leave me an instant's peace. If only there were some means of talking about them to someone. . . . I went into the big cellar and sat down beside Mr. Radnai. He shut his Heine and threw me a glance.

'What's the matter?' he asked. 'Are you ill?' Then he said: 'Come along, let's go up for a moment.'

He put his book in his pocket, as he made the suggestion.

We passed close by the bed where the Colonel's wife lay. She was moaning, in high fever. The Doctor was sitting at her bedside, looking profoundly thoughtful.

We went and saw the horses parked in the well of the staircase . . . . I noticed with horror that one of them was in process of nibbling the banisters and had already swallowed a morsel of wood. A bloody slaver drooled from its cracked lips and dribbled down over its chest.

'Not one bullet to put these poor beasts out of their misery,' said Mr. Radnai, as if he were rapping out an oath. 'An ammunition train blows up just beside us, the restaurant is crammed with high explosives, the metal of the cannons is melting – they're firing so much to use up the shells before the Russians arrive – and these wretched animals are going to perish of hunger and thirst!'

The horses surrounded us, whinnying as if in complaint, fixing us with their bloodshot eyes that started from their sockets. I could not endure their look and hung my head. One of the horses came up and gently nudged me in the back, as if to urge me to have pity on them, to bring them at last a little food, a little water. An intense, crushing despair overwhelmed me. I put my arm round the horse's neck and I burst into tears.

Mr. Radnai took my hand and drew me back towards the entrance to the cellar. Gently he stroked my hair.

'Poor little girl! Poor generation! . . . What a cruel shame it is!'

I stopped dead at the first step.

'No, I can't go back to the cellar,' I told Mr. Radnai. 'It'll collapse and bury us.'

'Don't be afraid . . . nothing more will happen now. Go down. . . .'

'Aren't you frightened, then?' I asked point-blank.

'But of course I'm frightened! I'm frightened of dying of suffocation, I've no idea what's happened to my family and my life depends on the whim of a few hysterical people. When are they going to denounce me . . . or give away my Jewish origin by some careless word?

'Don't be afraid of that,' I told him. 'No one has the faintest intention of harming you.'

We went down the steps in silence. Mr. Radnai took up his place again and took out his little suede-bound book. But I noticed that, instead of reading, he was staring fixedly in front of him.

Towards six, the men returned without having discovered the safety exit of the collapsed building. A young man and a young woman accompanied them. The girl must have been about twenty-two or twenty-three, she clutched her fur-lined coat round her, shivering, and never, for one second, let go the boy's hand. We contemplated them without saying a word. Who were they and what did they want of us?

It was Pista who spoke up: 'They come from the Vitez-utca. They had gone off to fetch water when the munitions train blew up, they're the only survivors. . . . They ought to stay here, they can't wander about the streets. I hope you'll take them in. . . . I'll manage to find food for them somehow. I'll wangle something, all right.'

We stared at them, petrified, as if they were ghosts. This young couple did not seem to belong to the real world. Like St. Thomas, we would have liked to touch them, to feel them, so as to assure ourselves that they truly were living beings.

Ilus, who was holding her baby on her arm, was the first to speak. She went up to them.

'Heavens,' she said, 'I can see that those two love each other . . . . How young they are . . . even death has had pity on them . . . . What is there I could do to help them? If there are still some things left whole in my flat, you can bring down anything you want. And I'll share my food with them, too.'

The banker's wife promised them cooking utensils, the restaurant keeper's wife offered them a tin of meat, the medical student asked them if they hadn't a pain anywhere.

A charitable impulse towards them surged up in every heart. It was as if this were the moment to settle for ever a debt of gratitude they owed to fate. Pista and the Doctor brought down a big divan and some blankets from Ilus's flat. Then they went off in search of a few provisions from the big grocery in the Fo-utca. It was the first time the Doctor had risked going out. The banker's widow called out from her corner:

'You might also bring a little meat to cook for a stew.'

The restaurant keeper's wife went white . . . this was a dig at her. But the old lady went on:

'The horse is an animal, just as the pig is. The only thing that matters is that the meat should be fresh. Personally, I'm not disgusted by it any more . . . I'm hungry. . . .'

The others said nothing, but these words were received by the couple of restaurant owners like an absolution. Ilus moved into our cellar, leaving her coal-bunker to the young couple, Eve and Gabriel.

Suddenly, through his delirium, the lawyer became aware of what was going on. From his bed, where he lay with his limbs outspread, like an old, sweating spider, he challenged Eve:

'Are you married, young lady? Normally, it is only married people who sleep together. . . .'

'But we're no longer living in a normal world,' retorted Radnai. 'Keep your temper and don't poke your nose into other people's affairs! . . .'

'We love each other,' said Gabriel softly. 'All round us, they're all dead.'

His features contorted and he drew Eve close to him.

'Good God! When I think I was so dead against your coming with me! . . .'

We no longer disputed their presence. It seemed to us as natural for them to be here as if they had lived with us for years. The thing that really mattered to me now was the *Peau de Chagrin*. Trying frantically to read it, I got too close to the sticky wick and my hair burst into flames. I gave a scream. My mother promptly flung a blanket over my head. But nothing remained of my curls which, till then, had hung down over my shoulders. My neck, too, displayed painful burns. They put some ointment on my ear and Pista, armed with an enormous pair of scissors, cut off the last uneven locks of my hair. A melancholy little lad stared back at me from the tarnished mirror I still possessed. I no longer even recognised myself

The days dragged by. Nights of fearful dreams, fights against a world of phantoms. My dream world had evaporated. Sleep no longer led me towards peace, but towards lunar landscapes of horror and evil.

Pista often disappeared for whole days on end but always returned smiling, like someone over whom even death had no dominion.

After one particular night, we waited, exhausted, for dawn to come. The explosions had followed one after another in an unbroken rhythm. Every time the house suffered a direct hit, the ground under our feet shuddered as if the earth too were inhabited by infernal powers.

At half-past six, Pista woke everybody up. He informed us that the Germans had, that very night, blown up all the bridges over the Danube.

We could not believe this stupefying news. We stared, unbelieving, at our informant; then, on a common impulse, we decided to go and verify his assertions with our own eyes. We filed up the great staircase one behind the other, making up a strange procession. The idea never even occurred to us that a bomb, falling without warning, might have torn us to shreds. The destruction of the bridges had thrust all our other fears into the background ... but this indifference was almost more alarming than anything else. We all gathered in the Colonel's flat. Pista forbade us to show ourselves, saying the crack Russian snipers on the other side of the river were aiming at every human silhouette. Huddled against the remains of the walls, we stared out through the ruined embrasures where the windows had been. The disembowelled bridges lay felled like trees in the troubled waters of the Danube.

Horrified, I studied the shattered Lanc-hid (the Chain Bridge), thinking of numberless times I had crossed over it with my father. I often used to go and meet him at the Lanc-hid Café and afterwards we would go for a walk. My dear old Lanc-hid, what had they done to you? And, over there in the distance, was the Elisabeth Bridge, also completely collapsed. It was swathed in the morning mist, as if to hide its huge, shattered body. In my mind I saw once again its light, graceful arch that linked Pest to Buda in a single span like a musical phrase, like a streamer flung over the rushing water by a playful hand.

The powerful river that, in the old days, used to carry pretty pleasure-steamers seemed to be infuriated by contact with the twisted ironwork; it seethed into giddy whirlpools and, in its impotent rage, hurled great blocks of ice against the quays on either bank.

A bomb quite close to us shook us out of our torpor. We went down to the cellar again. I lingered behind and threw one last look at the bridges which lay prone before me, like huge unburied corpses.

In the afternoon we went to fetch some water, but in vain. We returned with our buckets empty. The tap in the Kacsa-utca no longer yielded a single drop.

I'm thirsty.

Chapter Four

IT IS TWO days now since we have been able to get a drop of water. Ilus used the last half-glassful this very morning to make some warm gruel for the baby by adding a few remnants of dried milk to it. That poor child is so weak that he is incapable of sitting up; he lies there, day after endless day, quite flaccid, his head lolling and his plaintive wails stifled in his throat.

Towards midday, someone began to utter shrill cries in the cellar. I ran to see what had happened. It was the banker's widow, in her combinations.

'Look, I've found a louse!' she shrieked, gesticulating. 'It's really the last straw of this whole scandalous business that we can't even wash ourselves any more!' And she displayed, to anyone who cared to look, a sleepy louse on a scrap of old newspaper. We stood round the insect, staring at it. The event was so portentous that, for a few moments, it made us forget our thirst.

Outside, hell had once again broken loose. During the morning, the house had been hit seven times and we never stopped praising God for the solid vaulted cellars of this building which is nearly a hundred years old; what would have become of us in a modern house with cardboard walls? Even here, at a depth that equals the height of a whole storey, the ground never stopped trembling under our feet, as if an electric cable ran under the soil of the entire city of Budapest and we were continually walking on high-tension wires.

Lately I have taken to sitting on the edge of my bed with my legs tucked up under me. I shudder every time I have to take a few steps, I am so terrified of that lugubrious trembling.

* * *

24

Now that there is no more water, the caretaker and his wife no longer show themselves. They have accumulated stocks of everything and several people claim to have seen them taking a small cask down to the cellar, a cask which, from its appearance, ought to contain wine. At present, they keep themselves shut up in their private cellar so as not to share their treasures with any other human being.

This afternoon, however, the caretaker made an appearance when he went off, tottering at every step, to empty the sanitary pail in the courtyard. He seemed even paler and more shrunken than usual as he walked past with his head down and with such an unsteady gait that twice he let the excrements slop over from his bucket. No one, however, dared make the slightest reproach. Everyone knows that the caretaker is a Communist and the tenants are terrified that any remark may bring down his vengeance, once the Russians enter the town.

An unexpected silence occurred about four o'clock in the afternoon. The Germans, dragging their little gun mounted on an armoured car behind them, had left their post in front of the house and the street had suddenly assumed a calm and deserted aspect again.

Slowly, we went up into the courtyard. The horses had already gnawed the balustrade of the great staircase right up as far as the first floor and one of them had grown so feeble that all it could do now was to squat on its hind-quarters. It was the first time in my life that I had seen a horse sitting down. That one also would have been only too glad to get near the banisters so as to regale itself on them but it lacked the strength to do so and the others were sharing its portion amongst themselves. . . .

Bursting in unexpectedly as usual, Pista appeared, but, this time, with empty hands. We promptly surrounded him to ask his advice on the subject of the water. He declared that we had a chance of finding a little at the Turkish Baths, situated not far away, as these baths were not connected up with the city water supply.

Although this establishment was only about ten minutes away,

25

the distance suddenly seemed to us impossible to traverse. The idea of leaving the shelter of the cellar to walk through a street where, at any moment, a shell or a bomb might blow us to pieces, was intolerable. Pista affirmed that he was ready and willing to fetch the water but what would be the good of two pailfuls among twenty thirsty and dirty people?

'Personally, I'm going there,' announced the banker's widow, 'and, if there's the slightest possibility, I shall take a bath at once! It's really too much to get to the pitch of being verminous.'

These suggestions were followed by a discussion, which seemed endless, about who was to take part in the expedition. Finally, it was decided that everyone should go, with the exception of Mrs. Sarosi and Mr. Galamb who were told to keep guard over the cellar. We set off, armed with our pails, but, once we got into the street, each of us instinctively started to run.

'Keep calm!' shouted Pista, to assuage our fear. 'Running won't help you to dodge the shells!'

Those who were keeping a look-out under the porches of other houses plucked up courage at seeing us out-of-doors and our little bucket-laden group very soon swelled till it became a procession.

At a run, we soon reached the former Baths. A blast had torn the main door off its hinges: to enter, we had to climb over a big block of stone that barred the entrance. Inside, on the tiled floor of multicoloured mosaic, lay the corpses of two horses, their legs sticking up in the air and their stomachs swollen as if they were filled with water to bursting point. We circumvented these cautiously and slipped through the gaping opening, once a swing-door, that gave access to the galleries that ran alongside the sunk baths. This was the place, once adorned with palms and tropical plants in stone urns, where, in peacetime, the white-clad bath attendants used to receive their clients in an atmosphere of hot steam. If Pista had not accompanied us, we should certainly have lost ourselves in this icy, deserted labyrinth. It was a question of finding the main hydrant from which the baths received their boiling sulphurous water.

'We'll get there in a moment,' said Pista, taking the head of the procession. We followed him, but suddenly, as if paralysed with dismay, the entire troop stopped dead. Not understanding what could have happened, I stepped forwards to find out more about it. It was then that my gaze fell on the corpse at the bottom of the deep bath. He was floating, his eyes glassy and his mouth open, on the surface of water the colour of verdigris. The wet had so utterly ruined and mildewed his clothes that it was impossible to know whether he had been a Hungarian or a German, a soldier or a civilian. A startling example of the great justice dealt out by death who makes no distinction either between moral principles or between nationalities.

Above our heads, the roof had collapsed and we could see the sky: beams and tiles were heaped up on either side of the sunk bath and this pile of ruins presented an insurmountable obstacle.

'We can't possibly get as far as the water,' wailed someone in the crowd and Ilus burst into hysterical sobs.

'Wait a second,' said Pista, disappearing among the débris.

It was not long before he reappeared, straining with the effort of dragging a long plank behind him. After having placed it so that it bridged the two sides of the sunk bath, he stepped on to it and ran across.

'You can come over,' he called out. 'It'll easily hold under one person at a time.'

The melancholy procession resumed its march, keeping a gloomy silence. What a lamentable picture they presented, these unhappy townsfolk torn from their peaceful everyday life, advancing hesitantly across a narrow, slippery plank while, at the bottom of the bath, the dead man, staring skywards with his great, startled eyes, seemed to be counting their steps and watching their titubating walk.

The first arrivals gazed at us from the other side like the Blessed looking back at the souls still in purgatory. A single false step and the clumsy person would fall over and land beside the drowned man.

It was my turn to go over. My whole body was trembling.

They told me to wait till the others came back but the thought of being left all alone with the dead man filled me with horror. If my mother stayed behind with me, we should not have enough water and who knew when we might have another chance to come here again? I put one foot on the plank and it seemed to me that I was being forced to walk along a tightrope stretched above an immense precipice in the mountains. I had arrived nearly half-way when the plank shook from side to side. I gave a scream and fell on my knees, only to find myself exactly opposite the dead man. Pista was up to me in two bounds. He seized me in his arms and deposited me on the other side.

Suddenly, a wild desire made me forget everything for there, in front of me, were the water-taps. The pipes had been so badly damaged that the hot, sulphurous water was escaping everywhere, roaring like a waterfall. Nevertheless, we had to give up the idea of drinking it, for the first mouthful had been enough to burn our lips. The banker's widow stripped off her blouse and ran to put herself under a shower that, by some miracle, was still functioning.

'You'll scald yourself,' my mother shrieked to her.

'It's cold,' the other shrieked back to her.

We all rushed forwards to lap up the cold water of the shower. Nearly everyone had undressed. It was a truly voluptuous delight to bare our skins, dirty and itching with perspiration, to the jet of water.

A piece of soap went the rounds and looks full of gratitude were directed at Ilus who had brought it and was gladly lending it. All shame had vanished; the Colonel's wife, naked to the waist, was busy washing her combinations and Ilus was rubbing her feet and legs with her skirt pulled up well past her thighs.

Our joy suddenly changed to startled terror; a mine had just exploded quite close to where we were. We put our clothes on again at lightning speed and set off again, with our brimming pails, on the homeward journey. The bombs were falling thicker and thicker and Pista, with unfaltering agility, ran to and fro on the plank to help the weaker ones carry their buckets across. In the street, we ran, keeping close to the walls, and the precious liquid slopped over on the ground as we advanced.

In front of the house, the little cannon was already barking away. . . . What joy when, at last, we crossed the threshold of the street door, safe and sound! We seemed to forget that a single bomb would have been enough to bring the whole house down on us; the only thought in our heads was the certitude that these old walls would protect us from the machine-gun bullets and the splinters from bursting mines.

As I crossed the courtyard, going towards the cellar, a feeling stronger than myself impelled me towards the horses. My pails were still half-full. Never in my life shall I forget that moment, even if I am to live to an immense old age. First of all, I went up to the sitting horse and offered him the water. The happy whinnying that burst from him reminded me of our cries when we reached the bath. He shivered and drank up the water in great, endless mouthfuls. The other horses came forwards, stepping slowly and hesitantly. I had to go very carefully about the distribution, so that each one of them should have his share. In the looks the animals gave me there was an almost human expression of gratitude. The horses surrounded me, weak as they were; blood was flowing from their gums and suppurating tears ran out of their eyes.

As I went down to the cellar with my empty pails, I felt my heart as light and overflowing with joy as if, in the serenest days of peacetime, someone had just given me a magnificent present.

Chapter Five

LITTLE BY LITTLE, we have got into the way of running to Pista every time we need something. He succeeds in getting us almost everything we seriously want.

This morning we asked him to go and fetch a priest from the convent about half an hour's walk from where we live so that Mass could be celebrated here. Pista has acquired the reputation of an invulnerable being, like someone who carries a talisman and has only to wave his hand to ward off the mines and bombs raining all about him.

Our desire was realised more quickly than we had hoped. Barely two days went by before the soldier announced to us that Mass would be said in our cellar on the following morning. (It was truly strange to hear those words 'morning', 'afternoon' or 'evening' pronounced in the perpetual darkness of our cellar; our eyes, permanently red and watering, from peering in the feeble yellow light from the cooking-fat candles, could not measure nights and days. The only fixed point in our timetable was the night bomber that ended its work of destruction about four in the morning; after that, a comparative silence reigned till about six.)

The great day arrived. Everyone had been up and stirring since half-past three in the morning. It had snowed during the night and we were able to clean ourselves up a little with the snow in the courtyard. In the central cellar, a table had been covered with the last clean cloth we had been able to find and we noticed the astonishing fact that Mr. Radnai, the atheist, had shaved himself and put on a tie to adorn the neck of a shirt whose original colour it would have been hard to determine. The banker's widow removed the curl-papers from her hair with meticulous care and Ilus put a clean shirt on the baby. The day before, Pista had stolen some candles from a shop and had brought back six of them, as thick as one's arm. These were a treasure beyond price.

A few minutes after four, an old priest arrived, bringing the Blessed Sacrament in a golden pyx and the altar wine in a flask. A corner of Ilus's cellar had been transformed into a confessional; they had put a chair there for the confessor and a blanket on the ground for the penitents. Then we ranged ourselves one behind the other and the confessions began.

With his head bowed, avoiding all glances, Mr. Radnai too was queueing up. The caretaker and his wife were there, dressed as if they were going to attend High Mass in their own village. Eve never let go Gabriel's hand; the two of them stood a little apart from the rest of us. The Public Prosecutor had a temperature of 105 degrees; he was wandering in his mind and was going to receive the Last Sacraments. Stephen lit the candles on the improvised altar and the cellar was suddenly flooded with golden light. Shadows with bowed heads passed by me to go and pray in front of the altar. Pista smoothed out the last wrinkles in the cloth; then he too took his place in the line.

When it came to my turn, I felt my heart thumping violently.

'I don't want to die, Father,' I told him, almost in tears. 'I'm only fifteen and I'm horribly afraid of death. I want to go on living.'

The pale face with the lowered eyelids remained motionless opposite mine. How often he must have heard those very same words of rebellion, how often before someone must have clutched his hand, saying: 'Father, life still owes me so much. One can't perish in this darkness and filth when there are countries where the sun is shining, and people are walking about in the streets while we are besieged here in this city that has become nothing but a graveyard.' What I heard myself say was:

'Father, I'm terror-stricken every time I have to go out. You can't go anywhere now without treading on the dead. Wherever I go, they keep staring at me with their glassy eyes . . . they give me such accusing, reproachful looks because I'm still among the living. . . .'

'The fate of our body matters very little indeed,' said the priest gently. 'The death that we fear so much is only deliverance; it is only the moment when the soul escapes from its bodily prison to enter into eternity. And God loves us so much, my child! He welcomes us with an infinite, inexhaustible love. In His kingdom there are no wars – no death either. Sunshine, peace and sublime joy are waiting for us there. Can we be afraid of anything at all? As to the dead who are all about us here, don't imagine they're accusing us: on the contrary, they are sorry for us because we still have to endure the sufferings of this life. Don't forget that not one of those who have died here among the ruins is lost for life eternal. . . .'

As I came away, I was no longer aware of anyone about me. Through the warm mist of my tears, the light of the candles reflected all the colours of the rainbow; the walls had vanished to give place to a magnificent cathedral in which the light seemed to grow more and more radiant as if the golden flood of the sunbeams had mingled with it. Trembling voices were singing holy words and a feeling of pure bliss swept me away almost to the verge of ecstasy.

It was a long time before I came back to reality and saw that Eve and Gabriel were kneeling in front of the altar. The priest was solemnising their marriage. It was an unforgettable scene, that vow of faithfulness, as long as life should last, pronounced here on the brink of eternity and in the perpetual shadow of death.

The priest left us about seven in the morning, in the midst of a tremendous air raid. Everything led us to believe that today would be even more terrible than the preceding ones. The house had already been severely damaged and part of the corridor on the third floor was hurled down into the courtyard.

Everyone searched for some little present to give the young married couple. Mr. Radnai gave them an orange. He had hoarded this fruit, which was already completely dried up, for more than five weeks and had refrained from eating it, keeping it for still harder times. The caretaker had brought a glass of wine. Everyone was rejoicing at the sight of joy.

Later on, Eve came to look for Ilus in her little cellar and gave her the orange for the child.

Chapter Six

THE AFTERNOON WAS terrible. I stayed sitting on the edge of my bed without daring to put my feet to the ground, I had such a horror of that continual shuddering. The cooking-fat candle wavered as it gave out its yellowish light. I wanted to read but my eyes watered after a few moments. My mother never stops warning me that later on I shall have to wear spectacles.

Does one bother about the fate of one's eyes when one has only a few days to live? At this moment, I am no longer afraid of death, only of the passage from this life to eternal life. Shall we be killed by the bombs which will bring the house down over our heads and shall we perish by suffocation under the ruins or shall we be condemned to be burnt alive by the jet of the flame-throwers? If the Germans make us evacuate the house, we shall make the most magnificent of clay pigeons for the Russians posted on the opposite bank. They will shoot us down one after the other with the help of their telescopic rifles; they will even be able to enjoy our grimaces before they see us collapse in death.

Pista decided to go and steal a bridal veil for Eve. He said he remembered a dress shop in the neighbourhood where one could buy them before the siege. In the shop window, instead of the little feathered hats of the old days, there is now an unexploded bomb. But Pista was sure he would find a veil inside. We tried to dissuade him, but he laughed and his splendid healthy white teeth glittered in the light of the candles.

'I want this to be an unforgettable day for Eve,' was his obstinate refrain.

He did not go off alone, for the Doctor wanted to accompany

him. Famine had reached such a pitch in our household that the latter's decision was almost joyfully welcomed. We knew how expert the Doctor was at cutting up dead bodies; outside he would be sure to find the carcass of some horse and bring us back the best bits of it. The restaurant keeper's wife would make these into a nourishing soup and a meat dish.

Talking of this, our own horses are still alive. Those of us who are installed directly underneath the main staircase say they can hear them incessantly pawing the ground with their hooves. Pista tells us that the horse that used to sit on its haunches is so weak now that it lies stretched out full length and has only just enough strength to lift its head when anyone comes near it. I am waiting impatiently for the next chance to go and fetch some water so that I can give them something to drink.

'It's seven o'clock,' said Mr. Radnai, who had come to see us to have a chat with my father. 'Pista still hasn't returned.'

We began to grow more and more uneasy. Ilus, most of all, became desperately anxious for, if the young man did not return, the baby would have nothing to eat tomorrow: the last tin of dried milk was empty. . . .

'A quarter to eight,' said Mr. Radnai some time later, scratching his chin. 'Odd, the little mechanism of this watch,' he went on, as if he were thinking aloud. 'It was manufactured in Switzerland . . . I can hardly believe that country still exists . . . Switzerland . . . glaciers . . . pure air, winter sports, luxury hotels full of tourists, an obsequious head waiter asking if one would like lobster or prefer just some crayfish. . . .'

The smell of cooking wafted through the cellars . . . Good heavens! . . . Smell of cooking, what a marvellous, mouth-watering expression . . . Oh, we simply must eat! Eat? . . . No, engulf! Devour!

'No doubt you have travelled a great deal, Professor?'

'Yes,' said my father. But he gripped my arm, for I had just given a shriek of terror: an explosion, very near indeed, had shaken us all. The door of our cellar shot open, as if impelled by the blast of a bomb, but it was the caretaker who entered. He was livid and his trembling lips had barely enough strength to articulate these words:

'Come at once . . . he's just been brought back. . . .'

'Pista?' I gasped. A terrible presentiment tightened my throat.

We rushed into the passage, jostling each other. The Doctor unloaded Pista from his shoulders. They were both covered with blood as if they had been drenched in red paint.

'Is he unconscious?' asked a hoarse voice from the back.

'He's well and truly dead,' replied the Doctor timidly. His voice sounded almost as if he were apologising. 'We went a long way and a mine exploded right in front of him. The blast flung me against a wall. When the dust and smoke cleared away, I saw him again. But he was dead.'

The banker's widow was seized with nausea and stumbled out of the passage. The sweetish smell of blood penetrated into our very brains. Ilus burst into sobs.

'Here's his sack,' the Doctor went on. 'They're still in it . . . the things that were meant for you.'

He held out the sack to Ilus who took it with a nerveless gesture. She took an interminable time to untie the string, but no one helped her; we were all too petrified with horror. Bending over her task, she was already smeared with blood up to her elbows by the time she had at last managed to open the sack. Her shaking hands drew out of it three tins of condensed milk. She broke into a shrill laugh.

'Milk for the child . . . he's not going to die of hunger! Dear God, it's milk for the child! For my poor little child, lovely milkie for my baby. . . .'

It was some time before she could pull herself together. Then, fumbling in the bottom of the sack, she drew out a beautiful white veil.

'The bridal veil,' said Mr. Radnai in a toneless voice, while the little cannon at the corner of the street started barking again. Eve hid her face in her hands and shook her head obstinately.

'I don't want it – don't give it to me.'

At that, Ilus, holding the veil, went up to what had once been

36

Pista and covered it with the filmy white tulle. Her gesture was gentle and motherly, as if she were covering up her sleeping child.

'Thank you,' she kept whispering over and over again. 'Thank you. . . .'

The narrow passage was transformed into a mortuary chapel. We all knelt down and Eve said a prayer out loud. The veil slowly soaked up the blood and, outside, the shrapnel spattered down in burst after burst.

That night the air raids followed one after the other without a break.

At midday we had drunk all the water we had left. Now there was no more water, not a single drop of water. . . . Only blood, blood . . . everywhere blood. . . .

Chapter Seven

THE NEWS SPREAD that, at dawn, the Russians had occupied the barracks in the street next to ours. This was a building in which ten or a dozen Germans had been holding out for more than a fortnight against a host of assailants. So our liberation would not be much longer delayed. Once the Russians were there, we should be able to return to the upper storeys and abandon our infamous rat-like way of life.

It must have been barely seven o'clock when four Germans, armed to the teeth, burst noisily into the courtyard. They laid down their tommy-guns and forced themselves, with great difficulty, to drag a bazooka up the staircase. Then, loaded with heavy cases of ammunition, they invaded the few rooms on the first floor that were still more or less intact.

These manoeuvres left us perplexed. Everything seemed to point to their intention of transforming the house into a fortress and of holding out there to the bitter end.

It was becoming extremely improbable that we should manage to escape being killed for, once the house was besieged, the flame-throwers would very soon roast us alive.

With hardly a breath of strength left in him, he was so worn out and weakened by fever, the lawyer raised himself in his bed, gasping out in a raucous voice:

'Insolent dogs! They want to shoot from my flat! My wife's of Swiss nationality – I shall go and complain to the Minister. . . .'

His white beard flowed down over his nightshirt, dirty and clammy with sweat. Waving his bony arms, he looked like a skeleton in the winking light of the candles. The yapping sobs of the caretaker's wife nearly burst our eardrums, while Mr. Radnai managed to make himself heard, though he was speaking in a low voice:

'Look here, keep calm! As soon as the Russians appear, I shall put on the yellow star so that they'll understand that I'm a Jew. Then I shall be able to protect you just as you're protecting me now by hiding me from the Germans.'

The banker's wife retorted anxiously:

'You propose to stand up against fighting troops with a star? Do you think that will be the slightest use?

'Most certainly it will. The star is a symbol – it's the sign of the persecuted. And henceforth it will be the sign of the apotheosis of the martyrs.'

Ilus had come in, carrying the child wrapped up in blankets. An inexplicable feeling drove people to herd together, it was frightening to be alone.

My father, who had remained sitting in a corner, absorbed in his thoughts, exclaimed suddenly:

'I say . . . it looks as if that were water dripping down the wall!'

We clustered round him and noticed, in our turn, that glittering drops beaded the saltpetre-covered wall.

'Can one drink it?' asked someone in a faltering voice. 'We ought to get something to collect this water in.'

No one answered; we were staring at the wall, fascinated. The dripping increased; then we saw, to our horror, that a very thin, but ever-increasing layer of liquid was spreading over the floor. The water was invading the cellar on all sides.

'We must bale out this water at once,' said the Doctor excitedly. 'We'll make a chain with buckets that we'll empty outside, passing them along from one to the other. . . . But quick! Otherwise we'll be inundated!'

'Turn off the tap!' shouted the lawyer. 'Or send for the plumber . . . all the same, it's the limit!'

His breath gave out and he fell back on his cushions. We rushed off to get buckets and Ilus settled her whimpering baby down in the bed beside the lawyer so that she too could help in the task.

A line was formed from the cellar up to the street-door and the buckets passed from hand to hand as quickly as possible. The last in the line emptied them into the street.

The Germans had come downstairs and stood watching us at work.

'You're giving yourselves trouble for nothing,' said one of them. 'The wrecked bridges and the piled-up blocks of ice are obstructing the flow of the Danube. So the water's rising in the sewers exactly as it does in a lock. You don't imagine that just with these few pails you're going to get the Danube out of your cellar?'

We stared at him without wishing to understand him and our hands went on mechanically passing the buckets that were filled to the brim.

Meanwhile, the little cannon had begun to bark again in front of the house. That meant that the Russian fighter-planes wouldn't be long coming, either.

Those of us who were working in the dangerous spots were frequently relieved, for only the cellar and the stairs could offer some shelter. We went on relentlessly with our task for five hours, incessantly menaced by volleys of machine-gun fire and by exploding mines. We had no choice but between this perilous work, which could never produce a satisfactory result, and the prospect of being submerged by that stinking liquid which was rising in the cellar.

Towards noon, they sent up word that the water was going down; doubtless it had found another outflow. So the danger seemed momentarily averted.

We went down again, worn out, drenched with sweat and, above all, tortured by hunger. The cellar, which for so long had been our only refuge, now seemed to us icy-cold and horrible. The stench of the sewers had impregnated the blankets, the few bits of furniture and also what little flour we had left. That flour was our greatest delicacy and we used to eat a pinch of it from time to time as a treat.

We forced ourselves to behave as if nothing had happened.

The danger of flooding had vanished; the cellar still protected us from the volleys that rendered the upper floors uninhabitable, but a nameless fear gripped us by the throat. The caretaker's wife wept without stopping and her voice was no longer anything but the grating of a saw.

Early in the afternoon, the door of the cellar was suddenly opened and a German appeared with a tommy-gun in his fist.

'*Raus!*' he yelled. 'Everyone is to go up at once into the courtyard!'

We assailed him with questions. What had happened? Why must we leave the cellar?

But all he did was to keep saying that he pitied anyone who dawdled behind. The lawyer's wife thrust herself forwards.

'I'm quite willing to go up myself but my husband has just had a severe attack of pneumonia and he's an old man of eighty. Leave *him* in peace, at least.'

'Everyone's got to go,' insisted the German. 'I wouldn't care to be in the skin of anyone the C.O. finds here!'

We had to obey. The lawyer was helped, not to say carried, by his wife and the Doctor. Mr. Radnai had turned up his collar and walked with his head bowed. The banker's widow had hastily put on some lipstick. Eve and Gabriel walked arm-in-arm, radiant with a happiness that neither life nor death could touch.

The German opened the caretaker's door with a kick; the wife did not even raise her eyes. After the third summons, he seized her by the arm and dragged her out into the courtyard.

We were all together again and we waited in silence. The Doctor looked uneasy. Four Germans armed with their tommy-guns confronted us. Their Commanding Officer announced:

'The remains of our provisions have been stolen. Two men are going to search the cellar.'

The soldiers he indicated went down below. Several people wanted to speak and the Public Prosecutor declared indignantly that an accusation of theft was an insult. But the officer interrupted in a harsh voice:

'Silence!'

41

After a quarter of an hour, the two Germans reappeared and announced that they had found nothing. Their commander said to us, after consulting his watch:

'Listen, everybody: the ground floor is full of munitions. If, in five minutes, you do not give me back our provisions, I shall blow up the building. I shall not have to render account of this act to anyone, for I shall not leave Budapest alive. And, if the débris of this house blocks the street, the Russians will have that much more difficulty in getting through. . . . I shall now begin to count the five minutes!'

I felt my body go numb. It became as cold and strange as if I were already dead.

The Doctor burst into sobs. This man who cut up the carcasses of dead horses with the utmost detachment was weeping with emotion and terror.

'I've not stolen anything,' he moaned. 'Let me go!'

Ilus, exhausted from holding the child so long in her arms, let herself slide gently to the ground. Squatting on the dirty snow, she breathed on the baby's face to soften the rigour of the cold.

'Four minutes to go,' said the German.

The caretaker's wife, who had once been one of the fattest women in the capital and who had grown so much thinner since the death of her son as to make her unrecognisable, stared at us like someone counting the number of condemned men on the site of execution. Her sorrow seemed slightly appeased. Up to now, she had nourished a bitter hatred against the living but, now that we had only a few moments to live, all rancour seemed to have left her.

The banker's widow made a sudden gesture. She tore off the little bag of jewels which hung round her neck and, stepping forwards, she offered it to the Germans.

'Let me go and this fortune is yours.'

The soldiers remained perfectly still, without displaying the faintest interest. One might have supposed we were no longer dealing with men of flesh and blood but with robots.

My father and my mother were each holding one of my hands, gripping my fingers more and more tightly.

The lawyer screamed out that he wanted to go on living. I told myself that he had already lived eighty years and that *I* was only fifteen and had more reasons to weep than he had. . . .

It seemed to me that the great walls of the house had begun to sway. I could no longer see anything but the blurred outlines of the German soldiers in front of me. Only the fierce pressure of my father's and mother's hands kept me still holding on to life in the midst of this courtyard filled with ruins. . . . Then I heard some words spoken in German and I felt myself being hurled down into the depths of a dark abyss.

When, on returning to consciousness, I found myself once more in the cellar I hated so much and loved so much, I dissolved in tears. People gathered round me making a fuss of me. My sobs convulsed me like an electric current running through my whole body. They told me that, before the five minutes of grace were up, a Hungarian soldier had shouted from one of the windows on the second floor that he would give back the German army rations but demanded that the civilians should be left in peace.

He must have been a soldier of the disbanded troops, like Pista. No one ever knew what became of this man after his confession.

Chapter Eight

NIGHT HAD FALLEN and people who came down from the courtyard announced that the quays of the Danube were lit up by red flares. That is how the Russians mark out the places they are going to straddle with their artillery fire. This news aroused no emotion in any of us. We were too exhausted. The episode of that afternoon had taken away the last of our strength.

By eight o'clock, the battle was raging. The house received bomb after bomb and the bombers, whose continuous throbbing we could hear, were attacking the quarter, one after another, without respite.

At ten, the water began to flood in again. We watched its level rise from one second to the next. It was impossible to bale it all out with buckets; the only solution lay in flight. But where could we flee to? Where could we find a refuge that offered some sort of safety? We had no time for reflection; the water was already coming up to our knees. We stuffed our pockets with the few handfuls of dried beans we still had left and we rescued the blankets that we already had to hold high up so that they should not get wet. Mr. Radnai was hastily dressing himself and the water had already risen right up to his shirt tails. Ilus was wrapping up her child. The banker's widow was shrieking and gesticulating. Eve and Gabriel were helping all of us for they had no possessions to save.

We loaded our wretched belongings on our shoulders and marched off towards the staircase through the water which now came up to our waists.

The lawyer was riding pickaback on Mr. Radnai's shoulders and each of us clutched a precious grease candle.

A German wanted to make us go down into the cellar again but, as he shone the beam of his electric torch over the bottom of the staircase, he saw the black waves rushing up over the steps. He then indicated a door on the ground floor, saying that anyone who dared come out of there would get a bullet through his body.

We found ourselves in the caretaker's flat. The Public Prosecutor and the baby were tucked up together in the bed.

The first streaks of dawn were just appearing when, as if by magic, an absolute silence fell. We did not dare believe our ears and listened with our heads glued to the wall.

The Doctor declared that he was going to see what was happening outside. Everyone protested, for even to push the door a little way open would have been enough to expose him to a volley from a tommy-gun. But he shrugged his shoulders.

'Death's inevitable now and I'd rather be killed by a bullet than be burnt alive by a flame-thrower.'

He walked over to the door, turned the handle and went out. Trembling all over, I stuffed my fingers into my ears but the shots I was expecting with such terror did not occur. A few moments later, the Doctor's voice rang out through the silence.

'Hi, all of you in there! You can come out now – they've gone. Everyone's left the house!'

A frantic joy took possession of us. We burst out into shrieks and exclamations. The lawyer hopped about on one leg, yelling at the top of his voice:

'The Germans have gone! We're saved!'

It was he who rejoiced the most at this meagre hope of life: this man who was already eighty. . . .

Mr. Radnai's lips were still blue with fear but already he was affirming in a confident voice:

'I knew for certain that they were going to leave. You know, I have presentiments about that kind of thing.'

But no one paid any attention to him.

We staggered out into the courtyard. It was beginning to be

daylight and somewhere over in the east the sun was climbing towards the edge of the horizon to bathe the ruined city of Budapest in its rays.

The courtyard was full of machine-guns and arms of various kinds and littered with ammunition and empty cartridge-cases. In front of the street door lay a German soldier's cap and two cases of unused shells yawned open beside the deserted little cannon.

In this strange, murky glimmer, things no longer had any real existence: the courtyard, the street, the whole town, all blurred in a light that seemed to belong to another world, looked like a landscape on the moon. Everywhere there lay abandoned weapons. Opposite us, a house had collapsed on its inhabitants. Death had overtaken them in the course of the hideous struggle against suffocation. Over there, on the right, was the fragment of a fourth storey where a piano only stayed in place, thanks to a few bricks; of the neighbouring room, which must have been a bathroom, nothing remained but a wall with a towel-rail.

Everywhere, as far as the eye could see, ruins, ruins, and still more ruins.

In front of the confectioner's on the corner, lay the corpses of the three horses we had brought out from under the staircase. The sweetish smell of putrefaction assaulted our nostrils from all sides. We did not then know that the atmosphere of the town would be impregnated with this loathsome stench for many long weeks to come.

But wherever had the Germans gone to? One might have thought that they had evacuated the street. . . . But that was surely impossible. . . . Why was there this silence? Terror came over us. The silence became more and more oppressive. The banker's widow was of the opinion that the Russians must be here already because they had been holding the neighbouring quarter for the past three months. But where were they, then?

This uncertainty was appalling! We had the impression of watchful presences behind the walls, behind the ruins, even behind the corpses of the horses. The Russians must be very

46

close, perhaps even in the next building. Or did they think the Germans were still in our house and were they preparing a fresh assault?

A panic fear made us beat a retreat, first under the porch and then into the rooms on the ground floor.

After a quarter of an hour of anguished waiting, Ilus ran up, gasping for breath, and announced that they had just found a wounded German under the stairs. We rushed to the place. And there, indeed, in the space behind the great marble staircase, where in the old days, they used to keep the children's prams, a young soldier lay prone in a pool of blood.

'It only needed this,' exclaimed Mr. Radnai. If the Russians find us here, we shall all be executed.'

In a few moments, we were all standing round the wounded man who was losing quantities of blood.

'We ought to do something for him,' suggested Ilus in a hesitating voice. 'I'll go and get something to make a bandage with.'

'Don't be in such a hurry,' replied Mr. Radnai. 'This man would have had no scruples about letting us die like dogs in our cellar. And, if the Russians find out that we've given medical aid to a German, heaven help us!'

The lawyer had arrived on the scene, leaning on his wife.

'Gentlemen, we must dress this soldier's wounds. The Russians themselves would not act otherwise. First-aid to the wounded is a duty according to all the international conventions.'

The Doctor shrugged his shoulders and mumbled:

'The old man's talking through his hat. Where is any international convention respected these days? What's our beautiful city been turned into? A heap of stinking filth, with thousands of corpses left to rot.'

The banker's widow exclaimed impatiently:

'For goodness' sake, make up your minds one way or the other! The Russians may be here any moment now and you do nothing but argue. Personally, I'm getting out of this – I've seen nothing and I've heard nothing!'

47

The soldier had laboriously raised himself on his elbow and kept turning his eyes, dim with weakness and pain, towards whichever person was speaking. His gaze fastened on our lips, as if he had been deaf: he did not understand a word of Hungarian and fever made the trend of our discussion even more impossible to grasp. Nevertheless, he knew that it was being decided whether he should live or die.

His gaze became so embarrassing that soon we relapsed into complete silence – a silence that was like a thick fog muffling all sense of reality.

I no longer had the will-power to avert my eyes from that blood which seeped faster and faster through the torn uniform.

Suddenly, I had the impression that the ruins above our heads vanished and that, from the height of heaven, God was watching us to see how we were going to pass through this perilous ordeal, almost like death itself. In such an extremity, were we going to be capable of seeing nothing but a uniform and of letting a human life ooze away, drop by drop, under our very eyes? I was convinced that God was looking down at us with pity and that it was the impact of His look that made the Doctor shake himself abruptly.

'I'll go and get some bandages,' he said in a hoarse voice.

He came back a few moments later and applied dressing and bandages with quick, expert movements.

'He's severely wounded on the hip,' he told us. 'He won't last long. He must be in atrocious pain.'

Chapter Nine

THE PASTRY COOK who lived in the house next door slipped into our building. We received him as if he were a visitor from another planet.

'The Germans have abandoned the street,' he announced. 'One of them told me in confidence that they were expecting the attack and that they had abandoned their wounded because they foresaw a desperate battle. The road you have to take to go and fetch water is open at the moment but there's something far more interesting – the Germans have piled up any amount of valuable stuff in the building of the Law Courts. The doors have been forced and everyone can go and carry off anything he wants to!'

'We shall go and fetch water,' said my father gently, 'because that's an absolute necessity. The rest doesn't interest us . . . we haven't turned into thieves.'

'Thieves?' exclaimed the banker's widow, stung to the quick. 'Don't you think that's rather too strong an expression, Professor? Really, I do think, that, after spending three months in such conditions, we're entitled to look for some compensation!'

My father made no reply and we went off to fill our pails. Under the porches, bearded, yellow, filthy creatures stared at us, then ventured out into the open in greater and greater numbers. It was as if the cave-dwellers were assembling in a feast-day procession; a multitude, armed with empty sacks, marched forwards, over the mines and the corpses, in the direction of the Law Courts.

In the neighbourhood of the Baths, the sweetish stench of

putrefying corpses was so strong that it made me vomit and I had to stay outside. My parents managed to go right into the building by stopping their noses with their handkerchiefs. I was uneasy and terrified at the thought that they would have to cross the plank over the dead man.

And, as I was standing there, leaning against the wall, I saw a little old woman go into a stationer's shop through the shop front that had been blasted by an explosion. I watched her, fascinated, while she made her choice among the piled-up merchandise, like a fastidious customer. When my parents returned, she emerged with her arms loaded with innumerable rolls of toilet-paper and of Cellophane for covering jam pots. She disappeared behind a doorway, wearing a contented expression, exactly like someone who had just made an important purchase to their complete satisfaction.

One after the other, people were coming back from the Law Courts, bent under the weight of their loads. When they reached the narrow lane that gave on to the quays of the Danube, they flung themselves flat on the ground, as if obeying an order, and continued their way home, crawling on all fours.

We stared, dumbfounded, at the Public Prosecutor who in the old days, had only appeared at the most solemn trials, dragging himself along the ground, almost crushed under a heavy carpet. After him came Ilus, with a blue fox fur round her neck and a bundle in her hand. The banker's wife carried a violin case and a large bird-cage. Mr. Radnai brought up the rear, bowed under the weight of three rolls of Oriental rugs.

It was an interminable procession of ants pulling or dragging the most diverse objects. They advanced with difficulty among the dead bodies and, under their feet, the empty cartridge cases heaped up like dead leaves in autumn forests.

The sun began to shine. Its melancholy rays groped feebly among the ruins of the dead town and this March sunlight made the city a more ghastly sight than ever.

'There's every likelihood of epidemics,' observed my father.

We were thinking of the shelters dug out in the rocks under the royal palace where typhus had been raging for nearly a month.

The courtyard had taken on the aspect of a fair. The Colonel's wife had five Leica cameras hanging by straps on one arm. She was commenting at the top of her voice on the value of her find. Mr. Radnai was stroking his carpets like a merchant in an Oriental market.

'They're genuine Persians, I'm an expert in that line.'

Then a long argument arose between him and the Public Prosecutor for the latter was trying to prove that his own carpet was more valuable.

Ilus had brought back a sack full of silk stockings, and, in the kindness of her heart, proceeded to share them out. My mother forbade me to accept any and, at that, what with my trousers and my cropped, burnt-off hair, I felt betrayed and deserted. Who would have thought that it was precisely the fact of looking like a thin, lean-flanked little boy that was going to save me?

Towards midday, our companions were still busy arranging their various treasures when the silence, that was so alarming and lugubrious, was suddenly disturbed from outside. We rushed to the street door and saw the Russians arriving.

They were advancing in disorderly ranks, taking up the whole width of the street, holding their weapons in front of them, ready to aim. Their yellow great-coats were dirty and ragged. At each house, a group of soldiers detached itself from the main body. This human deluge swept closer and closer and, at last, a detachment entered our courtyard. The one in command, a Mongol with slanting eyes, yelled out to us, asking whether there were any Germans in the house. Several of us nodded our heads in the direction of the staircase.

The German was killed on the spot and Ilus, whom they had found by the wounded man, was violated beside the still-warm body.

From the first moment, we realised that what was happening

51

was very different from what we had hoped. Everything, from now on, was to be one long nightmare, made up of atrocities. Like an apocalyptic deluge, sweeping all before it, fresh tidal waves of soldiers kept invading the houses. An order from high up had forbidden anyone to bury the German dead: the corpses of the soldiers killed in the fighting, along with those of the prisoners massacred point-blank, were thrown out into the streets.

Chapter Ten

THAT NIGHT, SOMEONE knocked on our door. We listened, rigid with terror. The thought that it could not be the Russians reassured us a little for they did not knock before entering.

But whoever could be there? Mr. Radnai went to open it and surprise made him recoil a few steps. Three Germans entered. . . . Our faces were as white as if we had seen three ghosts. They were the soldiers who had wanted to blow up the house on account of their stolen provisions.

'What do you want of us?' gasped the restaurant keeper in a voice that sounded like a death rattle.

The Captain answered tonelessly:

'We don't want anything more at the moment, we simply want to ask you for something – civilian clothes. It's our one, very faint hope of being able to get out of all this. . . . If they find us in uniform, we shall suffer the same fate as the others, in front of these very houses. . . .'

It was the moment in which each one of us was able to estimate exactly how far Christian teaching had influenced his or her thoughts and actions, and also to estimate whether he or she could lay claim to any human dignity. We were face to face with the enemies who had destroyed our capital, with those responsible for all these ruins and for the fury of the Russians. But, here and now, there they stood, hesitant and anguished. They must have families somewhere in Germany; children, a wife, parents. All of those must undoubtedly be praying to see them again . . . for every soldier has someone who is waiting for his return . . . and everyone acts according to the orders of his superiors. . . .

We must all have had the same thoughts, for after a moment or two, we acted on a common impulse. The caretaker brought out a suit from his cupboard.

'It belonged to my son,' he muttered.

Timidly, looks were turned towards Mr. Radnai. He was wearing his yellow star these days. He was the one who had the heaviest reckoning against the Germans and now his word might have considerable weight with the Russians: a single denunciation might bring us to the gallows.

'I am a Jew,' he said in an icy voice. 'My entire family was deported. . . .'

At that, there was a silence. Only the bellowings of some Russian soldiers reached our ears.

'But, to prove to you that there still exists some human feeling, I will let you get away. . . .'

He turned away and, in a few seconds, we found enough clothes to fit out the Germans, who left the house, keeping close against the walls, with the little bundles, containing their uniforms, under their arms.

That night, the noise of the battle that was raging in the distance did not let us sleep.

The next day we learnt that some of the dispersed Germans had regrouped themselves and had attempted a counter-attack. They had been massacred to the last man.

The house was topsy-turvy for, every other minute, Russians kept coming in and going out. So Ilus decided to attempt to cross the Danube and rejoin her family. We went with her as far as the quay. There, where, in the old days, the most sumptuous houses in the town had stood, there was nothing left now but a pile of débris; the dirty grey river, cluttered up with the gigantic ironwork of the blown-up bridges where blocks of ice were still piling up, had completely flooded the wharves.

On the quays, Russian soldiers were demanding an astronomical fee for taking passengers over to the other side of the river in boats they had stolen. Ilus came to an understanding with one of them by giving him her wristwatch and an alarm clock. Along with the child and the soldier she installed herself in the rowing boat and they moved away from the bank. We followed them with our eyes. When the boat, with immense difficulty, had got as far as the swirling eddies in midstream, we noticed some Russian soldiers on the other bank gesticulating with all their might and firing into the air to attract attention.

No one understood the reason for their behaviour and the boat pursued its course. It had just grazed a pile of the fallen bridge when a tremendous detonation was heard. We were all shaken by the explosion. The boat, Ilus, the child and the Russian had disappeared for ever under the waves.

It was thus that we learnt that, to prevent the entire city being flooded, they were unblocking the course of the Danube by blowing up the piles of the bridges. Profoundly distressed, but dry-eyed, we remained where we were, petrified, until the soldiers came and drove us away.

With our hearts in mourning, we returned home, if one could still pretend that the mass of ruins, where the German soldier lay rotting under the staircase, was really a 'home'.

Everywhere, along the street, the corpses fastened their glassy eyes upon the living. The stench was becoming unbearable. My parents decided, at this point, to leave Budapest as soon as circumstances permitted and to go to our house in the country.

The night was barely closing in when the Russians arrived. They had come to requisition men for forced labour. My father had, just that moment, gone off to fetch water. Mr. Radnai made a negative sign with his head.

'I'm not going,' he said in Russian (he knew a few words of it).

We could not understand any of the conversation, only the tones and gestures. The Russian began to shout. Mr. Radnai replied in a calm voice. Finally, the soldier, red with rage, drew his revolver and emptied it to the last bullet into the stomach of our companion.

Never, never shall I be able to forget the expression on his face. His features reflected astonishment, terror and rage. He wanted to say something more but, when he opened his mouth nothing came out of it but a thick trickle of blood. He collapsed at our feet and his yellow star was stained with his blood.

The others went off to their forced labour without making the least objection and, when we bent over Mr. Radnai, he was already dead.

Chapter Eleven

BEFORE LEAVING BUDAPEST, we wanted to pay a visit to the friends who were installed in our villa in the Hüvösvölgy. Our mouths watered at the thought of all the food we had accumulated there and we told ourselves that, after two months, we would at last be able to eat our fill. The only risk was walking through the town. The Russians might requisition you at any moment for forced labour, and, once caught, it was difficult to get away again.

Finally, my father and I decided to make the venture. The two months of the siege of Budapest had left their mark on my father; he walked slightly bent now. As he had let his beard grow, there was something piteous about his appearance which was just as well nowadays. He armed himself with two empty buckets and we made a few rents in his jacket; like that, he would not strike a discordant note among the ruins and would fit in with the exigencies of the new régime. My mother arranged my hair like a boy's, someone found me a pair of spectacles and, for still more security, my right arm was put in a sling to make it look as if I were wounded. Thus arrayed, we set off, trusting in Providence.

Passing through Bem Street we reached the Margit Boulevard, floundering in the filth and the innumerable cartridge cases up to our knees. Russian soldiers were loitering all along the pavements. At a certain spot, they had rounded up the passers-by who had been stopped indiscriminately to be pressed into the forced-labour gangs. They let us pass without disturbing us. What use could an old man armed with pails and a wounded boy be in sweeping up the ruins? Our way ran past a big cinema; they were just bringing out some dead horses. On the outskirts of the Szena-ter, there were a great many dead German soldiers. It was here they had attempted a breakthrough, two days earlier. They had all been mown down; the tramlines were running with their blood.

Suddenly, my foot stepped on something flabby. It was a human arm. Torn from its trunk, it still wore the German uniform; a wedding ring glittered on one finger. My teeth chattered with horror. From that moment on, I walked with my eyes riveted to the ground. Near the Budagyongye tram stop, a soldier lay on his stomach, with his arms outstretched, like someone crucified. Near his inert right hand, the ground was strewn with photographs.

Had he, in his last agony, attempted to send some last message to his family by fixing his gaze on their features? It was as if, at the Budagyongye stop, he had been waiting for the arrival of some celestial, redeeming tram. . . . His soul seemed already very far away from that body abandoned on the pavement.

There were far fewer ruins in the quarter we were now passing through; these residential streets had been very quickly occupied by the Russians. It was from here that we had had to retrace our steps, two months ago. Two months which seemed to us, in reality, to have been twenty years.

As we drew nearer to the villa, the streets became more and more familiar. Dear Lord, if only the house were still intact! . . . If there were some of our provisions left, our worries would be over. And, besides, there were our relatives, those good friends who must have gone through so much anxiety on our behalf. It must be midday; we were positively giddy with hunger.

At last we came within sight of the house. What a relief! The bombardments had spared it. We went through the garden gate. On the terrace there were some tables and chairs. We advanced into the hall. The sound of voices reached us from the distance. Like blind people, we followed the voices which guided us to the kitchen. Our friends were all there; they were eating. They were eating round a properly laid table; a delicious smell wafted through the room. Aunt Julia, a tall, stout lady, froze stiff at the sight of us; the soup slopped out of her spoon. She challenged us in a hoarse, peremptory voice:

'What, you aren't dead, all the lot of you?'

'We're still alive,' I answered shyly, as if apologising.

It took them all some time to recover from their stupefaction but eventually they offered us seats at the table.

'Would you like something to eat, darling?' inquired Aunt Julia, and the word 'darling' fell from her lips like a muffled curse. She resented our being alive. She had grown comfortably accustomed to the idea of our being dead – perhaps she had even regretted us a little – and now she was angry at having mourned for nothing.

'We used to watch the bombings of the Danube quayside from the terrace,' said one of the boys, his lips all smeared with grease.

'They used to watch from the terrace,' I thought, and the mouthful of soup suddenly turned bitter as gall. My father said nothing.

Later on, when we were discussing the two months of famine endured in the cellar, he remarked:

'We'll take away a few provisions.'

'Provisions?' Aunt Julia blazed up at the suggestion. 'My dear man, I don't see how that's going to be possible, we've absolutely nothing left. We've used up practically all the food there was. . . . We needed a great deal for my big family – after all, you can't ration young people too strictly just when they're growing fastest. . . . Considering we'd been refugees since Kolozsvar, our own provisions had almost run out. . . .'

Without a word, we got up and proceeded to inspect the other rooms. The beds were made up with sheets embroidered with our initials and covered with our blankets. . . .

'We are saving our own,' explained Aunt Julia, fussing round us. 'After all, my dear, we thought you were all dead and didn't need anything any more. . . .'

'Except a coffin,' added my father drily.

'There isn't very much left of your silver,' the dear lady explained to us. 'The contents of your cases went down every time the Russians visited us. They've removed nearly all of it.'

We packed up what remained. Barely six pounds of flour was left out of two great sackfuls. But there was still a little sugar and a few tins of food. Tonight we would prepare a real feast.

We set off on our way home with empty hearts and weary bodies. A blazing sun darted its rays over the dead city that stretched out ahead of us. We almost shuddered at becoming aware of the eternal renewal of spring. Green shoots were already sprouting up, here between the fingers of a corpse, there pushing apart the thickly strewn cartridge cases with the frail but indomitable energy of grass blades.

The behaviour of our friends fitted in perfectly with the spectacle that the capital presented these days. It was neither repulsive nor inconceivable. All notions of morality had been completely turned upside down in this ruined city. Vice counted as virtue and hard hearts had more chances of surviving than soft ones.

A lorry overtook us, loaded with men dressed in leather jackets and armed with tommy-guns. Their vehicle only registered an imperceptible jolt as it ran over a corpse. Phantom-like creatures passed us on the pavement; they were all in disguise as if we were, all of us, protagonists in some Shakespearian drama – outlaws living on the margin of the normal world.

The tenants of our bombed house in Buda were anxiously watching out for our return. They told us they had seen quite a number of Russian women in uniform in the streets. These shook their heads in commiseration and declared that Budapest was now in a more lamentable state than Stalingrad. We had already seen some of these Russian women soldiers. They wore big rubber brassières and were heavily built, with legs like pillars. By way of compensation, they were probably hefty enough to lift a tank on their shoulders.

Life became more and more difficult; every single day raised a fresh problem. The bomb that had gone through my piano was

60

still embedded in the parquet floor and no one dared to touch it. The library no longer possessed either doors or windows; the draught blew in, lifting the manuscripts and scattering stray pages. In the drawing-room, the Russian soldiers had soiled the armchairs. We left everything as it was. There was no means of reinstalling ourselves. Everywhere was the same, whether in the most intimate recesses of our own flat or out in the open street; everything was littered with rubble and excrement. So we decided to leave Budapest and take up residence in our little country villa in Transdanubia.

As there were no longer any trains running on this side of the Danube, we should have to begin by getting over to Pest and then cross the river again at a point lower down. The Germans had blown up all the bridges but, at the railway station, they assured us that a floating bridge had been thrown across the river at Baja, downstream from the capital.

At the station of Soroksar, we succeeded in slipping into a cattle truck. We cleaned up the heap of dried dung as best we could and waited patiently. A crowd of about three thousand people had been sharing our wait since the morning. Towards eleven o'clock at night, it became evident that there was going to be no departure. Our teeth chattered in the chill night air and hunger gnawed at our entrails. The crowd hurled itself in a mass assault on the little village to find shelter for the night there. Seized with panic, the peasants barricaded themselves into their houses and shouted out of the windows that they had not anything left either, that the enemies had carried off everything down to their pillows. Nevertheless, a kindly carpenter took pity on us and we installed ourselves in his workshop. We stretched ourselves out on a bed of shavings. At dawn, we quenched our thirst at his well before returning to the station.

That day, the Russians made us get into another train from the one of the day before. We asked a railway employee if he knew what they were going to do with us and whether we should eventually depart.

He shrugged his shoulders.

'I haven't the least idea!'

Meanwhile, our truck had become filled to bursting with Russian soldiers and Russian women.

'That's a good sign,' said a white-faced man who was carrying a small child in a haversack. 'If the Russians get on board, the train will probably leave.'

'Who's going to defend me if they attack me tonight?' whimpered an old woman.

The man stared at her.

'Don't be frightened, good little mother, you're well past the dangerous age. . . . As a matter of fact, how old *are* you?'

'Seventy-three,' replied the old woman. 'Last week, five soldiers made use of my body, one after the other. . . .'

The man was silent. He could find no retort to *that*.

A young woman and her four children, a heavily made-up female of uncertain age and an old gentleman with a beard were travelling with us. We squeezed together into a corner of the truck to leave as much room as possible for the soldiers and to escape their attention. The crowded train waited a few more hours, then, after a sudden violent jolt, began slowly to move.

There was a commotion among the people who remained in the station. Some of them attempted a last-moment assault, screaming and clutching on to door handles or anything that stuck out from the coaches.

The train was moving out slowly and would soon be alongside a loading-platform that was very close to the track. All at once, a man detached himself from the crowd and jumped on to the step of a coach reserved for the Russian army and which was travelling empty, with its doors locked. The man frantically shook the handle of the door that gave access to it, his face convulsed with the effort, but all in vain. Suddenly the crowd began to yell like one man; the loading platform was so close to the rails that anyone standing on a carriage step would inevitably be swept off.

The man, struggling with the door, did not notice the danger. The cement wall caught him and sent him spinning against the side of the coach. The crowd stood paralysed, in a horrified silence. Above the metallic rattle of the train, one could distinctly hear the sinister cracking of crushed bones. With his face purple and swollen and blood spurting in rushes from his mouth, the human top lifted himself up, then fell back again, giving us the hope that, at last, he was going to fall to the ground. But the wall would not let him go and continued to mangle him for another dozen or more yards.

A great shout of pain and rebellion arose from the group of onlookers. With their clenched fists raised to heaven, people were screaming out curses: 'God, God, how can You allow a human being to be mangled like that by stone?' Some Russian soldiers, leaning out of one of the compartments, tried vainly to pull the victim up to them. The women sobbed and wrung their hands; tears ran down the faces of the hardened men; a Russian soldier covered his eyes and shot into the air as if to attract the attention of some divine power. At that moment, there were no longer victors and vanquished; the cruel fate of one nameless Hungarian had aroused the same feelings of pity and horror in both. When he reached the end of the loading platform, the mangled man, unconscious now, dropped beside the track like a yellow, bloodstained rag. The train moved round a curve and we were left numb and shattered by this tragic sight.

The convoy proceeded on its way at a speed of eighteen or twenty miles an hour. Those who were installed on the roofs of the coaches roasted by day and shivered by night. After travelling for twenty-four hours we were all dying of hunger and thirst. The first night in that cattle truck was really an ordeal.

At one point, the Russian soldiers held out a bottle to the mother of the four children. Smiling as they did so, they threatened her with their revolvers to force her to drink.

Her little girl of about five stretched out her arm.

'Mummy, I'm thirsty too. . . .'

The mother pushed the bottle away from the child but the Russian, still pointing his revolver, ordered her:

'Give your children some, too!'

He made the three older ones drink, only letting the baby off. Naturally, it made them all drunk. The children were sick and the mother spent the night singing. For twopence, she would have begun to dance, to the huge delight of the Russian soldiers who were doubled up with laughter. No one dared to mention thirst again.

We were sitting on our haversacks in the farthest corner of the wagon. A soldier, lying full-length in front of us, had propped his shoulder on my father's foot; all night long my father did not dare withdraw it.

Dawn was welcomed with a sigh of relief. We thought of our little house in the country, that haven of peace and serenity, to which we were now drawing near. Should we find it intact or should we see nothing but a heap of ruins?

Towards midday, the news spread that the convoy was going to change its route and that, instead of going down as far as Baja, it was to switch off to the left so as to carry us off into Russia by way of Roumania. It was the pale man who launched this rumour, assuring us that the Russian soldiers on the train were going home on leave. From that moment on, everyone was racking their brains to find a means of escaping. But the train that, up to now, had crawled along as slowly as a tortoise, suddenly accelerated. The soldiers began to sing and to fire shots through the windows.

During the afternoon, we really no longer knew whether we were free travellers or deported prisoners. In the evening, the train slowed down and stopped at a little, unknown village. We besieged the Russians and implored them to let us get off so as to satisfy certain natural needs. So as not to arouse suspicions, we left all our luggage in the truck before going off into the shelter of the bushes, which were luckily thick just there. A quarter of an hour later, we heard shouts and rifle shots let off to warn us the train was leaving. But not one of us went back to it.

To this very day, I still do not know if our fears were well founded or not. All the same, it was better not to risk finding ourselves in a Siberian internment camp at the end of the journey.

After a brief consultation, our whole group of refugees continued its journey on foot. A peasant informed us that it was about thirty-six miles to Baja.

It took us three days to get there. The first night, a peasant took us into his house; the other two, we were put up in stables. For food we had some bread and some milk. About seven in the evening, we arrived at the station in Baja. A railwayman told us what possibilities there were of crossing the Danube.

'There's a Bulgarian military train leaving the station in half an hour. It's transporting guns on flat trucks. Perhaps you could climb on to it. It's your only chance – the pontoon bridge is only allowed to be used by army convoys.'

Thanking our informant, we examined the train standing in the station. It was an impressive sight, for it seemed impossible that the wheels could support the weight of the huge cannons. A Bulgarian soldier, rifle in hand, was pacing up and down the platform. My father explained to him in German that it had taken us five days to accomplish a journey which would normally have taken five hours and that, if we could not get back to our house on the other side of the river, we were lost; we had no longer sufficient money or sufficient strength left to retrace our laborious road in the opposite direction.

The Bulgarian understood and thought things over for a considerable time. He was an undersized youth who could not have been more than twenty at the most. But his back was already slightly bent, as if under the excessive weight that destiny had imposed on his generation.

He looked at us again, this time very attentively, and signed to us to climb up on to the convoy.

'How much do I owe you for that?' inquired my father.

'Nothing,' he said quietly, and he helped my mother and myself to hoist ourselves up on to the truck. 'Whatever happens, keep calm. I'll fix things with my mates.'

Seated on a gun carriage, we proceeded, once again, to wait.

Some twenty minutes later, fifteen Bulgarian soldiers joined us and laid themselves down on the wooden floor without taking any notice of our presence.

The convoy moved off. It soon reached the bridge. But could it be called a bridge, this assembly of planks which seemed absurdly fragile and whose width practically coincided with the gauge of the rails? We were convinced that our days were going to end at the bottom of the Danube, along with the cannons. The heavily loaded convoy launched itself cautiously on to the floating bridge; the greenish-blue water swirled noisily and the wind that swept down the great river tore at our hair. At that moment, the soldiers began to sing. Carried by those male voices, the melody wafted sadly through the night. All about us, the water sucked and gurgled as the train rolled slowly on, shaking a little from side to side.

That moment, which drew us all together, shivering civilians and foreign soldiers perched alike on gun carriages, two feet above the Danube in the starless night, had something about its atmosphere that was almost sublime.

It was easy to believe that this journey was taking us into eternity, strange exiles as we were, rejected by either bank. The song rose higher and higher, as if it were beating on the gates of heaven to implore admission for a handful of souls. Their bodies would remain with the cannons, buried deep in the mud.

A brief jolt, and the convoy began laboriously to climb up a slope. We had reached the farther bank.

In the morning, we thanked the soldiers and set off along the main road on the last stage of our journey. After a few brief halts, we reached the end of it after three days' walking. Our house was intact and the great lake of Balaton lay calm and blue at the foot of the green hills, as if it wanted to know nothing of the tragic events that had taken place on its banks.

Chapter Twelve

FOR THREE YEARS, we lived modestly in the shelter of our little country house. We had grown more or less accustomed to our changed circumstances. But political persecution began to rage, exterminating people all around us, as if it had been an epidemic of small-pox. We had to make the decision to stake all we had and to get across the frontier before it was too late.

The day before our departure, I set off, on my bicycle, for a village, a long way from our home, where nobody knew me. I went into the little church, all gilded by the autumn sunlight, to say a prayer there. Since then, I have visited the most beautiful cathedrals in Europe but they have never made me forget that simple little house of God. The saints, painted by some unsophisticated hand, smiled down at me from the white walls; an old peasant woman was decorating the altar with fresh flowers, muttering prayers with her toothless mouth. Kneeling down in the last bench, I noticed that the parish priest was sitting in the confessional. Why did that let loose a flood of such violent feeling? As if I had touched a live wire, a sudden jolt ran through me, reviving all my memories at once: our life in the cellar, the marriage of Eve and Gabriel, the death of our good friend, Pista. And now, tomorrow, we were going to leave our beloved refuge. Sometimes fate forces the most peaceable of citizens to assume a heroic role. Almost unconsciously, I went and knelt down inside the deal confessional.

The priest shot me a brief glance, then covered his eyes with his hand. He was still young, and very pale.

'Father,' I whispered, 'I hadn't expected to go to confession. I haven't made any preparation; I haven't thought over my sins. It's something stronger than myself that's driving me to confide in you. If you knew me, I should not tell you that tomorrow I'm leaving with my family to cross the frontier. I should be too much afraid of compromising you. But I come from a long way away and I came in here by chance. So I can tell you what we are preparing ourselves for.

'I'm terribly frightened. I pray, but it's no good. There's nothing but a great blank behind my words. Why should God listen to me? My voice is so feeble, my cries can't possibly reach Him. And besides, I've sinned, because I've cried about all sorts of tiny, insignificant, frivolous things during these last three years. While men were dying all round us, I've been resentful because, for me, there haven't ever been any dances – because I've never been able to go anywhere, dressed in white and all flushed with excitement. At night, dead people come and sit by my bed and, instead of dreams, I have horrible visions. I don't know any more whether they were nightmares or whether the dead really appeared to me to drag me down into their dreadful dark world.

'Father, I've rebelled at not having known what it's like to be young and carefree. All the happy time of my childhood has been so completely blotted out of my mind that, when I try to piece together a few scraps, it's no good. It's all blackness, all round me. There's nothing – nothing at all except misery and anxiety. If someone stops in front of our house, I imagine it's a police officer. If I hear footsteps behind me, I think I'm being followed. All that's only illusion, but it tortures me. I would so much have liked to be happy. . . .'

'I don't know who you are or where you come from. One person among a thousand. It's as if you spoke in their name . . . to all of us. If you succeed in crossing the frontier, perhaps it may be your duty to tell what has gone on in this country. But remember this: justice and charity come before everything. In any case, what happens to us here on Earth is not so important as all that, because our true life is waiting for us Beyond. I am not going to give you any penance, but I enjoin you to pray every day with a deep faith. And I absolve you in the name of the Father and of the Son and of the Holy Ghost.'

The good little old woman had finished her pious task and was praying, kneeling under the oil lamps that burnt before the altar. I went out through the church door. The sun was setting and the shadow of the cross had grown so long that it seemed to stretch into the distance and cover the whole countryside.

Night had already fallen when I reached home. It was raining and the handle of the garden gate was icy cold. The touch of it made me shiver.

'Where have you been?' my father asked, as he came to meet me.

'I went for a walk,' I answered evasively. Then I sat down on a chair, staring straight in front of me.

My father held some papers in his hand; my mother was packing clothes into a suitcase. The doors of the cupboards were wide open and, in one corner, stood a packing case, with its lid raised, half filled with books.

'When do we leave?' I asked, with a little shudder at the thought of having to go out of the house in all this pouring rain.

'Tomorrow, my child,' said my mother, in a voice that sounded to me reproachful.

I sat there, huddled up near the stove, without either the strength or the wish to stir. The warmth had made me torpid and I felt as if I had been transported into a cinema where my parents were moving about on a gigantic screen. It was incredible, the amount of things we had!

When we arrived here, three years ago, we had had to set to work like pioneers in the Far West installing themselves on virgin soil. We had nailed up the broken doors. We had collected feathers, one by one, to stuff the burst pillows; we had gathered up the kitchen utensils that had been thrown out into the garden behind the house. It was there, too, that we had found some spoons and forks buried in the earth.

The peasants had, at first, regarded us with suspicion, as if we were not human beings but ghosts who had refused to vanish after an occult séance. When they passed us, you could see that they wanted to touch us, and that, behind our backs, they were whispering, with a mixture of fear and respect, that we were survivors from the Siege of Budapest. Eventually they grew used to the idea that we were living people and they became more friendly. One day, the man who used to sell us milk, before the war, had brought us a sitting hen and some eggs.

'How you've grown, young lady!' he had told me. It had astonished me, at that moment, to realise that I had grown taller in our cellar, instead of dying.

From time to time other people arrived, also from Budapest. They were famished creatures, most of whom had made the journey on the roof of railway carriages. With their eyes starting from their sockets, they had told us atrocious stories of the consequences of the warm weather and of the misdeeds of the sun which was decomposing the corpses. We fell silent then, as if we were ashamed of no longer being able to feel terror or shock or disgust.

Sometimes I was seized by an inner fear, but this fear was purely physical. At such moments, I had nothing in common with my body.

The days that had elapsed since the Siege had cheated and betrayed me. I had left the cellar filled with ardent expectation. A child had died there. She resumed life as a grown-up person. I would have liked someone to be delighted that I still existed. But men were interested in nothing but themselves and the sun caressed my thin arms and my pale face with as much indifference as if I had been a blade of grass. Time, for me, had drifted by in contemplating the lake and in waiting for the unknown man who would love me. Nothing whatever had happened. The seasons had merely passed, one after the other. . . .

When my parents announced to me that we were going to cross the frontier, this was a new ray of hope for me. Perhaps, at last, life was really going to begin.

As I stared about me, I asked myself what I could take away

with me. Before the Siege, I had been given a beautiful silk nightdress that came right down to the ground. It was my first piece of feminine lingerie. Never yet had I worn it. I decided to take it with me.

'What will become of the dog?' I asked suddenly.

At this question, my mother stopped dead, as if I had struck her.

The dog must have realised we were talking about him, for he came out of the corner, where he had been lying up till then, and wagged his tail. He belonged to no definite breed. He was a mongrel, but he was infinitely charming and intelligent. Every single one of his movements was a study in modesty, as if he wanted to apologise for his ugliness. He was watching us attentively and seemed to be smiling. He must have been convinced we were saying very nice things about him.

Betraying a dog is even more cruel than betraying a human being for he does not know what it is all about and can only judge by tones of voice and facial expressions. If you say the nastiest things to him, but say them in a gentle voice and smile as you do so, he comes and licks your hand gratefully. I did not want to betray our poor dog.

'What will become of the dog?' I asked again in an irritable, sharp voice, so that he should realise what was threatening him. But he did not stop wagging his tail.

'We'll have to give him to the notary,' said my mother, thinking out loud. But, no sooner had the words slipped out, than she realised that this was impossible, for we could not mention our departure to anyone. So, on what pretext could we confide this poor dog to someone?

The question remained unsolved. But it never stopped haunting us through all the bustle of packing-up.

I went to the cupboard and reviewed my possessions. I had a summer dress of white hand-woven linen. I should not take that, for we were in November and it was raining. I had a dress of claret-coloured velvet, cut out of a drawing-room curtain. How else could one have had any clothes at that period? That dress

71

invariably reminded me of the curtain and I had never been able to get used to wearing it. There remained my thick pullover and the skirt I wore every day here, also my school uniform. This last had become ridiculously short and tight; it constricted my chest. I had some high-heeled shoes that I had bought for the village dance. Tomorrow, we should have to walk. I should only need the flat shoes I usually wore. Then, at the bottom of the cupboard, there lay the exercise books in which I had kept my diary of the Siege. Should I take them or leave them? I still had time to decide. A whole night in which to think it over.

But, that night, we should go to bed late. The whole family was packing its bags as conscientiously as if we were setting off on a legitimate journey. The electric light became fainter and fainter and the curtains were carefully drawn so that no one could see in from outside.

Why did everything seem to me so strange and far away? It was as if I had no connection with the minutes through which I was living. My mother's features looked more and more hollow in the lamplight. It was only then that I realised that everything she had just packed into the suitcases would have to go back into the cupboards!

I watched this final farewell to possessions. I was sorry for my parents. The road that, tomorrow, would take us into the unknown, would be a harsh ordeal for them. And for me? I felt I should have to be reborn to be able to experience any emotion at all. At the moment, I was buried in a drowsy and obstinate inertia. The dog was asleep in his corner.

'What shall I do with the alarm clock?' inquired my mother, as if incapable of making a decision. 'Ought we to take it with us, too?'

'I don't know,' I replied.

My mother was holding a little lace collar in her hand.

'This came from Brussels,' she said. 'I kept it all through the Siege. I'm not going to leave it for *them*.'

'*Do* go to bed!'

It was the voice of my father, from the neighbouring room.

But he must have known perfectly well that his injunction was quite pointless at that moment.

At last, we really did go to bed. My pillow had grown hard ever since it had known we were going to leave. It was as if it had adopted a hostile attitude. Every time I moved, my heart fluttered anxiously. I thrashed about in my bed. I sat up. Was I still alive?

The morning brought with it a sense of brutal reality. Objects recovered their ordinary shapes and colours and even words seemed to have more meaning than they had had during the night. Only everything seemed much heavier than usual. I could hardly manage to hold my cup of coffee. My mother came in from the garden where she had gone to feed the hens and rabbits. We had kept some ever since we had come to live in the country. They were a necessity. Now they were to be left to their fate.

However hard I tried, I could not swallow my bread. It was as if I had a lump in my throat that got bigger every time I attempted to eat. We had to prepare something for luncheon. A chicken, possibly, so as to leave one less behind. I was so weary that I could not manage to catch one of the volatile creatures. They escaped, with a shrill cackling. In the end I gave up; the noise they made got on my nerves.

'Shall we have a guide?' I asked, about midday, in a detached voice.

'Yes,' my father replied. 'All we have to do is to be there in time to meet him.'

'Where?'

'At the appointed place.'

'Which town? Which village?'

'Better you shouldn't know any more.'

Of course, it would so happen that one of the notary's daughters turned up during the afternoon. She behaved as if we were still living in peacetime. She had come in just to have a chat; she was gay and we fluttered round her, like puppets jigging on strings. She and I made a plan to meet again in two days' time. I took a long time deciding exactly when, for she said five o'clock and I said a quarter past. I acted as if this difference of fifteen minutes were immensely important. I looked pleased when, at last, she accepted my time.

'But, whatever you do, don't keep me waiting,' she said, laughing.

Then she told us that her father found himself 'under observation'; that, often, they were disturbed at night, just to see whether they were at home.

'We're quite used to it now,' she said, laughing again. But her laugh got on my nerves, for it rang false, and I noticed that her eyes remained serious. The nose was a neutral point between the laughing mouth and chin and the grave forehead and eyes. What would happen if I were to tell her that, a few hours, from now, we should no longer be here? This thought excited me to such a pitch that I ran out, for a moment, into the garden and held up my face to the wind, so as to cool the inner fire that was burning my cheeks. If someone had been there beside me, I would have told even a perfect stranger that, in a few hours, we were setting off to cross the frontier. I wanted to share the secret that weighed on me. The dog rubbed himself against my legs. He had followed me and was arching his back like a cat.

I went back indoors, shivering. Our guest was taking her leave. She kissed me, and insisted:

'Don't forget – the day after tomorrow at quarter-past five.'

We held our breath till we heard the creak of the garden gate.

'What luck she didn't stay longer,' my mother said, at last. And she opened the door of a cupboard as if she were going to let out someone who had been hiding in it.

My father cautiously took out his watch.

'The train leaves at six and it is now five past four. It's time to get ourselves ready.'

I rushed to fetch the clothes I was taking with me. After having put on several layers of underclothes, the nightdress, well turned up, was fastened over them with safety-pins, along with the velvet dress. Over the whole lot went my pullover and my everyday skirt. It gave me a queer feeling to walk about stuffed out like this. I knew now how a very fat woman must feel in a crowded tram on a very hot day. My parents were rigged out in the same way for we must not dream of taking any luggage. What would people say? We dared not even take a little bag of food. We certainly ought to eat something before we left but not one of us felt capable of swallowing a morsel.

The dog who, up till then, had been very agitated, now went and seated himself on the doorstep, wagging his tail and displaying his narrow gums. He seemed to be smiling in a way that meant: 'I'm the first one ready – we can go now!'

Once again, I was overcome by a feeling of loneliness. No one would say goodbye to me, no one would wait for me down by the hedge to give me a farewell kiss as he swore to be faithful to me for ever. I had no one with whom I could arrange a way of corresponding in code, no one whom I could hope to meet again, however long hence.

I stood stock-still by the cupboard. I did not cry. History is so inhuman that it does not leave the smallest loophole of escape, even for a tear. Now I was only anxious for us to get away, at last. Every single minute more spent between those walls was making me weaker. My parents were not yet completely dressed. I waited. Before this journey into the unknown, I tried to compel myself to remember things. I would like to have carried away the memory of a few faces. But there was not a single one that lived on in me and it was then that I suddenly thought of those exercise books with my diary of the Siege. I pulled them hastily out of the cupboard, and tore out the pages covered with small, cramped writing. I folded them up and divided them among my pockets.

My mother was struggling to pull her fur coat on over several layers of dresses. She too found her movements severely hindered in all those clothes. At that, some odd little devil in me asked what was the point of all this? Why on earth did we have to leave? It was a mean and malicious question. Ever since we had left the cellar, the whole family had remained numb with fear. My parents had never spoken of it to me, as if, by silence, they could screen me from fate.

'This is the last minute for making the attempt to get across,' said my father quietly. Thus, involuntarily, he put an end to an argument, which, in fact, had never been started.

I dared to suggest:

'Your look gives you away. You ought to change it, because your eyes look terrified.'

'Nonsense,' objected my mother, but without conviction. She clutched the table as if she wanted to bring it with us. The whole house took on an air of consternation. Dragged by its own weight, the cupboard door swung open of its own accord. On the table lingered a crust of bread and a glass jug half full of water.

My mother wrapped the bread up in a napkin. 'So as it won't get dry,' she said, by way of excuse. Everywhere, order reigned; a meticulous order, a lifeless order. It was as if the house were already abandoned. Yet there we still were, swollen with clothing and undecided. Anyone at all could come in now and carry on the life we had led between those four walls. But would there be anyone who would want such an existence?

As we went out, we left the electric light on. We locked the door behind us.

'Let's keep the key,' my mother suggested. 'We might still be coming back.'

'If our plans succeed, we shan't need the key any more. And, if we fail, we shan't need it any more either. . . .'

My father's voice was mild and affected, as if he were reciting this phrase for the hundredth time. Then, with a sweeping gesture, he hurled the key into the garden, invisible in the darkness. We strained our ears but we did not even hear the little clink of its fall. It was as if an invisible hand had deftly caught the key in full flight.

Every one of our movements had been minutely studied for weeks. We knew exactly what answers to give if anyone questioned us. First of all, we were to go to the station. We were only to take tickets to the next station so that the booking-office clerk could not tell anyone where we were going. At the next

76

station, my father would take tickets as far as the frontier town. If, on the train, a patrol came and asked us what we were going to do in Ovaros, we should talk about Aunt Charlotte, a distant relative who lived there and who had invited us to visit her. When we arrived at Ovaros, we should try and get off the train as inconspicuously as possible and we should go to the house of the man who slipped people over the frontier, in an outlying part of the town. He would escort us to the station of the first Austrian village on the other side. From there, we should proceed to Vienna. We had enough money to pay the guide and to buy two thousand Austrian schillings. After that, we would see what happened. Such was our plan. There was nothing to do at the moment except to take care that everything went according to plan. Otherwise we might completely lose control of events and of ourselves. . . .

We went slowly down the main road. It was only round about five o'clock but it was already dark. It was raining. The dog bounded along in front of us. He would run on, then stop and retrace his steps to make certain he had not lost us. My father walked with difficulty; he did not see well in the dark. My mother held my arm. I was perspiring. My layers of garments stifled me.

We arrived at the station.

In the distance, the train was approaching with an ever-increasing din. At last it came into the station. We climbed up the steep iron steps to the compartment. The dog made despairing leaps to follow us and had managed to hoist himself up on to the lowest step when another passenger, an elderly man who was impatient to get in, brutally kicked him off. Not in the least discouraged, the dog jumped up again, but the doors were already shut. Standing in the corridor, I could not manage to get the window down; it was jammed, or too stiff. I pulled it with all my might and I felt one of the dresses I was wearing had split. Sweat was beginning to trickle down my back and I could feel tears running down on to my chin. I leant my face against the glass so that no one should notice I was crying, and, in despair,

77

I fixed my eyes on the deserted dog, staring with blurred eyes through the misted pane.

The train was moving and the dog was barking; he began to run along the platform, beside the coach. His thin, ugly little paws carried him at breakneck speed and I had the impression that he was catching us up, that he was going to leap on to the carriage step. But he grew smaller and smaller; already he had stopped barking, he had only enough strength left to run. And, then, he was no more than a little speck. The train had left the station and was steaming along between the dark fields.

I went into the compartment. Three people were installed in it besides my parents: two men and a woman. The silence was complete: you could hear nothing but the rattle of the wheels. Before the war, these coaches had been enlivened by the chatter of the passengers. Nowadays, no one dared to enter into conversation. Any sentence might be dangerous and it was impossible to know who might not be a police spy. This silent journey had something frightening about it. I hadn't brought a book with me. I shut my eyes and leant my head against the back of the seat. The gaze of the woman sitting opposite me burnt through my closed eyelids. I decided to gaze at her in turn; it was the only means of making her turn away her head.

The ticket collector appeared. He punched our tickets without saying a word.

'How many minutes do we stop at Belatelep?' inquired my father.

'We don't stop there at all,' said the ticket collector, suddenly becoming more talkative. 'It's two days now since they cut out that stop for the evening train.'

The woman with the piercing eyes began to stare at us again with interest. This time, it was my mother who extricated us from our tricky situation. She said to my father:

'Then it would be better to go and see them on the way back from Ovaros and not to break our journey now. You could take tickets on to there, couldn't you?'

'Is it possible to extend our tickets as far as Ovaros?' inquired my father.

The ticket collector nodded his head and dug out of his pouch a block interleaved with sheets of carbon paper. How complicated it is to take one's ticket on the train! The ticket collector had to make inscriptions in three separate places but, finally, everything was arranged and my father put the tickets in his pocket. We would have liked to take off our coats but we did not dare to, for the others would see our heavily-padded shapes. There was nothing, perforce, for us to do but to remain sitting in silence, motionless with suspense.

'I don't believe it's raining any more,' said my mother, after an endless lapse of time.

My father nodded, and let his cigar ash drop on his overcoat. He promptly brushed it off with scrupulous care. The train grew emptier and emptier the nearer we approached the frontier town. The disagreeable woman began to collect her things, so did the two men. It was only then that we realised they were travelling together. They had not spoken, any more than we had. At last, we saw them get out.

My father consulted his watch.

'The train's on time,' he affirmed.

We went out into the corridor. The train slowed down and ran into the station of Ovaros. We were the only people who got out. This was far from reassuring. It was half-past nine. Having sweated in the train, we now found ourselves shivering in the wind and the moonlight. A plate-layer was running along the track, a red lantern in his hand.

'If they ask us anything . . . Aunt Charlotte!" repeated my father, and, tickets in hand, we made our way to the exit. Finally, we found ourselves together again outside the station, in an almost deserted street. Two policemen were standing on the pavement opposite. They stared at us.

'Don't turn round,' my father told me. 'Let's walk faster.'

We followed him. He knew his way. He had prepared our flight with the utmost care. We left the centre of the town and went farther and farther away from it through a maze of little, narrow, ill-lit streets. When we reached the outskirts, my father knocked on the door of a house with dark windows. The door opened almost at once and a warm, unpleasant smell assailed our nostrils. A woman ushered us in and led us into a room lit by a blinding, high-powered bulb. The curtains were meticulously drawn. I gave a hasty glance round. On a cooking-stove, that gave out an infernal heat, a saucepan exhaled a thick steam reeking of onions. A fat man was sitting at a table, busy eating. He did not even get up when we came in, but merely signed to us to sit down.

'It's off for tonight!' he said, between two spoonfuls. His chin was fleshy and I should like to have seen his eyes but he kept them greedily fixed on his soup.

'But why?' asked my father, in consternation.

The man at last decided to look at us.

'Because of the moon, of course. Shines too much. Lights up everything. Can't possibly set off like that. Anyway, I don't want to risk my skin.'

The woman put another dish down on the table. I scrutinised the face of the guide. I listened so intensely to his explanations that the meaning of the sentences escaped me. I only understood one thing; it's off. Perhaps tomorrow. . . . It was nothing to do with him: *he* had no control over the moon. Then he gave us to understand that we must go away and come back at half-past nine the next night.

'But where can we spend the night and the whole of tomorrow?' asked my father. 'We can't go to a hotel – the police would be warned at once.'

He waited for the guide to suggest our spending the night in his house. But the fleshy-chinned peasant was positive and peremptory; he had undertaken to take us across the frontier: full stop. There was no question of staying in his house; the police made too many searches and they'd been keeping their eye on him for some time. He would only make the trip once or twice again, not more. This kind of business was getting too dangerous.

His wife added in a toneless voice:

'You'd do better to go at once. Come back tomorrow night.'

We definitely had to make up our minds. But where were we to go? I was hungry.

'Could you give me a little water?' I said, in the hopes of being offered something to eat.

With a brusque movement, the woman ran some water into a thick-rimmed cup. She thrust it into my hands. I only took two mouthfuls of it. The water was warm and smelt of disinfectant.

Chapter Thirteen

A FEW MOMENTS later, we found ourselves once more in the street. It was essential to start walking at once in a definite direction, as if we knew where we were going. Strollers were suspect, and if we were asked for explanations, all was lost. So we set off with a firm, decided step, like people afraid of arriving late at the place where they are expected.

'Where are we going?' I asked, panting.

The cold air I breathed in cut like a knife.

'There may still be one possible chance,' said my father. 'But, if that does not succeed, there's no other solution for us but to take a train again and to travel until tomorrow evening. Impossible to go to a hotel, and the station waiting-room is only too often raided by the police.'

We traversed unknown streets and arrived at last in front of a church. My father went up the steps and we followed him. The heavy door was not locked. We pushed it open. In the dense shadow, the sanctuary lamp gave out a faint glimmer before the invisible altar. Utterly worn out, my mother and I sat down in the last row of benches. As to my father, he disappeared. Were we to remain sitting here till daylight? And what were we to do for the whole of the rest of the day? We could not stay in a church for twenty-four hours. I ought to pray now, but I had not the strength to. I was cold, I was hungry, I was sleepy.

My father returned and touched us on the shoulder.

'Come,' he whispered.

We followed him. We walked down the nave and went into the sacristy. It was completely dark in there. But a gleam that filtered through the crack of a door allowed us to see a priest who was standing in front of us. He shook hands with us and invited us to follow him. He told us in a low voice:

'Be very careful, I implore you, and crouch well down as you walk, the moment you get into the room we're going to. The window has no curtains and a street lamp shines in from the street. The house opposite is a police station and the policemen can see everything that goes on inside. If we were to put up a curtain, it would rouse their curiosity.'

I wished I could see this priest's features so as to judge how much charity and how much fear there was in his make-up, but he had no face. He opened the door for us and we went into the room, bending down as low as possible. The lamp in the street outside swayed in the wind and its shadow swung to and fro on the wall. We sat down on the floor.

'We can stay here till tomorrow evening,' my father told us.

'However did you manage to arrange this?' asked my mother.

But the question remained unanswered.

'We must get undressed,' said I.

'Only our coats,' replied my father.

Never had I imagined it was so difficult to take off a coat while remaining squatting on the floor. We helped each other as best we could. My father was elderly and his blood-pressure was high, but he made no complaint. Outside, the wind redoubled its violence. The street lamp shot its beam of light on to the opposite wall, sent it dancing up to the ceiling where it disappeared in a flash; then, a moment later, the whole process began again. I was seized with giddiness, as if I were on a ship. I shut my eyes but the light hurt me, even through my eyelids. A strange sensation of sea-sickness came over me. My sweat soaked clothes were stifling me and my sick uneasiness was dragging me down to the land of nightmares. I wanted to open my eyes but the luminous pendulum, that kept swinging ever faster and wider, paralysed me. Then, in the dizzy vortex of anguish and drowsiness, a mouth appeared to me: a mouth with curving lips. To whom could that mouth belong and where could I have noticed it so clearly as to be sure I had seen it before? The mouth smiled and spoke to me, but I could not hear the words it uttered.

The night of torture dragged on. One moment, we were crossing the frontier, but the oscillations of the lamp brought me back to reality. It was two o'clock in the morning. My parents were asleep. To whom had that mouth belonged? Sleep overcame me once more. I was running along a dark road. A dead man came to meet me, one of those who had lain in front of our house in Budapest. He signed to me and smiled.

'They've stolen the wedding ring off my finger,' he told me, gaily. 'I'm going to reclaim it from the thief. No doubt he'll give me back my arm too.'

I noticed then that he had lost an arm and that a flower was growing out of the wound and getting bigger every moment until it finally blotted out the dead man's face.

At last it was daylight. We recovered the dregs of our strength as a wounded man does on the battlefield when dawn revives him enough to drag himself along, crawling, towards the village.

Crawling like that, we left the room.

In the passage, we stood upright and walked along to a narrow recess where we found what we needed to make a sketchy toilet. We still had to keep all our clothes on. Soon afterwards, we found ourselves squatting once more in the room where we had spent the night. An old priest, with an impassive face, brought us some coffee. He put the cups down on the floor as if that were the natural place to put them. He said nothing and behaved as if he scarcely noticed we were there. The time passed with atrocious slowness. Heaven grant there would be no moon tónight! So far, the weather was cold and rainy. The sky was muffled and grey.

We sat motionless for hours; then, once again, it was dark. The dance of the street lamp started up once more. Six o'clock. After an interminable time of waiting, at last it was eight o'clock. I hid my face in my hands to shield my eyes from the light. I had the feeling that I was pressing my face against someone else's hand. This feeling was not new to me, but whose hand was it and when had it stroked my face before?

84

At nine o'clock, we crept out of the room. The priest was standing there in the dusk and nodded us goodbye. We went through the sacristy, then, once again, we were in the church. The wan light of the sanctuary lamp made a faint red haze before my eyes. Then we were delivered up to the night. As we made our way, we kept anxiously scanning the sky. Thick clouds were heaped up so low that they looked near enough for one to touch them.

The door of the guide's house opened at the first knock. This time, the couple were more amiable. The wife was preparing some mulled wine for us.

'Wine? At this moment?' my father asked, incredulously.

'I make everyone have some before we set off' said the guide, with a grin. 'Gives 'em strength and raises their morale. I can't undertake anything with people who are frightened. And everyone's frightened on an empty stomach, even me. So come on, let's drink.'

He emptied a great mug of steaming wine. I raised mine to my lips and tasted this liquid. It was spiced and scalding hot. But my palate soon became accustomed to it and I emptied my mug avidly and resolutely. This drink warmed up our tired and famished bodies as if new blood had been injected into them. The room suddenly looked bigger to me and the guide's face rounder.

'I've drunk it all up,' I said thickly, giving a broad grin.

I had the impression that my mouth was split to the ears and that I should never manage to be serious again.

'Well done!' said my father. His spirits had risen, too. Then, with an elegant, airy gesture, he indicated the door.

'Can we leave, now?'

The guide took another draught.

'Too much,' said my mother, uneasily. 'Too much. If you drink too much, you'll lose your way.'

'And if he does lose it? What'll happen?' I said, with my mouth wide open as if for a guffaw. I wanted to cry, but I only laughed louder than ever.

The plump little peasant seemed suddenly to make up his mind.

'We'll be off,' he said, putting on his leather coat. He kissed his wife and gave us some instructions.

'Never walk one beside the other. Always in file, as if we weren't together. If I stop, you stop. If I lie down flat, you do the same. If I run, you run.'

My father interrupted good-naturedly:

'I'm sixty, my friend. It's not easy for me to run, you know.'

The peasant turned suddenly icy.

'Anyone who's running to save his life hasn't got any age,' he said, pulling in his belt. 'On your way!'

We went out into the blackness. The guide in front, my mother next, then myself. My father came last. We kept a distance of six or eight paces between us. It was a quarter to ten. The street was deserted. Our footsteps echoed as if we were walking under an arch. Soon we left the town and found ourselves in the vineyards. They were well-tended. But how difficult it was to walk there! The earth was rough and slippery. It was very dark. The guide went forwards at a rapid pace and, at all costs, we had to follow him. My father stumbled and uttered a stifled cry. The guide growled:

'Silence.'

My father was finding it difficult, walking in the dark; he kept slipping on the clods of earth. I longed to give him my arm but, among the vines, we could only advance in Indian file. At last, we arrived at the foot of a hill. A stream flowed in front of us and the rain had begun to fall again. It protected us, for it made visibility very poor. The frontier guards could see no better than we did.

The darkness was dissipating the effects of the alcohol. I stared at my feet and I listened to the dragging sound of footsteps. I was past knowing whether I was frightened or not. The moment was something beyond my grasp; events were too overwhelming for me, and I felt as if I had been swept beyond the limits of human comprehension. I went on walking.

The guide stopped abruptly and, with a motion of his hand, gave us the order to squat down. Panting, we sat down in the wet grass. How good it was to sit down for a little! It was eleven on the luminous dial of my watch.

Was it possible we had already been walking for an hour and a half? The sweat began to chill again on my back. I was thirsty.

The guide came up to us without raising himself upright.

'I don't know if they've already gone past,' he whispered. Then he added: 'I'm frightened.'

It was more irritating than alarming to hear him say he was frightened. What must we be feeling if *he* were afraid? We lay down in the soaking grass. Not far from us ran the main road. The asphalt showed pale and smooth in the darkness. It was nameless anguish to know that we would have to cross that broad, clear gap. How much longer should we have to stay here, waiting? The distant blast of a whistle rent the silence. Some instants later, a car went by. The shape of the guide reared up again.

'They've gone,' he said. 'We can try and get across.'

'Is the road the frontier?' I asked him.

He stressed his impatience with a little shake of his head.

'Of course not. The frontier's still a long way.'

Where was the frontier? What was the frontier like? We reached the edge of the road. The cemented surface spread before our eyes as if an invisible hand were widening it in front of us.

'Run!' ordered our guide.

My parents crossed the high road as if it were a skating rink. They wanted to run but all they could do was stumble. We were in the middle. An inner force urged me to run, but I followed the pace of my parents. The guide had already been on the other side for a long time. He gesticulated and muttered oaths.

'At last!' he said, when we arrived. 'Now there's a clearing – and then the forest begins.'

The road stretched behind us like a silver ribbon. We ran through the clearing and finally reached the trees. I leant against

87

the first damp trunk and got my breath back, pressing my face against the bark.

The guide never stopped grumbling:

'This is the very last time I ever do this job with old people. It's impossible. They creep along like slugs.'

We continued on our way, plunging into dead leaves up to our ankles. It was very dark. From time to time, a wet branch brushed against my face. And it was then that, suddenly, during that crazy journey, I realised to whom that nameless mouth and that caressing hand had belonged.

To Pista. I saw him again as I had seen him one day when he had said something to me, very close by the candle. I could not remember what he had said to me but I saw his mouth again and the gleam of his splendid white teeth. And the hand had belonged to him too, that hand that had helped me cross the plank above the drowned man. It was then that he had stroked my cheek. And I had only realised it at this moment. But, yes, at this very instant he was near me. He was holding my hand.

'Lie down,' hissed the guide. 'Lie down.'

We were lying full length in the leaves but, now, I no longer felt so abandoned. Pista was there to help me to surmount these last difficulties. The guide ordered us to go on. All I heard was his authoritative voice; all I felt was the contact of the wet soil; it was so dark, I could see nothing. I could hardly hear the laboured panting of the two tortured elderly people. We walked on. We walked fast, making an agonised effort and I did not feel strong enough even to glance at my watch.

The forest was growing less dense; the guide was becoming more and more uneasy and hostile.

'You'll have to pay more. For old ones like you, I shall ask extra.'

'You shall have all you want, but get us across the frontier,' said my father, and his voice reached me from very far away. Yet he was only a couple of steps from me.

We came to a clearing then, suddenly, the moon began to shine with all its brilliance, with all its celestial coldness. Our guide started swearing again. I no longer paid the least attention to him. Water was running all down my neck, my hair was soaked and my damp clothes imprisoned me like a cuirass. The dazzling moonlight flooded the black landscape with white.

'That's the frontier,' growled the guide. 'And that infernal moon has to shine! We'll have to run. . . . Go on – run – even if it kills you!'

Why had I always believed that a frontier must, of necessity, be a material obstacle? A barrier – or a wall like the ones that border certain mountain roads. And now I saw, as I ran, stupefied, and sobbing with the effort, that the frontier was only black grass and moonlight. I walked in the light as if drenched in a bath of silver and there where it shone most intensely, there where my hand and my hair and my heart were whitest – that was where the frontier lay.

I swathed myself in those enchanted rays.

Darkness suddenly asserted itself again, after the clearing. And I heard the voice of the guide, relaxed now:

'You can sit down; we're in no man's land.'

I collapsed beside my parents. I pressed one cheek against the earth, against that earth which belonged to no one and which was mine. This was where I was at home: here where spirits met again in the luminous void that stretched between the two parts of the world.

'Let's go on,' said the man, after that brief repose.

We were treading on Austrian soil. But the station we had to reach was still a long way off. My mother took off her shoes and wrapped her feet up in her silk scarf which she had just torn in two. She walked the rest of the way like that. My father lurched along, staggering, but his courage remained unshaken.

Dawn found us in a little Austrian station. Street vendors and men in short leather breeches occupied the waiting-room. They spoke a language I did not understand. It was the first time in my life that I had been in a foreign country. If I had begun to speak, people would have looked at me with astonishment. Our guide withdrew in company with my father; when he returned, he held out his hand to us.

'You're in luck. For the present, you're safe. Your train to Vienna leaves in ten minutes.'

And, having made this farewell, he disappeared into the crowd.

Here we were, alone together once more. My mother put on her shoes again. My one craving was an inexpressible longing to drink a cup of boiling-hot coffee.

'I bought two thousand Austrian schillings from him,' explained my father. 'He let me have them at a fair rate of exchange and he's taken tickets for us as far as Vienna. A thoroughly decent fellow! I only hope he gets back without any hitch.'

I asked:

'How long will these two thousand schillings last?'

My father considered.

'About two months. At least, I hope so.'

'And, after that, what will become of us?'

'After that, we shall have to begin our life all over again. . . .'

The waiting-room was becoming more and more animated. The women loaded themselves with their big baskets and bustled out on to the platform. We, whose limbs were quite benumbed, dragged ourselves along like half-unconscious survivors of a shipwreck who struggle against the undertow and reach dry land at their last gasp.

Stiff with sleep, we managed to sit upright on the wooden benches of the little local train. A sullen ticket collector punched our tickets with complete indifference. Opposite me, a man lit his pipe with ritual care. The nauseating smell of cheap tobacco turned my stomach. It began to rain again. The landscape melted into the grey sky. In the distance, factory chimneys went by, one after another. So did ruins, and still more ruins. I had the impression that I had been in this train for years, as if fate had nailed me to this hard wooden seat and forced me to travel unceasingly past endless ruins, in the company of silent beings. I had believed that, beyond the frontier, beyond Hungary, in the countries they called Occidental, the sky would be blue and the people happy. I had thought they would surround us joyfully and that their smile of welcome would make us forget the past. But, in this train, nobody smiled at all and the tobacco smoke became thicker and thicker and more and more unbearable.

We were getting near Vienna. I looked avidly out of the window. My heart beat fast. How many times my parents had talked to me of that enchanted city, always sparkling with gaiety. The train stopped in the midst of ruins. This must be the station, since everyone was getting out. We, too, got out. The rain trickled down the charred walls and dripped off the broken gutters. In a few seconds we were soaked to the skin. The crowd swept us along with it towards the exit. My coat was getting heavier and heavier and I would like to have split through that cocoon of wretched clothes I had worn for three days without being able to take them off. Suddenly I felt the fastenings that kept up my nightdress giving way. Impossible to stop it from unrolling its full length! There I stood, with the rain running down my face on to my grey coat, whose hem showed several inches of silk nightdress. I felt impotent and ridiculous. That light blue contrasted so sharply with the dingy grey that it was beginning to attract stares. People stopped and looked at me without the faintest smile. I rushed forwards, in tears, towards a nearby hut. The nightdress hindered my running, clinging to my ankles; the muddy water soaked through my shoes and splashed my clothes. When, at last, I got under cover, I had to wait till my hands stopped trembling. At first I wanted to tear the silk that had come down at such an awkward moment, but the material resisted. It was stronger than I was. There was no other solution but to pin it up. At last I was able to rejoin my parents and we left the station. The curtain of rain blocked our view. Where, oh where, was Vienna?

We set off walking at random. Chance brought us to the door of a café. We went into it. The waiter gave one glance at us, then resumed his chat with a customer. At another table, a couple was drinking coffee. The man occasionally spoke a few words; the woman never answered.

We sat down. The waiter came up and flicked a duster over the table.

'Three coffees and something to eat,' my father said in German.

We were so utterly exhausted that we could find nothing to say to each other. We sat, motionless, looking out into the street where the wind was now making the rain swirl. A stout old lady pushed open the door and entered, carrying a very fat dachshund in her arms. That reminded me of our own dog. Perhaps he was still running despairingly in pursuit of the train and of his faith in human beings.

The waiter brought the coffee and three minute grey rolls. I bent my head over the cup and closed my eyes. I drank. The beverage was only coffee in name, but it was scalding hot and it warmed both body and heart. Already, the street seemed to me less hostile. I devoured one of the little rolls. At that moment, I caught sight of myself in a mirror opposite me and I noticed that I was smiling.

'We've succeeded,' murmured my father.

He asked for the bill and drew out from his bundle of notes, a hundred-schilling one, which he laid on the table. The waiter came up and scrutinised the note, without touching it.

'It's out of date,' he said. 'All the money you've got there was withdrawn from circulation over a year ago. It's no longer worth anything at all.'

My heart began to beat so violently that each throb gave me a sharp pain, like a wound. My mother was terrified; my father had turned pale. We stared at the schillings on the table.

The waiter took up a hostile attitude.

'D'you mean you haven't anything to pay for your drinks with?'

His voice had become shrill, like a woman's voice. The man at the next table put down his newspaper, and observed the scene, leaning on his elbows. The taciturn couple turned round, too. The woman with the dog was watching us.

My mother took off her solitary ring – her last ring, the one that never left her and that she had worn ever since her marriage on the same finger as her wedding ring. A blue spark flashed up from the diamond, like a cry of distress. My mother held out the ring to the waiter.

'This is for the coffees. We didn't know that our money wasn't good any longer.'

The waiter took the ring mistrustfully.

'It's not a false stone?'

But the diamond sparkled so brilliantly that it needed no more to convince him.

'Don't give it to him,' I implored my mother, in Hungarian.

'We must, all the same,' said my father. 'God knows what may be waiting for us if he makes a scandal. We have just arrived illegally and our papers are not in order.'

'We'll come and redeem it,' said my mother to the waiter.

The man nodded, but, from that moment, we saw that he had made up his mind never to recognise us again and, if we ever did come back, to deny everything.

He held the ring in his palm wearing a thoughtful expression. Then he gave it a little toss, caught it again, and thrust it away in his pocket.

As he cleared away the cups, he said to us:

'You've only just arrived, haven't you?'

Then he withdrew to the far end of the room.

'And now what happens?' I said, in anguish.

My parents were silent. In those five minutes, they had aged several years.

An appalling despair came over me. I wanted to burst into sobs but my eyes remained dry.

And I asked myself; in the innermost depths of my being, whether life would one day have pity on me, whether it would consent, at last, to my having an existence of my own.

. . . How good that would be – to be born.

Part Two

Chapter Fourteen

AFTER THE SIEGE of Budapest, we had nothing left. The shells had made great holes in the front wall. I could have sat on our parquet floor, once so beautifully kept, and swung my legs out into empty space. The big house, divided up into flats, where I had spent fifteen years of my life had become a public danger. When the situation in Budapest had become stabilised and there were no longer any corpses in the streets, passers-by stepped off the pavement in front of our house and gave it a wide berth so as to avoid the risk of being crushed to death if it collapsed. The walls of my bedroom were full of cracks and those great black fissures affected me like open wounds.

We had not been able to save so much as a single object. The ruined remains of our old life were covered with an obscene deposit of filth. The vast rising tide of that bloody siege had withdrawn but it seemed to have left the city dirty for ever.

My mother's aunt used to wear a rose in her hair when she was young, but no photo of her survives. The only coffin she had was a pile of bricks and a mass of splintered glass. Towards the end of the war, the house where she lived collapsed on the tenants.

My aunt – I always called her that – was sixty-five and my uncle seventy, when I myself was six. I was a late arrival and only knew my grandparents from their photographs. On All Souls' Day, I used to be frightened when my parents took me to the cemetery. The sickly smell of the chrysanthemums, the little glass lamps, with their flickering flames, that everyone carried in their hands, filled me with inexplicable terror. For nights afterwards, I used to dream of ghosts and shiver under my blankets.

At seven, it seemed to me that everyone about me was old. I used to look long and thoughtfully at my mother's crow's feet and my father's greying hair.

My uncle and aunt lived on a fairly large pension. Their flat, on the gently rising heights of Buda, was full of souvenirs of their travels. They had never had any children. I often used to spend the weekend with them. A little room was always kept ready for me. I can see my bed again now, and also a huge cupboard full of sheets, slightly yellow with age, tied up with broad red silk ribbons. Between the folds, my aunt had put lavender sachets; for a long time, my childhood dreams were impregnated with that mysterious scent.

Number 3, Rue Notre Dame; that was their address. My aunt, who always dressed in black, could never look at the plate that bore the name of the street other than with a hostile eye. She had once been deeply wounded in the confessional and, ever since, her resentment had included the entire priesthood. Very much later, I learnt that, as my uncle had been divorced, she had not been able to have a religious marriage. Carried away by the fervour of a great love, my aunt would have liked to have had the Church as an ally and so secure both earthly happiness and the blessing of Heaven. But instead of a blessing, she had been given an ultimatum and ordered to leave the man she loved.

In the hothouse of my childhood, I was, at any rate, carefully shielded from all the misfortunes that overwhelm grown-up people. My parents were kind and indulgent and, in my aunt's home, I learnt to love old people

At eight years old, I was precocious enough to feel the depth of their love for each other in their looks and their gestures. They had a maid who was perfect in every respect, but it was always my aunt who helped my uncle on with his coat when he took me out for a walk. She would wait on the balcony till we emerged below into the street and her eyes would continue to follow us as we climbed the zigzag road. My uncle had a moustache that was beautifully groomed, though a trifle yellowed by the smoke of his eternal pipes. Dressed in black and carrying an elegant cane, he would stop at the turnings and explain to me that I must pay attention and give my whole mind to it. I would listen virtuously but I was enchanted when my hoop or my ball bounded away into the road and I had to make a breathless dash to retrieve them.

The Rue Notre Dame was lined with chestnut trees. In the spring, their flowers scented the air; in the autumn, the ground was strewn with their prickly husks with the chestnuts bursting out of them.

After lunch, my uncle and aunt used to lie down: my aunt in her blue bedroom; my uncle on the sofa in the study, with his grey cape over him. During that time, curled up still and silent in my armchair, I would read Dickens. In those early afternoons, I made the acquaintance of David Copperfield and Mr. Pickwick. The maid went about three; Saturday was her free day. She would shut the front door so softly that I was the only person who heard the little click. Once I went out on to the balcony on tiptoe to watch her go. There was a soldier in front of the house. They went off together, hand-in-hand, and, suddenly, the drowsing flat seemed to me empty.

After dinner, if it was fine, my uncle and aunt would play cards on the balcony. The scarlet geraniums, with their velvety leaves, gave out a moist, peppery smell. Insects from all the nearby gardens came flocking round my aunt's opalescent glass lamp. When the old people played cards, they always spoke English. I would listen, half-asleep, to the sound of their conversation and the rustle of the cards.

On Sunday mornings, my father came to fetch me and then he and I and Mother would go to church. My aunt always shut the windows; she detested the sound of the Sunday bells. All the morning of that day, she used to play the piano. Now and then, my uncle, in his study, would hum the melody she was playing.

My aunt had a small private fortune; my uncle had nothing

but his pension. But he possessed numerous greedy relatives whose visits my aunt, who was well-born and a trifle arrogant, regarded with extreme disfavour. Another thing depressed her; my confirmed hostility to the piano. Her long, silky fingers would fly lightly over the keys of her Steinway; when she played Chopin, my uncle would seat himself in an armchair and watch her.

For my tenth birthday, they made me a present of three books. One in Hungarian; the other two in English. What a birthday luncheon that was! My aunt had made some delicious ice cream for me herself. While she and my uncle were taking their siesta, I looked at my beautiful books. As my armchair was close to my uncle's sofa, I could watch him as he slept. His large hands, dry and wrinkled as parchment, rested on his grey cape. On his right hand, he had a large wedding ring; on his left, a heavy signet. I saw, from his watch, that it was ten minutes past four. I could hear my aunt's muffled footsteps as she got the ready in the drawing-room. I knew that, in a few minutes, she would come in and wake my uncle, and we should all have tea together. It would be a specially gay tea party – and I should be able to finish the ice cream from my festive lunch. Suddenly, it struck me that, on such an important occasion as my birthday, I had a perfect right to wake my uncle up. So I slid out of my chair, and, without taking my eyes off him, touched his hand. But he was sleeping deeply, with his face turned to the wall on which hung an Oriental carpet. The water for the tea was boiling. That made me more audacious still; I lifted the hand that wore the signet ring. Warm, and incredibly heavy, it slipped out of mine and fell back, inert. My heart began to beat so violently that each beat hurt me like a stab.

'Uncle! . . . Uncle! . . .'

I must have screamed, for, the next moment, my aunt appeared in the doorway.

She had never seemed so tall and so slender as she did in that wintry twilight. I had the impression that she would never be able to enter the study. She looked at her husband and began to call him in a metallic voice:

'Darling, won't you come and have tea? . . . Tea, darling!'

A minute or two later, she sat down beside him and took the hand that had dropped from mine between her own hands.

'What have you done?' she asked. 'How could you do that to me? Why didn't you wait to say goodbye to me? . . . You promised you would never go without saying goodbye to me. . . .'

I did not dare move. But it seemed to me that my uncle's lips had parted a little, as if for a last farewell.

My aunt began to move about with jerky, feverish gestures. She went into the bedroom, brought back a blanket and spread it over my uncle. Then she tried to telephone. But her fingers were trembling so much that she could not dial the number.

'Tell your parents to come over,' she said to me. I telephoned.

While I was talking to my mother, my aunt turned on all the lights in the flat.

Suddenly, I was seized with a violent nausea. In winter, the geraniums from the balcony were kept indoors in the dining-room and their sickening smell filled the entire flat. I wanted to open a window but I could not manage to turn the handle. Why had my parents not arrived yet?

My aunt wandered from room to room muttering incoherent words about the tea and about death. The crude light left my uncle's face naked of all shadow. The face that had been animated only that morning had turned smooth and yellow before my eyes. His wrinkles had vanished and the grey moustache looked strangely incongruous on those features that now seemed ageless.

Now I could imagine that even my uncle had, once upon a time, been young.

The doorbell rang. I ran to the door and flung myself into my mother's arms. As I smelt the faint scent of her shoulder, I burst into sobs. I would have liked to stay there for ever, with my eyes shut, hidden in her arms.

So my uncle had gone away, before my eyes, into eternity. 'You must always pay attention and give your whole mind to it,' he

101

used to say. But where was the elusive soul? I wondered. Where were his thoughts? Had he been dreaming before he died? What was there he might still have wanted to explain?

When I kissed his hand, it was already cold and lay crossed over the other on his breast.

After my uncle's funeral, I received a letter from my aunt. The black-bordered sheet was covered with her round, well-balanced handwriting.

'Dearest child,' she wrote, 'I want you to know that when I too am dead, like your uncle, all my possessions will belong to you. I should like you to keep the piano in the room you will have when you are a big girl. . . .'

I often went back to see her. The table was always laid for my uncle and the bottle of choice wine set beside his place.

The piano – she never played it again – remained silent and menacing in the middle of the big drawing-room. Like a coffin.

The last time I went into our own looted flat with my parents, I found something under some soiled books whose covers had been wrenched off. It was an engraving, almost undamaged in its frame, that showed the hill of Buda as it was at the beginning of 1900. Then I ventured into our dining-room that looked out on to the Fö-utca. I noticed a nail sticking out of the wall and I hung the engraving up on it.

Before our final departure, we stood for a moment in the street and looked up at our home for the last time. Through the gutted façade we could still see the engraving hanging up almost over empty space. Suddenly a brutal, impatient wind got up, scattering the grey dust. At that, we went away, our eyes full of ashes and tears.

In the little house of Fonyod, where I lived the life of a somnambulist, my one concern was to appear the typical growing girl who soon forgets troubles. I wanted to make things easier for my parents. I used to sing about the house to give them pleasure. With my mother's help, I cut myself out a summer dress from a flowered curtain. When my father said that everything was easier for the young, I agreed with him. In exchange for a pair of sheets, I managed to procure them a she-goat. The wrinkled peasant woman who agreed to this barter taught me to milk her. The she-goat, who was old and good-natured, allowed me to.

But at night, in my bedroom, I was restored to my true self; I dropped my mask of gaiety and returned to my books. Here, in the country, we had only some works by Scandinavian writers, a few Balzacs and one single Flaubert – *Madame Bovary*. My dreams were fantastic rides through a land of nightmares. Mademoiselle Julie was for me a dubious, almost treacherous friend. Sigrid Undset soaked me in an atmosphere of resigned melancholy that I found unbearable; once, when I was ill and feverish, I believed I was Ibsen's wild duck.

Pista, that young soldier who had been killed during the siege, often reappeared to me. But I was not frightened of him. Neither of him nor of my uncle. The peaceful death of an old man was, somehow or other, connected in my mind with the brutal death of a young one who had been bold and gay.

Every morning, life began afresh. The summers stretched out, stifling and interminable; the winters were rigid under the snow.

I remember one particular day in July. I had gone down to swim. The lake of Balaton carried me on its gilded blue back. Sometimes, looking behind me, I could see the dark-green tracks ploughed up in the still water by my swimming. Human beings were so far away from me that I had the impression of being utterly alone. As I went on swimming, I raised my head, as if to discover the invisible God. Suddenly, an unexpected wave slapped against my face. And that little wet smack of sunlit water struck through me like an electric shock. All at once, I became, for the first time, aware of my own body.

In one shiver, I became aware of the very movements I was making in swimming. Clumsy and frightened, I made sure that my schoolgirl's bathing-dress covered my just-developing breasts.

Almost completely out of breath, I hurriedly turned back towards the shore. I had become heavy with exhaustion and, in a moment of inadvertence, I swallowed a great mouthful of water.

At last, feeling the pebbles under my feet, I collapsed on the shore.

I was breathing violently, almost passionately. A little later, as I climbed up to the house again, I knew that my loneliness had become intolerable.

Chapter Fifteen

MY ARRIVAL IN Vienna had produced no impression on anyone . . . . We walked through the streets, less conscious of the torrential rain than of the cruel stare of the waiter in the café which had revealed that the Austrian schillings we had bought from our guide were worthless. Mamma had left him her last ring and now, urged on by fear, we were almost running, but with no idea of our destination.

At every turning, I expected to find some man or woman, with a kind smile, who would take us by the arm, conduct us into a warm room and then, with a discreet gesture, indicate the door of the bathroom to us.

Srutinising the faces of the passers-by, I could discover nothing but dull eyes and drawn features; all those gazes seemed to me to run over us like the raindrops.

'Suppose we go back to the station?' said my father.

'And take a train? Where to?' asked my mother.

'There's a hostel for refugees there. A Station Hostel. We'll sleep there tonight and, tomorrow, I'll organise something.'

As we had no money for a tram, we returned to the station on foot. There, we had to wait for my father while he went into the little office. I can still see that ruined station. Mamma was leaning back against a peeling wall: she looked so frail and vulnerable in this hostile dusk that I emerged from my little private world of dreams and vain expectation and kissed her thin face. She looked up at me with her blue eyes and smiled.

'The beginning of a new life is always very difficult, child. . . . But we are free.'

Papa was a long time coming. I looked at my mother's swollen legs; her slender ankles were now a shapeless, painful mass of flesh. And nowhere, in all that deserted station, was there so much as a bench on which to sit down. Beside us, the door of a waiting-room swung open of its own accord, but the room had no roof to it. An occasional plate-layer, with hunched shoulders, passed by us without paying any attention. I knelt down in front of Mamma and laid my hand on one of her legs; it was burning hot.

'Are you in great pain?'

'A little. . . .'

I had to make a great effort not to doze off. I could have gone to sleep then and there at Mamma's feet. Suddenly, as if they had sprung up out of the stone platform, we were surrounded by a crowd of passengers who were waiting for a train not yet signalled. I stood up. But I would have searched in vain for the faintest glimmer of interest in their eyes. I touched my own arm and ran my dirty fingers over my face. I wondered uneasily:

'Are we still visible? Perhaps we became transparent in that chilly moonlight? Perhaps our crossing the frontier was only a dream and I shall wake up at Fonyod again? . . .'

A harsh voice shouted: '*Barisnya burzsuj!*'

A huge Russian soldier had planted himself in front of us and was already pulling at my mother's fur coat.

The Russian made a sign to another soldier, pointed to my mother and kept repeating words we did not understand.

At that moment, Papa came back and told us to follow him.

We hurried after him, trembling, for the Russians were on our heels.

'I've just discovered that we are in the Russian zone,' said my father.

We followed him, white with terror.

At last, we were able to go back into the barrack-like building.

A man with greying hair was waiting for us.

'Come this way. . . .'

The Russians remained outside.

We stumbled the whole length of a dark corridor and

eventually arrived in a big room, lit by a single electric light bulb. Then, at last, the man spoke to us:

'Of all the mad things to do! You cross the frontier illicitly and you go and gad about without papers in the Russian zone! Why didn't you go to the American zone or the French one?'

'The last time I came to Vienna – in 1926 – I stayed at the Hotel Sacher,' replied my father, his face livid with weariness. 'How can you expect me to know the zones?'

The warden of the hostel, a colourless, melancholy person, promptly began to smile. The evocation of the Vienna of other days had a magical effect on him

'Obviously! The Sacher. . . . But times have changed. . . . Stay here till tomorrow morning. . . . At eight o'clock sharp, I will take you to the frontier of the zone. There you can sort things out with the Reception Centre; it deals with refugees' papers.'

In this great wooden room, rotten with rain, there were three long tables with benches along either side; the stove in the corner was heated red-hot.

'Sit down; they'll bring you some soup and some bread. The woman who will bring it must know nothing. If she asks any questions, tell her you've missed your train and haven't enough money to go to a hotel. Above all, don't undress in the dormitory. Here, in the Russian zone, there are any number of down-and-outs. Those are our night customers. . . .'

Unexpectedly, he held out his hand.

'Good night and good luck. . . . I'll see you again tomorrow morning.'

We sat down on a bench. A few minutes later, the sweat was trickling all down our backs. Mamma and I were wearing at least three dresses apiece and Papa had five shirts on. For three days, we had never had a chance of undressing.

'At least, let us take off our coats,' suggested Papa.

'No. The woman who brings the soup will see at once that we are wearing an abnormal amount of clothes.'

So we waited, continuing to perspire.

She soon arrived. She was in her forties. Her greasy chignon

107

clung to the nape of her neck like a bird's nest. She set a battered tray and three bowls of lentil soup before us, examining us with curiosity she did so.

'Bread as well?' she asked.

Mamma nodded her head without saying a word.

The woman brought three pieces of bread.

With her shoulders drooped and her gaze riveted on us, she sat down beside the stove. I expected to see her melt in that heat like a candle. As I ate my warm soup, I had the crazy idea that, if I had a long arm and an extinguisher at the end of it, I could put her out! I returned her stare insolently. When the soup was finished, a grey deposit remained at the bottom of our bowls. The bread stuck to one's palate and tasted of clay. When the woman saw that we had really finished with our spoons, she beckoned to us to follow her.

Stuffed out with clothes under our heavy coats and stiff as scarecrows, we filed out after her.

At the door of the dormitory she left us and was swallowed up in dark corridors. The atmosphere of the dormitory was thick and smelt as if stuffed with garlic; a blue light hovered in a corner, filtering through a sort of fog. Those feeble rays from a single bulb dimly lit up heaps of dark rags. These were the sleepers, wrapped in their verminous overcoats. This vast twenty-fifth class sleeping compartment possessed two rows of bunks. In the twilight, the top row seemed to me almost entirely empty; the passengers were clustered together in the lower one. We stepped forwards cautiously but every breath made us swallow a mouthful of that stinking air that tasted like mud.

After occasionally knocking ourselves against the wooden scaffolding we finally found two empty places in the lower tier and one in the upper.

Mamma took off her coat and sat down on the edge of one of the beds. Papa stood there, his hat in his hand, completely bewildered. He was amazed that we should be free yet shocked and disillusioned, in spite of himself, by all these sordid details. Eventually, he lay down in the lower tier and I climbed up to the place in the upper one.

Our moving about had caused trouble among the sleepers. I could hear muffled voices. Over the edge of my extremely uncomfortable nest, I suddenly saw the face of a bearded man looking up at me from below. His eyes glittered in the blue dusk; he was like an animal looking hungrily at a piece of meat. I drew back quickly and heaped the rough blankets over me. They smelt of suet; a cold, degraded wartime smell.

My skin was itching. I had the feeling of being devoured by a multitude of greedy, famished insects. I even thought I could feel the pricking of two sharp pincers on my knee. I felt about, with nervous disgust, but could find nothing.

All night long I was the prey of those imaginary insects. I economised my breath and only drew in tiny, prudent sips of air.

When we woke up, the dormitory was already empty. Heavy and drowsy from our suffocating night, we spoke very little.

In the big room, they gave us some more lentil soup; then the little man with the greying hair reappeared. His face was fresh and clean. He still had a dab of shaving cream under one ear.

He gave my father an extremely useful address.

He spoke of his aunt who had a house in the American zone and who let rooms to refugees who had no papers but who were trustworthy.

The little man then took us to the limit of the Russian zone. It was a little street like any other; the cool morning wind had dried its pavements. Under the plate bearing the street's name was a placard: 'Beginning of the American Zone'.

Papa said goodbye to him; we all shook hands with him and he went away.

'He's a good sort,' said Papa. 'Yesterday, when I told him about all our bad luck, he lent me twenty schillings. Now we can go somewhere and have a hot drink in peace.'

We went into a café in the Burgstrasse, the proprietress was still in process of sprinkling water on the dusty floor and sweeping it. Nevertheless she made us sit down and, a few minutes later, brought us the coffee.

I was delighted to know that we had twenty schillings.

'I'll leave you two here,' said Papa. 'I'll go to the Refugees' Reception Centre on my own.'

I went out with him and he brought me a morning paper. Then I returned to Mamma. We were both prepared for a long wait. Before I had said goodbye to my father, a vague idea had occurred to me.

'How could he possibly have lent you money?' I asked him. 'Was he so sure that you would come back.'

Papa had frowned a little.

'Of course he was sure, since he had my promise. And, besides, I showed him all our schillings. He was horrified at our situation that we would not be able to use them. He has kept them. He is going to a bank to see whether he can get something for them. He might be able to, as he is Austrian. Of his own accord, he gave me twenty new schillings for these two thousand out-of-date ones.'

I felt a rush of warmth and affection as I looked at my dear Papa who was so honest, so bound by the rules of a peaceful, bourgeois society that he was quite incapable of wondering, even for one second, whether this distinguished down-and-out might not have cheated him.

Mamma and I read the paper. The proprietress of the café was very friendly. Mamma told her that we had crossed the frontier two days ago. She could speak freely; we were in the American zone. The good woman brought us four slices of bread on which she had spread a little margarine – so little, you could hardly see it.

At a quarter to twelve Papa returned. We went off together to the Kleeblattgasse. At last, we were able to take a tram. Sitting just behind the driver, I saw my face, for the first time for three days, in his driving mirror. I was incredibly ugly and my tears during the night had turned me into an Indian squaw, rather pale, but decidedly warlike. A tall, fair, very young man was sitting beside me. His presence seemed to me like a challenge to death. I had seen so many dead young men in the streets of Budapest! I was already imagining him lying stiff and still in a

110

ragged uniform when he gave me a shy, friendly, almost frightened smile. Yes, he was alive, and so was I! But why was he smiling? Because I was ridiculous, unhappy, untidy and as heavy as a tortoise in my carapace of clothes? Or perhaps because I was twenty? I smiled too and turned my head towards the driving-mirror where I could see myself smiling. I wanted to say good morning to myself, too.

'We get off at the next stop,' said Papa.

Almost as soon as we stood on the pavement, we were struck by the sunshine and the blue of the sky. It was a little depressed, that sun, intimidated by the month of November. But its feeble rays were glimmering on a strange world – a living world.

Vienna was at last welcoming us. What was that city just then? A vast birthday cake cut into four slices; each of the four great Powers eating its own. Like ants who risked, at any moment, being crushed under the huge soles of army boots, the Viennese carried off only the crumbs of a former life.

I gave a little cry: 'Look, Mamma. . . .'

For the first time, in my life, I had just seen a black man. He was in uniform. My innocent astonishment had not escaped him; he smiled at me. It was the second smile of the day.

'Don't make any remarks,' advised my mother. 'Look, but don't say anything.'

We arrived in the Kleeblattgasse. It was a little old street, just near the Graben. We stopped in front of an ugly, but dignified house, with thick walls. Papa pulled the bell and we heard the sound echoing and drifting through the house. No one came. Mamma pulled the bell, in her turn, and the clamour started up again, ricocheting back from the well of the stairs.

The door opened at last. A dark-complexioned man was standing on the threshold. Papa put his question:

'Is Madame Wagner in? We have been sent by her nephew. . . .'

The man told us to come in.

The hall was dark and the ancient staircase creaked under our feet.

A woman came to meet us and made us sit down in a bright, warm kitchen on the first floor. Papa explained to her that we needed a room for a few weeks and that we should soon be leaving for Innsbruck.

The first thing she mentioned was money.

'Have you any money?'

'Yes.'

'How much?'

'How much are you asking for the room?'

'You haven't any papers?'

'Not yet.'

She shrugged her shoulders.

'The risks are very considerable, here in Vienna. . . .'

'How much a day?' my father went on, with gentle tenacity.

She named the sum.

Papa made a small, lightning calculation and said, 'Yes.'

Having received two weeks' rent in advance, Madame Wagner took us up to the third floor, opened a door and left the key in the lock.

'There's running water, too. . . .'

Papa asked for some soap. She promised to give us a piece.

The narrow room contained two beds, a cupboard and a washbasin. Without waiting a moment, we began to undress ourselves. At record speed, I tore off, one by one, my crumpled frocks and my jumpers that were damp with perspiration.

What a deliverance! But now the little room, with all our clothes in disorder, looked like a jumble sale. On the beds, dresses were mixed up, higgledy-piggledy, with Papa's shirts. Papa, standing, stripped to the waist, in the middle of the room was hunting for something.

'My hat was vanished,' he said. 'Haven't you seen it, darling?'

'Do you need it at this moment?'

'No,' replied Papa. 'But, all the same, I'd like to know where my hat is.'

In the pocket of my winter coat, I found one of my high-heeled shoes. But where was the other?

112

'You haven't seen my other shoe?'

'No,' said Mamma, who had become slim and frail again.

'What are we going to do with all this stuff?'

'We'll have to buy a suitcase,' said Papa, pouring water over his shoulders.

Madame Wagner brought us the soap. Mamma opened the door just wide enough to let her in.

Soon the room was full of water and soapsuds. Clean at last and wearing only the clothes we needed, we were aware of being ravenously hungry.

'We'll go and eat . . . and we'll buy a suitcase to put all these clothes in,' said Papa.

Out in the street, he added:

'But we won't buy the suitcase in the Russian zone. The journey would end in Siberia.'

It was half-past four. Already, the first lights of Vienna were beginning to wink. We had enough money for a small dinner. As we left the house, we noticed that not one of its windows was lit up. The little street hushed down in the darkness on its secrets and on our hopes.

While my parents were searching for their old Vienna, dressed up and mannered and peaceful; full of smiles and waltzes and the good smell of its famous coffee, I was looking avidly and excitedly at the Vienna of the present.

For Papa and Mamma, the city was a great actress, playing her last part. When her admirers came a little too close, she held a lace fan in front of her face to hide her deep wrinkles. But her voice, though slightly broken and hoarse from the smoke of the war, was still recognisable. It was a voice that went straight to the heart of those who had known genuine peacetimes and journeys without passports. . . .

What I saw was a Vienna full of soldiers of four nationalities, badly dressed people who were always shivering under the sleet, of shop windows that were brilliantly lit-up but almost empty. And I noticed how everyone was always in a feverish hurry to get back to their own homes.

113

When we left the Graben, we came to the Herrengasse. Mamma saw a church that was lit up inside.

'Let's go in,' she said.

We made our way towards the wide-open door.

On the pavement, a Salvation Army woman was singing. Her voice seemed to defy the ample harmonies of the organ. We looked into the interior of the church. The aisle blazed in the yellow, quivering light of the tall candles. In the distance, the priest was celebrating the afternoon Mass and you could see his gold-embroidered chasuble. The tabernacle reflected the light so brilliantly that we could see the glitter of its metal door from where we stood in the street.

I was seized with an inexplicable feeling of discomfort. The little woman in blue went on singing and her big bonnet tied with a broad bow under one ear made her look like an old-fashioned doll. Her clear, shrill voice asserted itself against the violent waves of the organ.

The Salvation Army man who accompanied her was seated on a stool, with the brass bowl for offerings on the pavement in front of him. He was trying to give his accordion the grave, swelling tones of the competing organ. The constant stream of passers-by, whether generous or indifferent, produced no change of expression on those two faces. The accordionist's was astonishingly young. His fixed, steady gaze seemed to see nothing of the people who poured past the brass bowl, now singly, now in groups. The woman sang with her eyes focused on some invisible point . . . a point above the heads of the crowd and lower than the sky. . . . Now and then, a fine, almost imperceptible rain made the asphalt glisten.

'Would you give me a few groschens?' I asked my father. He slipped two coins into my hand and I went up to the pair. With a swift, yet solemn gesture, as if I were voting for them, I deposited the money in the bowl.

We went into the church. The smell of incense enveloped me as if someone had flung an entangling veil over me. We found three places in the back bench and I watched, without the

114

slightest intention of praying. In those days we were always going into churches to find a refuge, to hide ourselves, to wait or to rest. My back easily adapted itself to the hard wooden backs of the benches. But that evening, an impression struck me. The faces seemed to be fixed in their aggressive outlines. They made me think of children's drawings where the pencil lines are gone over afterwards in black ink. And, suddenly, I felt I was stifling.

'When can we go?' I whispered into my mother's ear

'We're going in a moment,' she answered. 'Mass is almost over.'

All at once, the organ stopped. Thanks to this unexpected silence, a woman's voice penetrated into the nave. It was the Salvationist's voice but her frail song shattered almost at once against the marble pillars. She stopped singing.

I was moved. And hurriedly, with modest, trembling haste, I thought of my dreams and my desires. It was not praying; it was letting my thoughts run on unbridled. In the front row, people were already getting up and I, all at sea, still had so many things to express! How I should like to write a book, several books; how I should like to begin writing this very day and go on writing all my life! And how splendid it would be to have readers too . . . and, as well as all that, a great love.

My mother and father stood up and we left the church. But, as we were walking away from it, an idea struck me. I do not remember what excuse I made, but I returned to the church. It was already dark and empty. I wanted to feel God's presence and I almost whispered in His ear: 'I should also tremendously like to have a child. . . . My God, give me readers and give me children. . . .'

When I caught up with my parents, the rain was already falling heavily.

We looked for a cheap little restaurant. We found it on our way back to the Kleeblattgasse. It was marvellous, that little restaurant! A smiling waitress showed us to a tiny table covered with a paper cloth with a lacy border. Several people were dining and, from a nearby table, a smiling, made-up lady gave us an amiable nod.

'What does she want?' asked Papa uneasily. 'Is she a spy?'

I did not dare glance in her direction.

The waitress approached, removed the pencil from behind her ear, and prepared to take down our order. Then, as Papa looked at the handwritten menu, he turned white.

'We haven't these food tickets they insist on. . . .'

We bent over the menu in despair.

The waitress understood at once.

'If you can pay a supplement, you can have dinner all the same.

'Right,' said my father, 'but bring us something to eat quickly. . . .'

When the waitress had gone, he said:

'They gave me a little money at the Reception Centre. We can just get along for two weeks, but after that. . . .'

The waitress returned at last and we ate with a ferocious appetite.

The lentil soup was boiling hot. Ever since we had left Hungary, lentils pursued us! Afterwards, we each had a couple of thin, greyish Vienna sausages and a boiled potato.

I noticed an old gentleman near us who was eating with slow solemnity. He cut his little sausage into tiny, transparent slices and put a little mustard on each.

Just before we left Vienna, a kindly fellow who was showing us the way and who had realised we were refugees, had cursed the war all the time he was conducting us along with exquisite politeness.

'My sister died of starvation,' he told us. 'Now we have everything, but, before, it was famine. . . . It's along here, sir . . . this way, lady . . . the street you're looking for. . . .'

But that night, the dinner was incomparably rich.

I was entitled to have a cake, a tart that was a speciality of the restaurant. The jam was made of tomatoes and it was sweetened with saccharine instead of sugar. All the same, it was very good.

'You know,' Mamma told me. 'If you ask God for something the first time you go into a particular church, your prayers will certainly be answered.'

'I know,' I replied, radiant. 'I do know, and I asked. . . .'

'Well . . . may one know your secret?'

I revealed the one that was easiest to admit.

'I prayed to have a child.'

They were genuinely astonished.

A little later, when we were back in the street where our room was, Papa said to me:

'You ought to have asked for a passport for him too.'

'For whom?'

'For the child. . . .'

I laughed. It was a happy evening.

I rang the bell. A man we had not seen before opened the door. We went up to the peaceful little room and, a few minutes later, we were all sleeping in real beds, wearing nightclothes and feeling free people at last.

In the morning, I was awakened by a thought. My parents were still asleep but I felt extremely clearheaded. They were delivered over to me in their unconsciousness; their faces, abandoned to heavy sleep distressed me. The rhythm of their breathing, the total silence of that house, the stillness of our three bodies filled me with a violent despair. That day was my twentieth birthday. I had not mentioned the fact the day before, not even during dinner. I almost wanted them to forget this date; I was already prepared for a bitter disappointment. Events had gone too fast for me; I wanted to stop and recover my breath

Perhaps, downstairs, a letter had arrived for me. A letter with a lot of stamps and several postmarks; a letter that had come from a long way off. From what country? I had no idea. A letter that had been written while we were crossing the frontier. A love letter, a letter of waiting and hoping; a letter full of promises. I imagined an impatient, eager man, somewhere in this great world. A man who had been waiting for me for years, who had been following from afar all my adolescent joys and sorrows, a man building his life on my life. The image of the man and the image of the child became strangely intermingled. Sometimes, in my wild dreams, I was leaning over a cradle in which lay a child with a grown-up's face; a face I had composed out of a thousand details.

Saturated with analytical novels, I had often fled from an imaginary house, repeating to myself the arguments of Ibsen's Nora. And, while we were still at Fonyod, when I used to go and swim in Lake Balaton, I would often be Flaubert's gentle Emma waiting for her lover as I walked through the steep wood that led down to the shore. I invented daring dialogues. I repulsed the treacherous advances of invisible gallants who pursued me and, at the end, I flung myself into the lake as one flings oneself into a great adventure.

But the reality was very different. Before we left Fonyod, I had wanted to go to a dance organised by the young people of the village. Alas, all my pre-war clothes appeared to have shrunk. The fact was, it was I who had grown. The flowered chintz curtain which adorned our rustic dining-room was converted into a dress for me. It was the first one that did not constrict my chest. My mother gave me her only pair of high-heeled shoes.

I knew already that our exile by the lake was drawing to its close. The project of our departure, long ago conceived, cherished and ripened, was our daily topic of conversation. Nevertheless, I wanted to dance just once more in Hungary. I also wanted to be nicely bronzed for the evening and I spent the entire day on the lake shore, basking like a lizard in the warm, fine sand. But a violent sunstroke gave me a high temperature and I had to spend that much-looked-forward-to evening in bed. The days that followed were thoroughly wretched. The only diversion that remained to me was to retire completely into my dreams. I no longer went to Budapest; now that I had finished my studies, what reason was there for me to go? The doors of the future had been hermetically sealed again; even my parents' old friends looked on me as a ghost from the past. It was no longer possible to say or to hear a personal, human word. The sense of my utter uselessness in other people's lives left me absolutely crippled and helpless.

Between my own experiences concerning life, love and death there were certainly amazing discrepancies. By now I had acquired the habit of dreading every moment I dreaded people's faces; I dreaded lips that might utter cruel words. I dreaded the darkness that brought nightmares. I had seen decomposition at work. For ten days, in front of our house in Budapest, I had watched the faces of corpses gradually becoming covered with scales like the backs of fishes. I had seen the despairing expression and the weeping eyes of the horses in Budapest, dying, inch by inch, of thirst as the days went by. I had also lived through the crazy, meaningless hours of the great bombardments when the concrete shuddered and the walls collapsed. I had seen a baby sucking at the empty, dried-up breasts of its mother. All this was mingled together in my mind. And if someone had asked me the question: 'Who is the woman you would wish to be like?' I should have answered, without hesitation, 'Madame Bovary!' But when a boy kissed me for the first time, I had nearly fainted; the sensation of a stranger's lips on my own had utterly overwhelmed me. . . .

And now, here I was in Vienna. I was twenty years old and everyone around me was asleep!

I got out of bed and dressed. I went down to the kitchen where Madame Wagner was already bustling about by her gas-stove. It had been agreed that she should give us breakfast.

'Good morning, madame,' I said, sitting down on a chair.

'Good morning, mademoiselle,' she replied amiably, but without a smile. 'Would you like your coffee?'

'Yes, please.'

No sooner had I sat down to it, than I realised I was hungry. From time to time, the door opened. At first, it was a man of about fifty who spoke Polish with Madame Wagner. He glanced at me furtively and with some distrust. Madame Wagner must have told him I was Hungarian and did not know a word of

Polish for he seemed appeased and went on talking volubly without bothering about me. I then concentrated on eating as slowly as possible so as to see as much as I could of the life of this strange house.

There was also a taciturn young man whose nationality I could not guess as he did not utter a word.

Definitely the most interesting was a young woman with flaming red hair, blue eyes shaded with long lashes and a magnificent body, heavy yet graceful, like a Roman statue.

After having sized me up, she smiled at me. But it was not a friendly smile; it was the smile of a woman who wants to display her teeth to another woman. I was enchanted to be the other woman.

'Just passing through Vienna?' she threw out casually, though the question was pointless.

'We don't know yet whether we're staying permanently or whether we are going on somewhere else,' I answered, my heart beating.

'You speak German very well,' she went on, as she drank her black, unsweetened coffee.

'I learnt it at school. . . .

At that moment, my parents arrived, tense and anxious.

'How *could* you leave the room like that without warning us?' scolded my father.

'I haven't stirred out of the house,' I answered, more sharply than I meant to.

Meanwhile Madame Wagner had introduced the young red-haired woman to my mother, who looked slightly mistrustful.

'You see, madame, little Wanda is the daughter of one of my Czech cousins. She is a Czech too, and a refugee like yourselves. The poor girl lost her husband during the war. She is engaged to a charming American who is a great consolation to her and who is going to take her to New York. . . .'

'Delighted. . . .' said Mamma, remaining strictly within the bounds of conventional politeness.

Wanda presided over my parents' breakfast. She put her

120

elbows on the table and never once removed her advertising smile.

'I'll be back in a moment,' I whispered to my father. I ran down the stairs. I wanted at least just to look in the letterbox. But, in this old door, there was no slit for letters. And suddenly I thought that, here, everyone was in transit like ourselves. No one had any papers nor any real address.

I went up to the kitchen again and, at last, for the first time, I saw some trace of real life. On the first floor, a child was looking out from a door that stood ajar next to the kitchen and watching the staircase.

'What language do you speak?' I asked in German.

By way of answer, he shut the door.

Well, that was that. . . . I went up to our room pausing for a moment on the second floor where there were three doors. I overheard scraps of conversation in Polish. Then I retired into our own room I looked out through the window; the street was quiet, as usual. A solitary, idle dog was sniffing into corners; he was hesitating, unable to make up his mind. . . .

Later on, when we went out, my parents told me that Madame Wagner had invited us to have tea with her. She had promised to tell them where they could get papers to leave Vienna and cross the frontier at Linz. We were in the American zone of Vienna but the city itself was surrounded by the Russian zone of Austria; the whole country, in fact, was divided up in the same way as its capital. Our aim was to get to the real West and therefore to leave the Russian-occupied territories. Madame Wagner had told Mamma that a night train, leaving Vienna in the evening, stopped, round about midnight, at Linz. There, the Russians rigorously scrutinised the passengers' papers. Those who had Austrian identity cards could proceed on their way unmolested, but with the papers handed out to refugees, it was impossible to get through. There were thus only two solutions. Either once again to have a guide who would take us on foot and then in a boat, or to procure ourselves forged Austrian papers. Both solutions required money – the money we did not possess.

We had lunch in the same little restaurant. The friendly waitress gave us extra rations of potatoes and sausage.

'Will you still be here the day after tomorrow?' she inquired.

'Yes, alas,' my father replied mechanically. 'Where else could we be?'

'You're brave, considering your situation,' said the waitress admiringly. 'Very brave. . . .'

'It was more difficult crossing the frontier than it is living here,' explained my mother.

The waitress nodded.

'All the same, you're very brave. . . .'

Papa lost patience.

'All right, then, we *are* brave. But why keep on saying so?'

'Because, from the day after tomorrow, we shall be in the Russian zone,' declared the girl. 'For a month.'

Papa dropped his cigar.

'They change the zones?'

'Every six months.'

At such a moment, I felt myself completely detached from what was going on. I felt like a builder standing on the outer scaffolding of a house and amusing himself by watching the inmates through the window. I saw my parents turn pale and the waitress's face became so definite, so clear in all its details that I can still see her long nose, her thin, nervous mouth and her frizzy hair, dull and dry from cheap permanent waves.

'Yes, indeed, my good sir,' she repeated. 'That's the way it is.'

We swallowed our lunch very quickly and returned to the house.

Madame Wagner, in her warm kitchen, huddled against her stove, was not surprised to see us. She was knitting and her needles devoured the grey wool at disconcerting speed.

Papa asked her to return us the money we had given her for the two weeks in advance.

She shook her head.

'Impossible,' she muttered. 'Impossible.'

And we could see from her face that this refusal distressed her even more than it distressed us.

122

'But we have absolutely no resources,' my father explained gently, emphasising the words as if he were speaking to a backwards child.

'And I have no resources either. A poor widow who fends for herself as best she can. . . . All my tenants are leaving tomorrow night. For me, that is a catastrophe. . . .'

Half an hour later, it was my father who was comforting *her*.

'But, Madame Wagner, why didn't you tell us yesterday about this change? You must have foreseen it.'

She was snivelling, but her eyes were dry.

'How can you expect me to foresee History? And I don't like getting mixed up in high politics. In any case, I *should* have warned you, tomorrow afternoon.'

Finally my father demanded:

'But where are we going to live?'

There was a malicious little gleam in her eyes as she replied:

'At the Station Hostel. . . .'

'You are too kind, Madame Wagner,' my father answered dryly.

She continued to knit without flinching. Then she added, suddenly timid and helpless:

'You could go into the French zone. It's quite close, near the Graben. Go to the French, they'll help you. . . .'

Half an hour later, my father had left the house. And mother and I stayed on in the warm kitchen, silent and motionless, like objects forgotten in a corner. Mamma was reading the *Wiener-zeitung*, turning over the pages with a sharp flick. Each time she did so, the sound of the paper made Madame Wagner start. She found our hostility hard to bear; she kept giving little sighs and letting her work slip off her lap. Finally she got up and began to get the tea. Out of the corner of my eye, I noticed the number of cups on the table. When my mother saw these preparations, she stood up.

'We'll go upstairs and wait for your father there.'

Madame Wagner flung herself in front of the kitchen door.

'You can't do that to me! Refuse the tea I'm getting ready for you. . . . We mustn't part in anger. In this life, you never know when we may need each other. . . .'

In our hearts, we were frightened of her. We were completely at her mercy for, if Papa could obtain no help from the French authorities, it was she who would have to get us out of our troubles!

We stayed. Later, Wanda arrived, accompanied by a thin little American who was eclipsed by his uniform as if it were a costume for a fancy-dress ball. We shook hands and Wanda made him sit beside her and filled his teacup for him.

The economical Madame Wagner did not switch on the electric light and we remained physically and morally stupefied in the soft dusk. The shadows gradually grew deeper and deeper, as if our own gloomy words and thoughts were increasing them. Wanda was impressive; her eyes shone and she lavished every possible attention on the American, who muttered incomprehensible words in the depths of his throat. Wanda presided over this strange tea party. I admired her. She was the first *femme fatale* I had seen; she must have had a very murky past. She talked to Madame Wagner; her red hair, with its metallic sheen, framed a face that, expressive as it was, never gave a real smile. Afterwards, the American told a long story of which I did not understand a single word. At the beginning of it, I paid attention; I wanted to be the well-educated girl who had not spent eight years learning English for nothing. Unfortunately, I had to realise that my studies had been completely useless. He spoke in a way so different from my teacher that it amounted to another language.

The tea that Madame poured us out from time to time was becoming extremely strong. I was aware of that stale taste of tea leaves that have been soaking for a long time in hot water; that musky taste that curdles one's saliva, coats one's palate, puts one's teeth on edge and accelerates one's heartbeats. But I went on drinking all the same, like someone drinking innumerable toasts to their own projects. I knew that I should write a novel about Wanda, about her mysterious, shoddy life. I could feel episodes and details springing up in my mind; I had already decided that she should have a golden-haired friend of her own type; the type of adventuress who is resolved to retire, as soon as she is thirty, into a corner of what is called 'decent' society.

She was the adventuress who wears her own body like armour and who 'settles down' as soon as she sees the first dints in it: the crow's feet, the slackening chin, the breasts growing less voluptuous as they grow heavier. At that point she finds the eternal, simple-minded soldier who is capable of confusing love with the body and taking patience for tenderness. This little American here who was carrying off his European wife to one of the great cities of his own country, as one carries off a piece of loot, would never know that it was she who had made the good haul. I was already thinking about the fate of their children and trying in my mind to describe their faces. I could have warmed up the cold tea by holding the cup between my burning palms. I had divined the source of my own secret; I was at once feverish and rapturous. It was then, in the gathering dusk of that crucial afternoon, that I first drew my invisible line, my magic circle. I divided all the human beings I had known up till then into two camps: those whom I would keep as vague, floating memories and those who would take shape again, recreated or modelled by myself, on blank paper. I had completely lost all sense of reality. I was ensconced in the middle of a chapter I should one day write . . . wanting to get away from this atmosphere of charming ghosts, I rose from my chair and said to my mother:

'I'm going up to my room.'

'I'll join you in a few minutes,' she replied.

Hurriedly, I said goodbye. Wanda's hand was warm and flabby; it was already the hand of the little bourgeoise she would soon be. The American also produced some presumably friendly words out of his throat. At last I was outside the door. I ran up the dark staircase and plunged into our room. I switched on the light and, as I passed the glass that hung over the washbasin, I looked at myself. I was transformed. I studied myself for a long time, and suddenly, my own face became a stranger's; I had to sustain the gaze of someone who looked astonishingly like me. When I left my double, I looked feverishly for my winter coat. It was in the cupboard, on a hanger. I took it out and flung it on the bed. I had no scissors, so I tore open the stitches of the hem with my nails. Before we left Hungary, I had slipped two school exercise books into the lining. It was part of the diary I had kept during the siege of Budapest and which I had so often meant to burn at Fonyod. But, though I was frightened of keeping a text that might be dangerous, I had never mustered up sufficient resolution to destroy it. And now, my exercise books were here in Vienna, at liberty! I stroked the blue paper covers which still displayed their white labels bearing my name. Once, a very short time before his death, Pista had taken one of my note books . . . I don't remember which one . . . and said: 'You're always writing, mademoiselle. You mustn't ruin your pretty eyes.' It was the first real compliment I had received in my life.

When my mother came in, I slipped the exercise books under my pillow.

'My poor child, I haven't kissed you today, and today's your birthday!'

'It doesn't matter a bit,' I replied, feeling full of generosity. I had quite forgotten my bitter resentment of the morning. 'It doesn't matter a bit. . . .'

She was close to me, sitting on the bed; weighed down with care, anxiously listening for my father's footsteps. She looked small, fragile and immensely tired. My secret was on the tip of my tongue.

Before I had time to regret it, I announced:

'I'm going to write a novel, Mamma. For me, Wanda is Vienna. I've already got at least fifteen characters. Just imagine, how marvellous to write the life of a woman who changes her lovers with the zones! What do you think of the idea?'

'Appalling . . . terrible . . . disgusting. . . .'

She was on the defensive now and thanks to that shred of experience I had gained in the kitchen, I wanted to shock my mother.

'There are things one mustn't say and one mustn't write,' she added, firm and decisive.

But I was gay and sure of myself. I improvised, so as to shatter her still more.

'I shall have a black man in this book too. He'll kill, like a sort of modern Othello.'

My mother had all her hackles up when my father arrived. He brought very good news. The Refugee Aid department of the French zone had accepted us. They were going to lodge us in one of the hotels placed at their disposition and they would give us papers to cross the demarcation line at Linz.

'They're charming,' repeated my father. 'Charming.'

After dinner, in a half-dream, I was already imagining a French fiancé for Wanda.

That night, I slept dreamlessly, with the quiet conscience of one who has accomplished a task.

Chapter Sixteen

THE FOLLOWING MORNING, I was dreamy, absent-minded and highly irritating to my parents. We set off very early to the Mariahilferstrasse and, in a shop, we found a cheap cardboard suitcase. It was shiny but it had a spurious elegance and it was adorned with two locks of some anæmic metal. My father was submerged in his worries. We had to leave Madame Wagner's house that very afternoon to install ourselves in the Hotel Graben. I carried the suitcase and thought of the ones we had had before the war in Budapest. They were of pigskin; their size and weight and their solid brass fittings made them a curse to porters. Those suitcases were little portable wardrobes, worthy of our slow, stately journeys. I shall never forget those journeys, or myself, a shy, spoilt child in a first-class carriage with my nose against the window and the metallic taste of tunnels in my mouth. My imagination would play round the small, silent houses the train overtook, spitting out simultaneously smoke, soot and the throbbing fury of its engine. How pretty they were, the Hungarian stations! They awaited us in the hollows of valleys, on the shore of the lake, in the heart of the cornfields, among sheaves stacked in the shape of a cross. If I had got off the train blindfold, I should have known each place just by its smell. The smell of pines and streams announced the mountains; the damp mists that tasted like tears, meant Kolozsvar. The smell of shells and wet seaweed, that little wind carrying drops of spray, that was the lake. In yet another place, the station was surrounded by ripe cornfields and sweet with the scent of acacia honey.

'What a sleepwalker!' cried Mamma because, in crossing a road, I had looked neither to left nor right. 'Wake up, child!'

'Heedless youth,' sighed my father, shrugging his shoulders.

I shut myself up in my silence, without looking at the swarming streets. They were full of people, terrified of the Russians, who were hurriedly moving house and seeking refuge in what, for the next few months, would be the Western zone.

We crossed the Burg: already the Russian soldiers were appearing in the park full of naked trees.

'And you're dreaming,' my father went on. 'You forget that we are in Vienna, with a few schillings in our pockets, faced with an uncertain future. . . .'

No, I was far from forgetting that we were in Vienna. I was thinking about Wanda and about my decision of last night to write a book about her. But I had a great problem. How could I depict an amorous life with no experience except that one kiss whose disturbing memory was still with me? However, to reassure myself, I thought of Emily Brontë. She had been able to write *Wuthering Heights*, shut away in a vicarage, out of her virgin violence and hatred.

We arrived back in the Kleeblattgasse. Madame Wagner could not be found. My father knocked at her door for several minutes without obtaining any answer. Soon afterwards, we left the house, with the suitcase loaded with our clothes.

The Graben Hotel was in a quiet, elegant street near the Herrengasse. The great vestibule smelt of dust. The reception desk, with its empty pigeonholes and bunches of motionless keys, was as sad as the blank gaze of a victim of amnesia vainly trying to recall his memories. The porter lowered his newspaper and watched our approach; then he took the permit my father held out to him. While he was reading it, I noticed that his hand shook slightly. At the bidding of an unseen hand, the lift set itself in motion with a mechanical sigh and slowly vanished in its cage.

'What is your nationality?' inquired the porter.

'Hungarian,' my father answered, mistrustful.

Behind the rimless spectacles, the moist eyes softened.

'I was in Budapest in 1912,' said the man.

He got up and spent a long time searching for a key. Key in

hand, he returned from the reception desk and signed to us to follow him. He was small and bent and he questioned us with tenacious obstinacy.

'So the French have sent you here. . . . Will you be staying long?'

Papa did not answer.

On the third floor, he turned to the right and we followed him in silence. The great faded red carpet muffled the sound of our footsteps. The porter's gesture, as he opened the door of Room 43 was that of a servant, but his voice was full of contempt as he said:

'If you're not warm, tell the French to give *us* some coal too – and not only the hotel guests!'

He walked over towards the window, pulled the curtain and opened a door.

'You've got a bathroom as well, This was a fine room before the war. An expensive room. . . .'

My father, suddenly irritated, dismissed him.

'All right, my good man, we'll find everything we need. . . .'

The porter had gone. So I took the key that was still hanging outside in the lock. That key had promoted us to occupants! . . .

Mamma arranged our possessions in enormous wardrobes that contained at least fifty hangers and fifteen drawers.

I shut myself up in the bathroom with a piece of soap. By a miracle, the water was very hot. I stood, naked, on the little mat that bore the name of the hotel, waiting for the bath to fill and, after a few minutes, I immersed myself up to the neck in the water. It was an extraordinary sensation; an almost painful delight. With my eyes shut and my hair drenched, I lay in the bath, covered with this wet, caressing warmth. I had the feeling that this bath was going to deliver me from all physical misery. For over a week, I had been soaked in sweat, which had sometimes run down my face mingled with tears. Now my feet, tired from long walks, stretched themselves out joyously. I could hear the nervous beating of my heart, like a far-off disquieting tom-tom.

When I came out of my bath, Mamma wanted me to lie down for a little. My father had gone out. I huddled up under the eiderdown, meaning to get up as soon as my mother had had her bath.

I did not wake up till seven o'clock in the evening. Papa was writing, bending over the table in the pink glow of the bedside lamp. His tired, absorbed face softened my heart.

'Papa. . . .'

He turned towards me, smiling.

'You've slept well, my child. . . .'

'Where's Mamma?'

'She's downstairs, in the hotel kitchen. She can make us tea or coffee for after dinner. They've given her permission.'

I shall always remember my stay at the Graben Hotel. What a strange, indefinite life we led there! Our bodies, at long last, had revolted. They had borne up well during the period of high tension but here, in this semi-repose in which we had nothing to do but to wait for our identity papers, they manifested their displeasure. My mother's ankles were so swollen that she stayed in bed for four days. My father, with his livid face, was a prey to insomnia and I myself was constantly battling against terrible dreams. The physical and moral shock we had sustained revealed itself in this general loosening-up.

My father who, even during our exile on the shore of the lake, had been able to provide for the family needs by giving lessons was now entirely at the mercy of organisations. From morning to night, he filled up forms and interminable questionnaires. Our aim was to leave Vienna for good. We wanted to get to Innsbruck, in the French zone. The officer who dealt with our affairs thought they would accept us in the Refugee Camp at Kufstein, fifty kilometres from Innsbruck. But we first had to get into the zone occupied by the Western Powers and, to do this, we had to cross the demarcation line of Enz. This was a little river near Linz. The railway bridge was guarded on one side by the Russians, on the other, by the Americans. To choose liberty as the principle of a normal life, to say that liberty is an

131

elementary human right, is easy. The immense difficulty begins the moment one begins to take those words seriously.

In those days, at least, I did not yet know that any human being labelled with the name of 'refugee' was destined to be a clown, that he was cast as the buffoon of a disintegrated Europe. He was the wretched stage character who talks and tells stories, who tries to persuade people; the optimistic hawker who believes in his merchandise and cries it to almost deaf ears.

What remains in my mind of Vienna? The raw, healthily intoxicating sensation of a discovery. The discovery of my first foreign city. As a child, I had been the prisoner of a small estate and great traditions. My parents travelled while I remained in Hungary. I had the baptism of the West without passport or luggage. I could have recited whole passages of *Undine*, which was marvellously translated into Hungarian, but the fact that everyone around me spoke a language different from my own, enchanted me. Vienna without her waltzes, Vienna famished for food, was still charming Vienna to us – and our time there was a time of hopes that did not yet contain any seeds of bitterness.

I was able to buy a few sheets of white paper and a pencil. And, while my parents made the rounds of the offices and the various organisations, I stayed in the hotel bedroom. I wanted to write the novel about Wanda. I cherished her and cursed her; she sat there beside me, invisible, mocking me with her voluptuous smile, proudly confident of her beauty. Everything of which I lacked experience – the whole of life, in fact – I replaced by brutality. I revenged myself on her, too. I had her nightdress torn to shreds by a jealous Negro; she was knocked about by an American who, of course, had Indian blood in his veins; she was to be deserted by a Frenchman and raped by a Czech. I made remorseless demands on her in the way of parting embraces, savage kisses and base betrayals. I jotted down notes for all these episodes but the list of my future chapters was so formidable that, before my parents returned, I tore it up and disposed of it down the lavatory.

To escape on my own was anything but easy. For my parents, a great city in the period just after a war, was the headquarters of the white slave traffic where bandits laid hidden traps for pure, innocent young girls. Oh, how they exasperated me with those old, out-of-date stories of theirs! I wanted a tête-à-tête with my own Vienna, an assignation with its romantic little squares, the memory of a moment that belonged only to the two of us. After my purchases of paper, I had three schillings left over. One afternoon, I went off without telling my parents. All on my own, I saw everything with a different eye. And, in the glass of a shop window, I saw myself . . . fair-haired, frail-looking and unsure of myself. If I had had some red on my lips, I should, I thought, have been almost pretty. . . .

I went into a little café and I ordered a Viennese coffee. It was there I smoked my first cigarette since our departure from Hungary. It was a Hungarian cigarette; it was half empty, because the tobacco had come out in my pocket. Opposite me was an old woman who was feeding her dog with the crumbs of her cake. Half an hour later, I left and returned to the hotel at a run.

'We were already beginning to get anxious. . . .'

I suddenly lost my temper. . . .

'Oh, Lord, do let me alone with your eternal fussing. . . .'

I have always regretted since that I was so impatient with my parents, but it is so difficult being twenty.

The next day, we went off to have ourselves photographed. It was the first automatic apparatus I had seen. A smiling Fraülein made me sit down in a tiny, violently lit cage. She took my head in her hands and turned me towards a slanting mirror situated at the end of this species of box.

'Smile!'

I did not want to smile. I was alarmed at the idea of seeing my face fixed on shiny paper. I had spent those dead years by the lake without once having my photograph taken. I used to avoid looking glasses; it seemed to me that, if I did not ever see myself, I should suffer less from loneliness. But here I was the prey of this glittering wild beast that wanted to burn and devour me with its blinding light! I endured six clicks and then it was my parents' turn.

Ten minutes later, they handed us the little photos in a transparent envelope. I was confronted with the velvet collar of my old winter coat and, above that collar, a drawn face in cruel relief, obstinately fair hair and black eyebrows.

My parents were executed in the same manner. Three heads of criminals; three faces of morons; three grotesque profiles. It was the new technique.

Two days later, we received three forged Austrian identity cards. I saw my photo again; it bore the name of Elise Meyer. Neither the face nor the name belonged to me. Were we free or had we lost our memories?

I was the daughter of this Meyer family. At all costs, we must avoid uttering a word in the train. We were Austrians, going to stay with friends of theirs in Innsbruck. 'Don't give yourselves away by your accent. The Russians are strict; it's their last chance of controlling people's movements. They're hard; they look suspiciously at all the passengers and their papers. Naturally, you're taking a considerable risk. If you're lucky. . . . If not, they'll hand you over to the Hungarian authorities.'

Fear rendered us silent. On the evening of our departure, we crept down the stairs with a cat-like tread.

'Are you leaving?' the porter shot at us. 'Haven't made a long stay, have you?'

We walked along the icy street to the tramway. We still did not say a word. Our lives were in danger. But if, the next morning, we were at Innsbruck, it would be real freedom at last!

Silently, I said goodbye to Vienna, with my eyes full of tears. I was at the beginning of those years when they filled with tears at the slightest provocation.

At eight o'clock precisely we were on the platform, jammed in the middle of quite a large crowd. There were some American Negro soldiers; near us stood a grave nun, with an enormous starched butterfly on her head and, farther away, two Russian soldiers.

134

The train arrived, throbbing and clanking, and we took our place in a compartment. There was room for three on the wooden seats. I sat beside my mother, near the window and the nun made up the third. Papa took the place opposite me; next to him were two civilians – a seedy man and a woman with a big basket on her knees. I was aware of an obstinate little pain in my neck. It was a vein that was throbbing hard, as if I had another heart under my left ear. The real heart was drumming against my chest with heavy, irregular thuds. I wanted to be sick. I would have liked to tell my parents that it would be better to get off the train and go back to our vegetative life at the hotel, for this tension was unendurable. I could not even ask what time it was, because, once installed in the train, I could no longer put the question either in Hungarian or in my German whose accent would betray me. I knew that the train left at half-past eight and that we should reach the crucial bridge twenty minutes before midnight. Three hours and forty minutes of travelling.

The train left the station without a jolt, as if it were sliding down a slope. That sensation of accelerated speed went right through my whole body. I closed my eyes, wanting to sleep or, at least, pretend to sleep, but it was impossible. Condemned to silence, I was brimming over with ideas. . . . I could have kept up a feverish and excited conversation all through the night. How humiliating it was to be so frightened and to be holding blindly to luck with a kind of inward imploration. And all that for a displacement of a few kilometres. One was an occupier or a liberator, according to whether one were born in the East or the West. But, between the two, there was only a shifting waste of waters that ebbed and flowed at the mercy of the political tide. As I sat there, with my eyes open and my face against the window fogged by my breath, I felt nothing but hatred for the train. Outside, the universe was black. I could not discern a single light. To think that, if the Russians discovered us, it meant returning to Hungary! When we had crossed the frontier on foot, and were too exhausted to go on, we had at least been able to lie down on the wet earth and hide our faces in a heap of dead leaves. But this train was rushing along at a crazy speed like a travelling morgue with its corpses sitting on wooden benches. I looked down mechanically at my feet. If only I could slip under the seat and hide myself!

Mamma was dozing or, rather, pretending to doze. There was a nervous tic in her left eyelid; the spasm had a rhythm of its own and made her whole face quiver. My father was staring at some invisible point; I was in his field of vision but he was looking right through me. If only the real Austrians with us did not notice our terror! . . . What could this respectable Meyer family be frightened of? The thin man beside my father had finished reading his paper; he folded it up and, absent-mindedly, let it slip to the floor. I did not dare either to pick it up or to ask if I could look at it, though the time would have passed more quickly with that paper. The door of the compartment opened with a creak and an Austrian inspector walked through, leaving the opposite door open too. Wasn't that a sign that we should soon be there? Mamma opened her eyes, but her left eyelid went on rebelliously twitching. The man picked up his paper, and the nun clutched the crucifix of her big, heavy rosary between her fingers. The man opposite began chatting with the woman beside him, who was peeling an apple over her basket. Mamma looked at me; she was hungry too. The woman shared the apple with the man, who ate it greedily. They were all talking now and this buzz of voices seemed to emphasise our muteness.

Outside, there suddenly appeared lights. The train slowed down; then stopped. Words of command, yelled out by the Russians, rent the night. Once again, those voices, *their* voices. They made us shudder in a European train; they made us feel alone in the midst of a crowd and turned a journey into a nightmare. My father slipped his hand inside his jacket, no doubt meaning to take his identity card out of his pocket; he did not see my mother's disapproving glance and she had to say, in German:

'Wait . . . not yet. . . . Wait till they ask for it. . . .'

The man opposite stared at us as if he had noticed our

presence for the first time and the nun looked at her rosary.

The critical, agonising moment arrived. The Russians came into our carriage. The one who was examining the identity cards wore a fur cap; his eyes ran indifferently over the passengers, comparing faces with photographs. When he came to our row, he glanced at mine, then down at the identity card. He found the likeness perfect. Afterwards, he took my mother's papers, then my father's. Everything was in order. The man beside my father was holding another apple in his left hand. Suddenly, I realised that he was eating because he was frightened. The Russian took his card, looked at it and said a few rapid words to the other Russian. The man, frozen like a statue with half his apple in his hand, waited, as if hypnotised. The buzz in the compartment had stopped; everyone was silent, everyone was listening but no one dared turn their head or even look. The Russian made a sign to the man and said to him, in German:

'Get out. . . .'

The man stood up, his face livid. His eye-sockets were dark, like septic wounds; his gaze fastened on us avidly; he trembled like an animal caught in a trap. I thought he was going to jump out of the window, even right through the glass pane, if that was the river out there in the darkness.

'*Davaj*,' said the Russian, and, pulling down the window, he yelled something to the others outside, standing by the train. It was the scream of the bird of prey, swooping down on its victim.

The man left the train, accompanied by a soldier, and the inspection went on. We remained in our places, utterly spent, like puppets whose invisible manipulating strings have been cut. The nun was praying; her thin lips were shaping words. For whom was she praying? For the unknown man?

This eternity of waiting plunged me into a state of trance I had never experienced before. The sweat ran down my back and my face was damp all over. I did not want to go on seeing my parents' ravaged faces. I shut my eyes so that I could abandon myself completely to my dreams. I would have liked to go to a country where there were no more controls. In any case, I wanted to leave Europe. At Kufstein, we should have the possibility of choosing a country as one chooses a fabric in a shop. Perhaps the solid island upheld by the pillars of a great tradition, England. . . . Or far from Europe; Australia or South America.

The train started off again, slowly and jerkily, like an invalid making his first tentative steps. We were on the bridge; the flickering lights of Linz were drawing nearer. It was evident that we really were saved.

The train stopped again. The nun turned her head towards me. I risked a faint, shy smile. She smiled back at me.

The door of the compartment opened and the three representatives of the three Powers entered. The French officer saluted everyone, just brushing his finger against his cap. The English one held out his hand for our papers and the huge American unscrewed a large oblong tin. Without warning us, he sprinkled us as if we were herrings to be salted. He pulled my father's coat open and threw a little more of this yellow dust inside it. Papa was so much surprised by this that he did not even make an instinctive gesture of annoyance. The nun's shoulders turned yellow too. Mamma received most of the powder on her back and the rest on the bodice of her dress. The American could shake the D.D.T. without risk to himself for he was wearing gloves. He undid the top button of my winter coat and I received the cold, stinging powder on my neck. I must have given a sudden jerk, for my cheek too was covered with D.D.T. It was the last straw and my resistance completely gave way. I buried my head on Mamma's shoulder and burst into tears.

Later, when the train was safely running through the American zone, we ventured out into the corridor so as to be able to talk, but, since the disinfecting process, we had nothing left to say to each other. We were on the soil of a free Europe; the train had become friendly, almost a trusted ally. I opened the window; the cold air was like a bath in pleasant, refreshing reality. Back in the compartment, I huddled into my corner and, utterly tired and worn-out, I tried to sleep. A passenger switched off the main light and we sat motionless, like embalmed corpses, faintly lit by a mysterious blue glimmer, like the night light in a hospital ward. After all, what were we but hospital cases on the long sick list of History?

A young couple, who had got into the train at Linz, were already asleep. For both of them, it was an ordinary, uneventful journey; they had not had to cross the Styx to find happiness again. The pregnant wife held her large, soft hands over her stomach to protect the sleep of the unknown human being who was going to be born. How miserable that journey was for *me*, with my clothes sticking to my uneasy body, with those blue shadows on my face that had never known any real girlhood and the dull aching of a mind that was already inclined to melancholy! . . . In the dimness, my father's features composed a strange mask in which old age mingled with startled surprise. My mother, in her sleep, was clinging pathetically to her dream, as if she realised she must not move in case she woke up. So as not to crush her starched *cornette*, the nun kept very upright as she dozed, but every now and then she felt herself swaying forwards. This gave her a kind of fright, but she promptly recovered her balance.

Outside, the night betrayed none of its secrets. Outside there was liberty, but it was vague and featureless. What were we seeking here? Where had we come from and whither were we going? In my half-sleep, I was all incertitude. I should have liked to twenty years older, to have formed definite opinions and habits. I should have liked to call up my memories but there was nothing in me but an immense avidity. I was at once rebellious and thankful; I reached out towards everything, ready to taste and savour and touch. I wanted to chase away the shadows and replace them by sharp, physical impressions.

And then, miraculously, outside it began to be day. At first it was only a little grey rift, infinitely far away. Then the train was galloping in the heart of a rosy mist; the dawning colours seemed to be pasted against the damp pane; the blue lamp lost its malevolent power and the sleeping faces became marvellously

139

young; free of wrinkles and free of thoughts. It was as if angelic, brainless children were travelling in a blue and silver tunnel. The nun leant back, relaxed, against the hard wooden seat; she was dreaming; her pearly, transparent skin had a soft blue shimmer on it like reflections from a sapphire. Everything gleamed and shone; it was the festival of the dawn.

The young husband, opposite me, stretched and yawned. But the miracle had been accomplished. It did not matter that the magic had gone out of the atmosphere; I knew, I had seen with my own eyes that there were daybreaks like that. . . . And so, from that day on, I have loved the dawn. . . .

Chapter Seventeen

THE REAL MORNING, grey, cold and hostile, overtook us in the midst of immense mountains. The horizon had shrunk till it was no wider than the railway track. The Inn, green, capricious and turbulent, with its fierce torrents and its waves edged with white foam, followed the train, which was going at full speed. Sometimes, on the top of a proud peak, the ruins of a fortified castle would appear. The atmosphere of the compartment was thick and poisonous with stale breath. The future mother, heavy in her pregnancy, was visibly hungry; she was nibbling a biscuit and trying not to lose a crumb of it. All the faces were swollen from a bad night's sleep; I looked at my hands; they were dirty. My fingers were hurting me; it was a grumbling pain, discreet but obstinate. I owed it to the damp cellar where I had lived during the siege of Budapest; the water ran down the walls stained with saltpetre. I had never felt the cold, impressive contact of a valuable ring, but that pain that I carried in my joints, that went with me everywhere and that woke me up took the place of the ring.

At last, we arrived at Innsbruck. Mamma stepped down from the train as nervously as a shipwrecked passenger having to climb down a rope ladder to reach the lifeboat. As we left the station, which stood in the centre of the town, I felt crushed by those assertive overpowering mountains that encircle Innsbruck. In Hungary, you have to travel for a whole day to catch sight, far away, of the bluish chain of mountains; you have time to get used to them. But here they were right on top of us, as cold and indifferent in their whiteness as enormous sugar loaves.

It was very cold. The sun shone on the snow-covered peaks.

The streets were bustling and full of tourists. A band of youths passed by us; they were carrying skis on their shoulders. A girl looked at us with interest; her red pullover was as vivid as a scarlet poppy. In my winter coat, which was black, I felt like a crow in all this immaculate whiteness. But soon the snow melted under our feet. After that, we floundered in puddles of greyish water. Near the station, we hastily swallowed a cup of coffee; we had to get as soon as possible to the office that registered and placed the refugees. We had to reach the camp at Kufstein that very afternoon.

Then began a perfect orgy of questioning and interrogations. We filled up forms till we had cramp in our fingers. The offices were well heated; the employees all had the same monotonous voice; it was a soporific atmosphere after a sleepless night. How difficult it was to reconstruct how one had spent one's time during the last ten years! . . . Where were you in 1938? . . . At school . . . I was nine and a half at that time. . . . Of which party were you a member? . . . I was a Girl Guide. . . . What have been your principal changes of abode since that year? . . . The space for the answers was very limited; one had to invent another, more concentrated language in order to satisfy the authorities. I could say yes; I could say no; I could cross out something that did not apply. But there was no room for any of the finer shades! These questionnaires demanded an answer in morse code; a biography in telegraphese.

About four o'clock in the afternoon, the official gave us new identity cards. He put a pad in front of us and indicated the empty square under the photos.

'Your fingerprints, please. . . .'

Feeling suddenly very hot, I brushed my thumb lightly over the pad. The official saw that we were novices at the job of being refugees. He helped me by taking my thumb in his cold hand and forced me to rub it hard on the greasy pad. While my parents in their turn were performing the same operations, I studied the design of my thumb. There were wavy, parallel lines that formed concentric rings in the middle. Did the fingerprint of a criminal differ greatly from mine? This paper also bore witness to the fact that we had been disinfected. As we left the office, I had a fit of giddiness and Mamma had to sit down on the bench in the corridor. We had had nothing to eat since this morning and it was now half-past four. In three-quarters of an hour, our train left for Kufstein. How often we had heard of that little town at school! This was because the Hapsburgs had imprisoned a great many Hungarian patriots in its castle.

Soon we found ourselves back in the street leading to the station. Only a little while ago, the weather had been marvellous; weather for winter sports and scarlet pullovers, just as the prospectuses announced. But now dirty, ragged clouds covered the sky and a spiteful wind flung hail full in our faces. It was refugees' weather. . . .

An ill-heated little train took us to Kufstein, where we arrived at half-past seven, in a snowstorm. Outside the station, a railwayman showed us the way to the camp and we set off through the badly lit streets. I walked with my teeth clenched and kept blowing my nose to stop it from freezing. We did not say a word to each other. In the misty light of the street lamps, I looked out for a sign post or an arrow indicating the way to the camp.

And then the moment came when we found ourselves in front of a lowered barrier. We had reached our goal. A sentry came out of his box, examined our papers in the light of his pocket torch and said something to us in Russian. It produced a very disagreeable impression. Here, too? Were we not far enough away, even now? The man pointed out a distant, lit-up hut, raised the barrier and we crossed the frontier of the camp of Kufstein. In that snowstorm we could only just make out the multitude of sombre buildings; only here and there did a window show a light. Soaked to our very bones, we entered the office of the camp where a woman official received us. We stood in front of her; she had red hair and wore spectacles with metal frames

'You're Hungarian, all three of you, aren't you?' she said.

'Yes.'

143

'I'll call the head of the Hungarian section at once.'

She spoke German with a strong accent and, at last, she made us sit down. I could still go on living, but I no longer wanted to. I wanted to go to sleep here permanently, in this still warmth. I was no longer even hungry.

The Hungarian, who came in, shook the snow off his shoes, said 'Good evening' to the woman, and held out his hand.

'You've arrived late,' he said. 'Have you had anything to eat?'

'No.'

'I'm going to take you over to the canteen so that you can at least have some soup tonight.'

We followed him. The canteen resembled the one at the Station Hostel and the woman who gave us the soup spoke Russian. . . .

'Why are there so many Russians here?' inquired my mother.

Our new friend shrugged his shoulders.

'They're Ukrainians; most of them were in Vlassov's army.'

I did not know who Vlassov was and I had no desire to know.

After we had had some very hot soup, we went out once more into the snowstorm. The Commandant walked in front of us, with a torch in his hand. I could feel the water running inside my shoes; the soles had already been so thin in Vienna! He walked the length of a row of huts; the feeble lights were not bright enough to outline the mysterious shapes that were blotted out by the whirling snow.

'Here we are,' he said, making his way into one of the huts.

We found ourselves in an immense, dark corridor, crammed with doors on either side and buzzing with various noises. Here, everything smelt of onions and urine. The man tried to open the seventh door on the right. The rebellious key went on turning round and round endlessly in the lock. It needed ten minutes' work before we could go in. What we entered then was a cold room, with three iron bedsteads, meagrely lit by a feeble bulb fixed to the ceiling. There was also a wardrobe. In the middle stood a table stained with large, oily smears, and two chairs.

'You're extremely lucky,' he observed. 'Your predecessors, who went away a week ago, have left you a stove.'

The stove was indeed there, huddled in a corner, like a sick animal.

Our guide made a slight gesture and said, in an uncertain voice:

'I forgot to introduce myself. My name is Karpai . . . Colonel Karpai. . . .'

My mother nodded and smiled, but, a moment later, she asked:

'Do you really think one can live here?'

My father stood there, motionless; he was still carrying the suitcase. Everything was so dirty that he still did not dare put it down.

The Colonel was optimistic.

'It's always difficult when one first arrives, madame, but tomorrow, I'll help you. . . . You must set about organising your future life. . . . The shops are only open in the morning. . . .'

'The shops?' repeated my father ironically. 'We have no money.'

'Then so much the better,' replied Karpai, 'so much the better. You'll get everything you need here free. I'll say good night to you now. Don't forget that, at last, you have no more troubles . . . you're at home. . . . The water is at the end of the corridor, by the W.C.'

He went away and we remained in our 'home'.

Mamma sat down on one of the grey mattresses; it was all covered with stains. With disgust, she fingered the blankets that were stiff with the chilled sweat of other people. My father examined the surroundings as if he were looking for some lost article. It was at that moment that we heard, for the first time, the close, almost confidential voice of an unknown woman. The woman was humming, but where was she? Mechanically, I glanced under the beds. I opened the cupboard; there was nothing but some grey blankets. The voice followed my movements; it was humming a sentimental song: 'Lili Marlene'. And, now, a man was speaking:

'I've told you already you mustn't lick the knife. . . .'

145

We listened, paralysed. How could one lick a knife and hum at the same time?

The man became annoyed.

'If you go on sucking that knife, I'll slap you. . . .'

There was some muttering, then the woman began to sing, articulating the words very clearly.

'*Uber der kaserne, in dem grossen Tal. Steht eine Laterne. . . .*'

There came the noise of a resounding slap. A child howled and the woman went on:

'*Wie einst, Lili Marlene . . . wie einst, Lili Marlene. . . .*'

A second feminine voice intruded on the scene.

'If you smack Géza again, you just see what I'll do!'

'I *shall* smack him, because he's insufferable. And you won't do a thing. . . .'

And, once again, the indefatigable singer repeated:

'*Wie einst, Lili Marlene. . . .*'

She was our neighbour on the right. The family, where a child was licking a knife, were our neighbours on the left.

'She hasn't a large repertoire,' said Papa, lighting the remains of a cigar.

How far away morning seemed! Should we ever get to it?

I stood up on one of the chairs and hung a blanket up on some big rusty nails in the embrasure of the window. Under my bed, I discovered a little heap of coal and some wood, wrapped up in an old newspaper.

While mother was fussing round the beds, I lit the fire. But, two minutes later, the stove belched out whirling gusts of dense smoke. Instead of being warmed, we had to open everything so as to make a draught. We left the room a prey to the savage wind and took refuge, shivering, in the corridor. The neighbouring family's door opened and a young woman came out, carrying a chamberpot. She stared at us and vanished in the direction of the W.C. A few minutes later, she returned.

'Are you, by any chance, Hungarian?' she asked us, hiding the empty chamberpot behind her back.

'Alas, we are,' said my father.

146

I could see he was at the end of his tether.

'Wait a moment,' said the woman. She went into her room and reappeared, two minutes later.

'Come into our room for a little. . . .'

We accepted her invitation joyfully. In their home, it was warm. A small, kindly man shook hands with us. A little boy, just beginning to walk, climbed up on the bed with disconcerting speed. Mechanically, I looked round for the knife.

Then our neighbours offered us their boiling-hot coffee and their open hearts with the spontaneous generosity of Hungarians. He was a shoemaker in Budapest; they had come there a year ago with the child asleep under a drug. They explained the rules of our new life to us; they promised to leave us all the things they did not need any more; they were going off, in three days, to Venezuela.

We stayed talking to them for a long time. The child fell asleep in his mother's arms. We spoke in low voices, as if we were afraid life would overhear us during these indefinite moments when we were waiting on the brink of events. Stupefied by the warmth and the unexpected peace, I looked at them all. The faces were drawn by a giant hand that, by preference, used black shadows but emphasised eyes and foreheads with patches of white light. The shoemaker was telling us about Venezuela; his wife listened devotedly; the child, pink and heavy, slept with parted lips, from which a trickle of saliva drooled.

'What a fate! . . .'

Who had said those words? Words and faces melted away into a soft, unreal blur.

'Let's go . . . you're almost asleep,' said my mother.

We returned to our own icy room and lay down on the beds, wearing our winter coats and with our hats pulled down over our ears. I was shivering so much that I drew one of the dirty blankets over my head.

'Dear God, make the morning come soon . . . make the morning come soon. . . .'

147

Chapter Eighteen

OUR FIRST DAYS at Kufstein were like a nightmare. If we did not have to make a fire by rubbing two sticks together, it was thanks to our friends who guided us through the labyrinth of the camp. During the war, this sinister city of huts had belonged to the German army and, after the war, it had become the haven of the refugees. Kufstein, in my eyes, was an enormous orphanage, in which the children abandoned by their unnatural mother, Europe, could begin their life again in the artificial incubator of an international organisation. All these elderly orphans were fed, clothed, registered and examined in precisely the same way. I was not at all ungrateful to Fate for, at that period, the quality of all our personal feelings depended entirely on a comparison that was easy to make. The freedom of the West was, for us, a living miracle and Hungary no longer appeared as anything but a vast prison. But the fact that Hungary was no longer anything but a prison and that life compelled us to live as parasites was a tragedy. We kept saying to each other, in the same breath: 'What a joy to be here. . . .' and 'We're reduced to *this* place. . . .' I simply let myself drift aimlessly on the tide of events.

The medical examination had established that I was in good health; a little under-nourished but, then, who was not? . . . Fragile in appearance, but robust enough for work. I can still feel on my back the cold touch of the fingers that sounded me. I felt convinced that I should retain blue bruises for the rest of my life. The X-ray photograph demonstrated that I had a heart and lungs of iron. The oculist stared into my eyes with a little lighted mirror. The room was dark and he held my head with one hand and bent over my eye with the intense curiosity of someone spying on a secret through a keyhole. I could smell his breath and a blinding bead of white light wandered about inside my brain. Suddenly, I had the terrifying notion that what he was really doing was spying on my soul. A little later, when I tried to read the illuminated letters on his blackboard, I discovered that my eyes had grown weaker in the cellar; I had written too much by the light of a single candle.

All those eyes staring at the blackboard, how habituated they all were to gazing on grief! . . . The camp spent a great deal of money on glasses and Lithuanians, Ukrainians, Hungarians, Spaniards and Russians contemplated their liberty through steel-rimmed spectacles.

The countries that seemed most accessible were full of reservations about us. Australia had a great weakness for teeth. She did not like them to have stoppings in them. Australia wanted strong, vigorous beings, full of *joie-de-vivre*, with white teeth solidly planted in impeccable jaws. Australia repelled the unmarried with disgust; to be welcomed there, you had to have a wedding ring. I got all the information I could about England. The island that was so high in my esteem and so misty in my imagination was lacking in nurses for mental hospitals. England had a definite preference for male nurses because, as I learnt, the insane are extremely strong when they are enraged, which they frequently are. There was still another possibility, to be a miner. As for emigration to America, it was conditioned by so many rules and regulations that the mere list of the main questions and the essential conditions to be complied with made up a thick little book. I had to think about learning a trade. But, in our hearts, we had no desire to emigrate. We were fated to be Europeans and my parents were glad that they had passed the age limit for the exodus. Here, at Kufstein, there was the name of a different country on every lip. . . .

Thanks to our friend the shoemaker, we had become capitalists. He and his wife had given us an enormous number of useful things before they left. So we were able to bring back our lunch and our dinner from the canteen and eat them in our room, and, with the aid of the electric heater, we made our breakfast ourselves.

I had become incredibly sensitive and thin-skinned and my reflexes were so instantaneous that the mere contact of an object or even the mere awareness of a look was enough to make me tremble. I was tense and restless in this false security and I had not the bliss of being alone, since I was shut up in the same room with my parents. How miserable and detestable it was to have to dress and undress while the others turned their backs! And, besides, one was always being woken up during the night by noises coming from all over the place. Our neighbour on the right, the indefatigable singer, was a mad Lithuanian woman who had seen her entire family executed and who had been planted here by chance or by a pitiful fate. She related her story to everyone. When I caught sight of her, I fled; her blue eyes that looked like a hunted animal's gave me gooseflesh. The room that had belonged to the family who had gone to Venezuela was now occupied by a young Jugoslav couple. They appeared to make love from morning till night, and from night till morning with the same rhythm and the same moanings. Those intolerably long winter days took away from me any impulse and even the very power to smile.

My parents had made the acquaintance of the Hungarian colony and, one after the other, all these people told their story: 'When I crossed the frontier . . . the moon . . . the dogs. . . . Was the barbed wire already up when you crossed? . . . The guide. . . . But, of course, we're going . . . to the Argentine, perhaps . . . the country of the future. . . . My son is an engineer . . . that is, he has still one more year to do at Innsbruck University. . . .

The young man in question always appeared at Kufstein on Saturday nights. He was tall, clumsy, already beginning to grow bald, and in sight of his diploma. He wanted to get married before he went abroad. All these youths had the same fixed idea: to select a continent and a wife. . . . What was I doing in their midst? . . . A medical student also wanted to marry me because he had picked Australia. How I loathed myself, seeing myself

150

through their eyes! Dressed in clothes from unknown donors, I felt like a grotesque mannequin in a dress parade of charity garments.

Those garments arrived regularly in great corded, disinfected bales and they brought us friendly messages from all the peaceful corners of the earth. Once, I spent a whole afternoon helping to distribute them. I shall never forget that mountain of shoes, all new, but dating from the First World War. They were museum pieces that had aged without ever being worn, preserved alike from sunshine and from rain. There were ladies' shoes in yellow kid, trimmed with white doeskin; there were bootees; there were gaiters with little black buttons, and boots for slim ankles hidden under softly rustling skirts. When a pair of mauve satin boots appeared, the feeble electric bulb in the hut lost its yellow light and began to glitter like a chandelier and I could see an enormous golden circus ring and a blonde, voluptuous bareback rider who went through her act, dreaming of those lilac boots. The factory must have gone bankrupt before she could buy them and, twenty years later, the boots were resuming their interrupted career at the camp of Kufstein. But who would wear them?

The dresses with their waists round their hips came out of those old Charlie Chaplin films in which the heroines had heart-shaped mouths and foreheads covered with coy little curls under hats pulled down over their ears. But those dresses were not new. Under their arms, stained half moons indiscreetly bore witness to emotions of long ago; to other people's heat and other people's sweat. All this stuff had been disinfected by the passage of time and by the foresight of the authorities. Nevertheless, I handled those clothes with the deliberate stoicism of a nurse, who uses her reason to master her disgust, in the name of science, so as to preserve her self-control. After the free shop in the camp was closed, I dressed myself up à la Mae West under the amused eyes of a fat Ukrainian woman who was in charge of the shop that week. I put on long suede shoes and tried to balance my weight on their fantastically high heels. I put on one of the outmoded vamp's dresses – the metallic smell of the disinfectant filled my nostrils – and, for want of a glass, I looked at myself in the smoked surface of the window pane.

The woman looked at me too, her cunning eyes taking in every detail of my appearance. She had three long white hairs on her chin and her yellowish false teeth behind her bloodless lips made her look like an old she-cat waiting to pounce on the last mouse of her life. She came close to me and suddenly put her big, bony hands round my waist. I recoiled, startled, and she told me, in a few words of German, that I was pretty. I hastily put on my ordinary clothes again, and, leaving the shop in disorder, I hurried back to our room. Later on, we received some modern clothes but I wanted to keep my Budapest winter coat. It had been made by an admirable tailor for my fifteenth birthday; it was well nipped-in at the waist, there was a double row of buttons down the front and the collar and cuffs were of navy-blue velvet. More or less well-equipped with these worn garments, and with a shy smile on our lips, we took part in the life of the camp. My father found a lending-library in the little town of Kufstein so, at least, we were able to read. I often went to the little chapel that had been set up in one of the huts, and, with despairing tenacity, I tried to find some relief, some feeling of peace in it. But my trouble was elsewhere and neither the wheezy harmonium nor my forced fervour allayed it completely.

Spring was coming and I had the stifling sense of not having caught up with life. Dawn was lighter and, by four o'clock, I was already awake. Restrained by my parents' breathing, I would lie motionless on my mattress with my eyes open, waiting. I was incubating an undefined love as one incubates an illness. I wanted to love someone. But whom? Whom could I love? Like a captive, I wanted to go away with the daylight to some other life. In the seeming immobility of those sorrowful days, I was preparing my own escape.

With the pocket money the camp gave its grown-up orphans, I went off for a day in Innsbruck. I wanted to breathe freely, to be away from my parents and to see the French Consulate at close quarters.

From the age of five, I had learnt to love France as one loves a distant, brilliant, radiantly kind relative. At fourteen, Balzac had been for me the rich, solid nourishment that strengthens the adolescent mind and makes it grow; I was swallowed up in that monumental work. Afterwards, came the lightning stroke of Stendhal; then I ventured into the unknown territory of Maupassant and came to love the pages of Giraudoux as one loves the memory of a man who died young. Mamma sometimes used to sing Lucienne Boyer's songs – *Je me sens dans tes bras, si petite, si petite auprès de toi* – and, with many tremors, I read *Les Thibault*. At ten, I saw the harsh face of Jouvet; he was the hero of a film that was certainly unsuitable for children. Nor shall I ever forget those great evenings in the theatre, when I was hidden in a corner of the box, and the marvellous moment when the curtain rose on *Madame Sans-Gêne* or on *La Dame aux Camélias*. And how I loved *Les Femmes Savantes* and *Tartuffe* too. It was all this that I wanted to find again in the French Consulate at Innsbruck.

In the little entrance hall, the lethargic receptionist made me sit down at a little table with two questionnaires to fill up. It was there that I saw Georges for the first time. He was sitting very upright on a bench, wearing a high-necked pullover and there was something pathetic about his oval face and fair hair. He was looking at me with his grey eyes and holding a passport in his hand. As I began to study my questionnaires again, I was aware of his gaze.

He got up and came over to me.

'Would you like me to help you to fill up the questionnaire?'

'How did you know I was Hungarian?' I asked without looking at him.

'By your accent. . . . When you spoke to the receptionist. . . . If I can be of any use. . . .'

The door of the office opened and a woman called him in. He disappeared.

I was left alone with the two forms and I filled them in in block letters. I explained that I wanted a job in France and that I should be an ideal children's governess. After a while, Georges returned and it was my turn to be summoned into the office. I was very soon made aware that I was nursing a ridiculous hope in trying to settle in France. Had I been a miner or a farm labourer, it would have been child's play, but, according to the woman who interviewed me, France was overflowing with governesses. I had a mental vision of an army of foreign girls – Swedish, English, Irish, Dutch – marching on Paris under the special banner of nursery governesses. Without a nationality, what chance should I have in this avalanche of women? The bourgeoisie does not like stateless nurses.

'But we're in the French zone,' I dared to point out. 'I thought it was easier to get to Paris from the French zone.'

'It's not a question of zone, mademoiselle. The principles of a country that is defending its integrity are always honourable. . . . You must realise that, if we let everyone come in. . . .'

I left her with the extremely unpleasant feeling of being defeated.

Georges was waiting for me in the entrance hall and among the draughts of chill spring wind he introduced himself with as much easy grace as if he had been in a drawing-room in Budapest. I learnt his name and his surname.

'May I walk along with you?'

'I'm going to the station; I must get back to Kufstein by the five o'clock train.'

We walked towards the station in the fine rain.

'Are you going to France?' he inquired.

'I should have liked to go, but it's too complicated.'

The lights of Innsbruck were coming on and the asphalt gleamed.

In a moment of absent-mindedness, I looked at Georges. He was a charming boy. He told me that he was soon going off to Peru, where his best friend, with whom he had been at school for eight years, had found a silver mine.

154

In the rain that had begun to fall, the enormous mountains were being blotted out by thick, grey clouds. I was once more conscious of the dampness. I had been given some Australian shoes at the camp shop, but I had put on my Budapest ones to come to the Consulate

'It's very hot in Lima,' he told me. 'I shall have a horse and a riding whip and Indian servants.'

'How old are you?'

'Twenty-three. . . .'

'And what did you do in Budapest?'

'I was a law student. I was supposed to become a high-up in the Diplomatic like my father and law is essential for that career . . . . But I've left Hungary for good and I'm going to Peru. . . .'

We arrived at the station. I took out my return ticket and showed it to the collector. Georges returned with a platform ticket. I held out my hand to him:

'Goodbye, and have a good journey. . . .'

'Thank you,' he said, and he remained standing there in the rain. I watched him through the train window.

That night, at Kufstein, I was very depressed. My father knew of this boy's family; he said his father was a well-known man. Before I went to sleep I thought that, if he had not been going to Peru, I might have loved him.

During the Siege, I had seen so many dead young men lying on the pavements of Budapest and had such a vivid recollection of those astonished, glassy-eyed faces and those wide-open mouths, frozen in the effort of snatching one last breath, that it would have been hard for me to be insensible to Georges's living charm. The very time we were living in was his ally. His youth was not a mere detail, but a positive merit. The rolled collar of his pullover added the necessary imaginative touch and his plan of going off to Peru lent him an aureole of unflinching courage. There was a discreet, romantic elegance about his gesture of farewell as he stood on the platform with his golden head bare in the rain.

I had told him my name before the train left, so he was able to write to me. His first letter arrived a week later, from Paris. I had a strange shock, almost a feeling of faintness when I saw his writing. The letter, insignificant in itself, assumed the importance of a message from beyond the grave. Georges's handwriting was exactly like my uncle's. How many times, on his desk in the Rue Notre Dame, I had seen similar well-balanced lines that looked almost engraved in the very black ink on the white paper. It was a handwriting full of wisdom and kindliness, whose round letters were linked by tiny, subtle curves. Those little signs, obedient bearers of calm thoughts and historical references, invariably grew smaller towards the end of a page and resumed their normal size at the beginning of the next. My uncle wrote to me frequently. I was pleased and proud when I received cards from him announcing presents and agreeable surprises.

The outmoded handwriting of this almost unknown young man spoke of Paris and his approaching departure. The result of that letter was that I took to drawing his profile, gilded by a foreign sun, everywhere and on everything. I needed neither pencil nor paper; I traced its invisible contours on the darkness of night, against the green leaves of a late spring and, when I went to the lending library, on the very road before my feet.

This unexpected letter, whose passport was the resemblance between the two handwritings, produced quite a sensational effect on my parents. 'What? . . . You got into conversation with a total stranger and he has the audacity to write to you? What impertinence – and what times we live in! . . . Yes, the father is a remarkable man, but that doesn't prove the son is too! . . . All the same, there is no doubt that he is decent and honourable because his handwriting is really good, extraordinarily good. . . . An astonishing resemblance. . . .'

I listened to all this with unfeigned indifference, even with a slight contempt, and, according to my capricious moods, I now loved, now hated my parents. My frustrated, inwardly seething life, had destroyed my capacity to smile politely and say friendly nothings. I was always on the defensive and in a state of suspended animation; I knew that the mere fact of having survived a world disaster meant nothing whatever in terms of personal happiness. Time passed. I wrote little odds and ends of news and Georges, who, in my mind, was already far away, became my one and only living memory.

I could no longer endure the presence of my parents. I saw in them the obstacle to the future I might build up and, to frighten them and to show them that I was conscious of being twenty, I kept bringing up different projects every day.

'I shall go to Australia and start a publishing house in Melbourne. . . .' or else: 'I've got a unique opportunity; England will accept two nurses from Kufstein; I could be over there in three weeks' time.'

'Are you mad?' asked my mother, as if this were a relevant question.

'No,' I answered, 'but I shall soon be seeing mad people at close quarters. Apparently, the severe cases wet their beds. . . . I shall write a novel about an asylum over there . . . in English, naturally.'

When my father told me I ought to be careful in the little lanes of the camp after dusk, I was overwhelmed by a feeling of despair. Obviously, I should never be able to overcome them. I was imprisoned in the vicious circle of the insane love of parents who no longer had anything to do except to love me. And I wanted to be loved in a different way. I loathed all the details of my childhood that I knew by heart; that I had been adorable, that I had learnt to read when other darling babies, my contemporaries, were only just beginning to walk. My hatred of the piano had turned into a caprice of fate that had prevented the 'infant genius' from becoming a great pianist. Equally often, I heard how rare it was for a young girl to be as pure as myself and how very, very careful I must be not to lose this purity that had been so well safeguarded! I wanted to scream with rage when my father made a Latin quotation and I paced round and round the narrow room like a caged animal. From sheer despair, I put myself down for a dressmaking course. But, instead of seeing needles and thread, I saw a geometrical diagram on the blackboard. When the teacher, a charming woman, explained that this parallelogram was none other than the drawing of a pattern, I promptly made my escape. I had never had anything but a deep, unsurmountable loathing for all forms of mathematics!

The miracle, like all miracles, came unexpectedly, simply and without any fuss. I was vaguely friendly with a woman in the camp and sometimes took refuge in her company. She had taught French in Budapest and she often talked about her youth in Paris and about the friends who had remained faithful to her. She was making preparations for her voyage to South America; she had left Hungary at the same time as ourselves – towards the end of November 1948. At my request, she had written to one of her French friends who lived at Versailles and who, for a long time, had been looking for a nursery-governess for her charming little girl of seven.

The letter engaging me arrived one evening at the end of May. I showed it to my parents with the victorious air of a young Indian brave presenting his first scalp to his elders. My parents found the whole thing impossible, theatrical and ill-considered.

'You want to go and work among total strangers? Heaven knows what a trap may be awaiting you! What you should do, is ask for a scholarship grant and go to the Sorbonne. . . .'

'I can do that over there. . . . I don't want to stay here any longer. . . . And, besides, why strangers? She knows them very well. . . . No, but honestly, I'd rather die than go on like this . . . I want a room whose door is shut by *me* and no one else and where I'll be alone. I want a cupboard with things in it that I've bought out of my own salary. I want to perfect my French. . . . I'm fond of children. . . . A little girl of seven, that's easy. . . . You'll kill me if you keep me here. . . . Every generation. . . . the rights of youth. . . . White slave traffickers have other fish to fry . . . they won't be watching and waiting for *me*. . . . But, of course, I'll be careful. . . . You simply *must* realise you're being unreasonable. . . . A well-brought-up girl can't be in Paris on her own? In the first place, I shan't be on my own, I shall be looking after a child. Besides, since when have well-brought-up girls crossed frontiers illicitly without passports? I find that much more shocking, walking on all fours and being frightened of the moon and of being hunted down by dogs, and crying with your face buried in dead leaves. . . . And is it correct for a well-brought-up girl to tread on an arm that has come away from a corpse? Come away because it's decomposing . . . a well-brought-up girl eating horse flesh from horses blown to bits by bombs. . . . When I was taking my exams in Budapest and I felt someone walking behind me, I shivered with fright. I didn't know what they were tracking me for . . . my slim ankles or my bourgeois origin. . . . What else do you want from me? . . . And if these times *are* nothing but danger and suffering, let's go ahead all the same. . . . But, look here, I'm twenty and a half . . . yes, even the months count. . . . Heaven knows how long I've been grown-up . . . but you know it as well as I do! . . . A little girl of seven, it'll be just as if she were my little sister . . . in fact, why *haven't* I a little sister?'

I celebrated my liberation by taking the train for Paris. But I was poisoned by all the advice and all those wearisome unproductive conversations. I had used up all my breath during those endless evenings and, once I was actually on the train, my one desire was to leave everything I had known and felt up to that moment, as quickly as possible. My father accompanied me into the compartment; he put the suitcase we had bought in Vienna into the luggage rack and kissed me. Then he rejoined my mother on the platform. I had still five minutes to get through. I was trembling with feverish impatience; I kept looking at the Kufstein station clock. But, one minute before the hand reached the appointed time, my eyes met the eyes of my parents. And, suddenly overwhelmed with an immense fear and a wild rush of tenderness, I wanted to get out of the train and throw myself into their arms and explain everything, twenty and a half years of love for them – in a single gesture. At that precise moment, my mother's face was lit up by a tearful smile. I think she wanted to tell me, in sixty seconds, everything a mother can tell her daughter who is going off to conquer an infinitesimal corner of the world. My nature was not given to making confidences: I was naturally taciturn. It was at my mother's side that I had made the acquaintance of death in Budapest but we never spoke of birth, pain, love and women's secrets. Such reserve was extremely reassuring, and, in the padded shelter of this feigned indifference, I had been able to go calmly through all the crises and the unanswerable questions that beset the transitions from one age to another. This affectionate hostility was my refuge and when, in one of Pearl Buck's books, I read the description of the sufferings of a Chinese woman in labour on the fruitful earth and encountered, for the first time, that warm atmosphere of blood and tears, it was like my revenge for having crossed that frontier alone and unaided.

. . . But now that the train was slowly beginning to move, my mother walked along beside it. 'Be careful, my child,' she said, and her face told me that she could have gone on talking to me for hours. My father, too, came up close. 'Be *very* careful,' he said, in his turn. The train began to move faster and faster. I leant out through the window. They were far away and I shouted: 'I love you tremendously, I'll come back soon . . . I love you tremendously. . . .'

Swallowed up by a tunnel, the train gave a death rattle, and I burst into tears.

Chapter Nineteen

IT HAD BEEN arranged that Madame Bruller should meet me at the Gare de l'Est. I had sent her my photo from Kufstein so that she could recognise me easily. But I think that, even without a photo, she would have made no mistake. I had prepared a serious, conscientious nurse's face; the face of a girl who would be attentive to her employer's wishes; in fact, a very correct little person who would not let herself be carried away by her own youth. Rumpled from a sleepless night, my hands damp with stage fright, I watched Paris coming nearer and nearer. The station was swarming with porters; it was almost impossible to avoid them, and I lingered in front of my compartment with my Budapest winter coat over my arm and the cardboard suitcase at my feet. My heart was beating fit to burst my chest and I was convinced I had a black smudge on my forehead for I had been sitting by the window whose frame, in the morning, was covered with a thick layer of soot. I watched the people going past and I was so strung-up by this waiting that I did not notice the young woman who had touched my arm.

'Mademoiselle?'

I said, 'How d'you do' with a start.

'My car's in front of the station; come along. . . . Not too tired?'

I answered with a sigh:

'Terribly. Travelling's always. . . .'

But I did not dare go on, for she looked so worried.

'As tired as all that?'

'Oh, but not in the least,' I corrected myself. 'Not in the least.'

'You know,' she said the moment we were in the car, 'the maid had an attack of appendicitis last night; she was operated on this morning. . . .'

'But I'll help you, madame.'

Now that she had mentioned the maid's illness, she fell silent like someone entirely intent on their driving.

I was sitting beside her and the blinding sun put a curtain of light between Paris and myself. The windscreen was dirty and the metallic rays of this unexpected heat were blurred by the layer of dust. Madame Bruller had an obstinate chin, sharp as a sarcastic retort, a heavy lipstick, a delicate shiny nose, eyes fixed on the road in front of her and black hair drawn into a tight chignon that I longed to touch to find out if it were real. Without looking at me, she asked for news of her friend, the teacher.

'She's very well. I think her boat leaves on the 29th for Rio de Janeiro.'

Madame Bruller jerked a sentence at me in the cryptic manner of a dice-player.

'But for her, you wouldn't have been able to come to us. . . . However, she's given the necessary references.'

'I've certainly got a smut somewhere,' I thought, 'and that smut makes me look suspicious. Otherwise she wouldn't have made that irrelevant remark.' I tried to catch a glimpse of myself in the driving mirror, but without success.

'Where is little Monique?' I asked, risking my self hesitantly on unknown territory. 'Is she at school?'

'No. In bed. She's ill. . . . Have you had chicken pox?'

I just managed not to exclaim: 'So she's ill, too!' and said:

'Yes, madame. I had chicken pox when I was still in Budapest.'

She looked at me suddenly; she was able to do so, we were safely on the motor highway.

'In Budapest?'

She said this with so much incredulity that I mechanically touched the little hole beside my ear, invisible to anyone but myself, that the chicken-pox had left me.

'In Budapest? . . .'

After a few moments' silence she went on:

'You'll have quite a lot to do in the first few days. You must stop the child from scratching herself. . . . It itches a great deal.'

The tone she used to me was that of a tired teacher repeating the same thing innumerable times to a mental defective. I should have liked to say that chicken pox itched in Budapest too, but judged it wiser to keep silent.

'I held her little hands all night long; my husband has been sitting up with her for the last two days. . . .'

And the maid, when had that happened? But I did not ask the question.

'I had gloves when I had chicken pox. . . .'

She shrugged her shoulders:

'It's better to hold her and make sure. . . .'

I had seen the houses of Versailles appearing but, before we arrived in the town itself, she took a by-road and soon we stopped in front of an old, two-storeyed house. It was covered with ivy and the garden was overgrown with weeds; the wrought-iron gate, rusted by the rain of years, stood half-open. Later, I realised it was impossible to close it.

She opened the front door. The hall was astonishingly small, with two doors to the right, one to the left, and the staircase leading to the upper floor. I put down my coat and my suitcase and followed her. On the first floor there were four bedrooms of which one was occupied by the little invalid and a neighbour who was looking after her, a kindly woman with grey hair.

'Thank you, my dear,' said Madame Bruller, bending over the child.

I went up close and I saw a red swollen blotch of a face, completely distorted by a crop of pimples.

'This is Monique, little Monique.'

At the sound of her mother's voice, the child let out a yell.

I bent over her and I was aware of the two women watching me keenly. Not a movement, not a sound of my anxious, jerky breathing escaped them. I felt as heavy and clumsy as if they had

163

tied invisible weights to my limbs before I entered the room. I sought the child's eyes. I wanted to feel the first contact which, even if hostile, would be exclusively our own. And if I could make her stop screaming with a smile, I should already have scored a success. I did not love her yet. It is impossible to love out of duty, but I was full of goodwill and, suppressing a spasm of disgust, I lightly touched one of the small hands that was red and damp with saliva. In the distorted face, the eyes were replaced by two slits filled with a black stare, swimming with tears, and the smell of that tortured skin, burning with fever, filled my nostrils and went right down to the bottom of my throat.

The neighbour went on whispering to Madame Bruller. I stood awkwardly by the bed. I must do something or other to please them. I looked in vain for a glass of water I could offer with the classic gesture of nurses. The blanket was well tucked in; there was no point in touching it. The child never stopped moaning; she had placed her voice like an actress who has to keep it up for the five acts to follow. She moaned rhythmically; I hoped one would manage to get accustomed to it, like the tick of a noisy alarm clock. I sat down on the edge of the bed; the child was quiet from sheer astonishment and the two women slipped out of the room as swiftly and silently as smoke rings escape from an expert mouth. They had only been waiting for me to sit down, a captive for an unspecified time. When Monique wanted to touch her face, I seized her hands and caught them on the wing. I could not take my eyes off her; her movements were too unexpected. It was hide-and-seek of the reflexes and I was always quicker than she was. The window of the room was scrupulously closed. The curtain let a pale light filter through. I had no watch; the last time I had looked at a clock was at the station. I tried to define the distant noises in the house; downstairs they were opening and shutting doors. A woman's voice – Madame Bruller's perhaps – was speaking on the telephone: I could hear an occasional 'Of course', and 'Naturally. . . .' I floated in this stifling twilight atmosphere. Monique grew tired before I did; I saw her struggling with a ray

164

of light like a midge on a fly-paper trying to pull off its delicate legs one by one. At last Monique was stuck fast in a kindly sleep; she stopped moaning and, behind the mask of the childish malady, I could see the suffering face that had not even the advantage of charming or moving one by its pallor. I got up and, at last, looked at the room, like a sleepwalker rudely awakened at the very peak of his trance to find himself in his nightclothes on the roof of a five-storeyed house. This room was fairly large. Beside the wardrobe, there was a divan; then came a few toys scattered on some shelves, a chest-of-drawers with its two bottom drawers open, a locked door, and a moth-eaten carpet. And, everywhere, in the gilded shafts of the banished sun, motes of dust danced in a perpetual ballet; the curtain was not properly drawn. I tiptoed over to the window. The garden below was tranquil. A white, silent hen was walking about and pecking for worms. She plunged her tiny head into the grass like an unaccustomed bather who only likes getting wet up to her shoulders.

'Is she asleep?'

Madame Bruller's whispering voice struck me in the back and took my breath away.

'Yes, she's asleep. . . .'

'Then what are you waiting for? Come and have lunch, you must be hungry.'

I went down with her to the ground floor. The smell of hot oil and freshly roasted meat filled the house.

'I'd like to wash my hands.'

The request seemed natural to her and she indicated a door, with an impatient gesture. At last I saw myself in a glass. I rubbed my hands with a piece of soap and looked at myself. There was no black smudge on my forehead but my eyes had dark rings of weariness round them. Those nights of tense waiting at Kufstein and sixteen hours on the train without any sleep, made my face look drawn. I cast a furtive glance round the bathroom. How well I was to come to know every corner of it! There were two dressing-gowns made of towelling hanging up on hooks. They

165

were worn and weary from too much service; the enamel of the bath was chipped and the geyser bore black traces of flames that were either irregular or over-greedy. On the shelf was a tube of toothpaste, some battered toothbrushes and a pink plastic beaker with the imprint of lips on it. But here, too, there was a window looking out on the garden. I also noticed two pairs of slippers. The man's slippers conjured up the thought of Monsieur Bruller. He must exist and, judging from his slippers, he was tall and heavy; a hundred kilogrammes of malice bundled into a striped jacket. I imagined him as fat and overwhelming. I emerged from the bathroom and Madame Bruller led me into the dining-room where a thin, frail man was reading a paper that lay on his plate.

'This is Christine,' said Madame and I felt a certain disquiet that she did not add the exact definition: 'Christine, the nurse.' Reduced to being only Christine, the horizon of diverse tasks seemed to me vast, almost limitless.

'Did you have a good journey?'

Monsieur held out his small soft hand to me as he asked the question. But he did not wait for my reply and plunged back into his newspaper.

Madame Bruller indicated my place, as if she were showing me a town she wanted to present to me.

'You're going to eat with us, like one of the family. . . . Would you mind putting your paper down, darling?

The man did not stir. The new tone she had adopted on my account was so unexpected that her husband had not even realised that she was speaking to him.

'Your paper. . . .'

Her true voice struck him like the explosion of a bomb. He put it down by his plate and we attacked a stew, accompanied by boiled potatoes.

'Would you bring the salt, Christine?'

I stood up.

'Where is the kitchen?

'The door on the left. You'll find it on the table.'

The kitchen was in a disastrous state. A regiment of saucepans was piled up on the floor along with plates, cutlery and glasses, a whole bridal dowry, complete with the wedding presents! The fleeting ghost of the maid gave me an outsize grin; it had the impertinence of beings who have never existed. I found the salt. The Brullers looked at me. They wanted to see my reaction to the vision of the kitchen printed on my face. They pressed round me as poor relations press round the doctor who is watching over the last moments of the rich aunt on her death bed. I pretended to have seen nothing.

'You left Hungary when?'

'Seven months ago.'

Madame Bruller inquired:

'So late? Why did you wait till 1948?'

Monsieur Bruller did not want to be left out.

'Must be no joke, what's going on over there. . . .'

'Oh no. . . .'

'Were you in Budapest all the time?'

'Up to taking my Higher Certificate.'

'It's all so dreadfully sad,' went on Madame Bruller, then added:

'You'll help me wash up after lunch, won't you?'

'Of course, madame. With pleasure.'

Monsieur Bruller said pleasantly:

'I did not think Hungarian girls were fair. I imagined them with long black plaits, sometimes right down to their ankles.'

'It's rather unusual,' I replied evasively.

They left the table very hurriedly. Madame Bruller had explained to me that she would take advantage of the child's sleep to snatch a little rest. . . .

'My husband is going back to his office in Paris . . . I'll leave you on your own. . . . You'll find all the cleaning things you need . . . . Afterwards, I'll show you your room. . . . But during these next few difficult days, you'll sleep on the divan in the child's room. . . .'

I heard Monsieur's car start up and I was left helpless on this raft, floating on a sea of ill-kept lawn. How far away Paris was! 'Write to us at once,' my mother had said. . . . 'The very day you arrive!'

In the silent house, abandoned in the midst of mountains of dirty crockery, I felt I was living in a dream from which I could waken at will. But it was no use thinking. I must begin to collect the necessary things for the washing-up. I heated the water in a clothes-copper. I found a brush but it was very worn-out and was shedding its bristles as a sick dog sheds its hair. I had to heat up three lots of water to vanquish the pile of washing-up. When everything was sparkling, and at the very moment when I had an irresistible desire to sit down, Madame Bruller called me:

'Christine, come here, quick. . . .'

I ran; she called down from the floor above:

'Would you make me some very weak tea and some warm milk for Monique?'

After that monster cleaning-up, I already knew where to find tea and milk . . . and despair.

Till evening, it was a constant whirlwind of orders.

'Christine, would you mind airing the bedroom? I've taken the blanket off the bed, you might make it up again. . . . If you've got a minute, then do wash Monique's little bits and pieces that I've put in a heap on the bathroom; as a rule, I send everything to the laundry, but the child's nightgowns are too fragile. . . . Don't you think there's a lot of dust in the living-room? . . . If you're used to having *goûter*, do get yourself some. . . .

I began with Monsieur's and Madame's bed. It was the first time I had seen a vast French bed and Madame told me to tuck the blankets in smoothly and tightly. To begin with I stripped off everything and removed the imprints of the two bodies, the lean one and the flabby one, united in the holy bonds of matrimony. Madame decided that the sheets were dirty already and gave me some clean ones. I perceived that she had decided to make a fresh start in life and 'put everything in order at last'. Monique moaned again; her voice was fresh, full of vigour and expression. The enormous mattress confronted me like a warrior, heavy when I lifted it but becoming horribly pliable when I wanted to master it. It was impossible to turn it; it remained bent double on the bed like a giant with stomach-ache. But at last I succeeded and the room was soon tidy. During a minute when Madame had her eye off me, I glanced out into the garden and I saw the hen just in front of the window; her head was bent over to the right as she stared at an invisible point; her white feathers looked yellow in the twilight; she wore her delicate red comb like a diadem. She raised her head towards me and her eyes seemed full of kindly curiosity, and, to show her favour, she winked her left eye, drawing up her eyelid from below. We looked at each other; we were already accomplices and I decided I would call her Undine. In her knowing silence, she was like a fairy on the dark green grass.

'Christine; what are you doing?'

What, in fact, *was* I doing? Nothing. And I answered, like my own echo:

'Nothing, madame.'

'Are you tired?'

'A little, madame.'

'Come along, we must go and get dinner ready. My husband will be home in half an hour.'

Before going down to the ground floor I went into Monique's bedroom. She was sitting propped up against her pillows and reading a child's picture book.

'Will you tell me a story?'

I would gladly have stayed but Madame was already impatient.

'Christine, aren't you coming?'

'Stay here,' whimpered Monique. 'Tell me a story.'

Monique howled: I went downstairs and Madame said:

'You mustn't make a child in that state cry.'

'I didn't mean to make her cry. She called me and I went into her room. She wanted me to tell her a story.'

Madame Bruller became severe.

'You mustn't spoil her. Whatever you do, don't spoil her. . . .'

169

I laid the table. I peeled unknown vegetables, great menacing black roots. Madame gave me a chance to escape.

'When you go out of the house, turn right and go round to the back – you'll find a cage. We have a hen who lays an egg every day – that's Monique's egg.'

I was enchanted and I went out of the house with a great sigh of relief. The little street in front of it was deserted; the shadows were already lengthening under the trees; the warm air caressed my face. I found the cage beside two bushes covered with buds. The little cage was open and on the yellow straw I saw a dazzlingly white egg; I touched it, it was warm; Undine could not be far away. She appeared, with her crooked diadem, swaying as she walked. I held out some crumbs to her on the palm of my hand; she looked at them with interest but was still too hesitant to accept them and retired into her cage as if into a sedan chair. I closed the little door and went back to the house with the egg.

Dinner was anything but tranquil. I had to go upstairs twice to Monique and afterwards I hurriedly swallowed the food that had gone cold on my plate. Madame gave me some sheets and, feeling extremely depressed, I made up my bed on the divan in Monique's room. How much I should have liked a room to myself! But perhaps, in a few days, I should have the maid's since they now no longer even mentioned her.

I had no dressing-gown so I had to dress again completely in the bathroom to walk the few steps to Monique's bedroom. With the aid of a sedative, she had gone to sleep again and Madame said I had been extraordinarily lucky to have arrived at the end of this disagreeable illness.

Monsieur came home very late. I heard the brakes of his car in a troubled half-sleep. My blanket was too short and I had to double myself up to keep warm. The pillow exhaled a faint, almost imperceptible smell of mildew. From where had she unearthed that pillow for me? I went to sleep with my knees huddled up. I was too weary to cry.

* * *

170

Sharing the intimate life of other people is terrible. After I had been there four weeks, I knew their faces, the words they used, the way they walked that deformed their slippers, the peevish mood that dominated the morning, the insipid taste of their cooking. Monique, convalescent now, displayed a face that was pale once more and stared insistently at me with her large eyes during meals. She expressed openly what her parents dared not say; she had full liberty, since she was only a child. I do not say she hated me; her feeling about me was something subtler and more refined. She would stare at me coldly; she would burst into yells and tears, and then be suddenly silent, awaiting her opportunity.

'Why have you got an accent? Is Hungary like China? Why do you have meals with us? The maids always had theirs in the kitchen. . . .'

The father would intervene, as diplomat and humanist:

'But, Monique, you know quite well Christine isn't a maid, she's your nurse.'

Monique was not embarrassed.

'Up to now I didn't have a nurse, only a maid. . . . Why do you call her something else?'

'You talk too much, child,' said the mother. 'Eat up your. food nicely and then Christine will put you to bed.'

Putting her to bed was a struggle over every single article of clothing she wore. Unbuttoning her innumerable jerseys and undoing her shoe laces were major operations. To perform them, I knelt down in front of her. I also told stories; I told them very badly; I yawned as soon as I began a story. It's not my fault, but children's stories bore me to death. If only I could talk about Wanda! . . . Wanda will have a Negro lover. . . .

'Is it nice to have a lover?' But my mother's menacing face banished the word 'lover'; I purified my thoughts and asked myself the question again: 'Is it nice to have a husband?'

'Oh do hurry up and begin,' Monique would say.

'Once upon a time. . . .'

I imagined Georges in his silver mine. I saw him walking up

to his ankles in the liquid silver that ran like an underground river.

'If you don't tell me a story, I shall tell Mamma.'

'What shall you tell Mamma, my precious?' inquired Madame Bruller, appearing in the doorway, her face covered with thick cream and her hair tied up in a scarf. Her face was so shiny that her features had lost their definition; nose, eyebrows and mouth were all blurred under the oily mask. Her dressing-gown was open a little at the neck; she was already in her nightdress. I could hear Monsieur Bruller bustling to and fro. The sight of his wife almost made me pity him. Kissing her must be like kissing a lump of lard!

'But, Christine, you've no imagination! The poor little thing's *so* fond of fairy tales. . . .'

At last, they had all gone to bed. Tomorrow they would have a long lie-in and *I* should be free. Tomorrow, Sunday, I was going to Paris. Apparently there was a special Mass for the Hungarians. Since I had been there, I hadn't had a Sunday to myself, and, tomorrow, I was going to have a whole day. I would leave at nine so as to arrive in time for the eleven o'clock Mass.

Chapter Twenty

I WOKE UP very early and had to wait, lying perfectly still, for the hours to pass. At night, by Madame Bruller's orders, the windows were hermetically sealed for she had an almost hysterical fear of burglars and draughts. Towards dawn, the house was always full of the stuffy smell of heavy sleep. I got up about half-past seven and tiptoed to the bathroom; I shuddered with apprehension when the gurgling of the tap sounded very loud. I turned it down to a very thin trickle of water and shut the door with infinite precaution. At last, I left it all behind me, and went out to take Undine some drinking water. She was standing on one of her yellow feet, with her head tucked under her wing; when she saw me, she shook herself and avidly pecked the crumbs from my palm. I had the feeling that her pecks were sharp, affectionate little kisses, a manifestation of primeval sympathy, a sign from that other world beyond the human one. That morning, everything was reaching out expectantly to a new awakening of life. The buds, all those tight green little knots, had unfolded during the night and the frail young leaves were scattered with dewdrops.

I set off in the direction of the station. I was wearing a little blue woollen dress and my hair hung loose on my shoulders: the Kufstein missal was so big that I could not shut my handbag. The late June sun was already hot and the sleepers of Versailles would be throwing off their blankets in their feverish doze. I imagined the families behind the closed shutters. But none of them had the faces of Monsieur or Madame Bruller. With a logical, conscious tenacity, I wanted to preserve that image of France I had made for myself years ago. I knew that Monsieur and Madame were no more than a disagreeable detail. The day before, I had sent a letter to my parents, a restrained letter, expressed with considerable reserve: 'I am very well and I am glad to be in France.'

Moreover, I was always thrilled when, as 'sender', I could inscribe Versailles on the back of the envelope. Not for a fortune would I have admitted that the crazy rhythm of my work had prevented me up to now from seeing the palace, the gardens and the shade of Marie Antoinette whom I loved on account of Fersen. Even when one is a Republican, one forgives all in a queen who had the capacity to love. It was Stefan Zweig who had told me all I knew about her and told it with infinite art, at once compassionate and indiscreet. Stefan Zweig's book on Marie Antoinette had seemed to me like the literary speech for the defence of a barrister who was in love with his client and was no longer bound by professional secrecy.

That morning, the dead streets of Versailles were embalmed by a youthful, radiant sun. I walked in silence and a golden haze. I caught the train at the last minute and, leaning back against the hard wooden seat, I was overwhelmed with inexplicable terror. I was going to see Paris. How I should have loved to see it in different circumstances – with a passport in order in my pocket, a blue beret on my head, a portable typewriter in my hand and a book of traveller's cheques in my handbag! When I was building up my plans in Budapest, that was how I had imagined arriving in Paris.

When I gave up my ticket at the barrier, I realised, that very instant, that my hands were rough and my nails broken. I did too much washing and scrubbing in Madame's kitchen with products that were cruel to the skin. In the waiting-room, I saw the map of the métro. I went straight down into it, without going out into the street, like a swimmer who goes faster under water. The kindly women ticket collectors helped me to find the place on the Left Bank where the church was situated. I left the métro and found myself in front of the building and, crossing a courtyard, I went into a chapel that was still empty.

174

I knelt down on a prie-dieu, and, with my chin on my piously clasped hands, I observed the people who were coming in in little groups and dispersing themselves in the nave. A smell of cold incense floated in the air and I felt that, in a few minutes, I should be very hungry indeed; I had left Versailles without having any breakfast.

I was extremely distracted during the religious service; I only caught a few words of the sermon in Hungarian: 'Be good, hardworking and kind.' And, after that, I plunged back into my own thoughts like someone falling into unconsciousness. Towards the end, I went out into the little courtyard where my compatriots were already chatting. Later, I realised that this was the regular meeting place where they saw each other once a week. I did not know a soul. I waited aimlessly in a corner, simply to pass a little time and, suddenly, something gave me a shock as violent as that of the first pain that heralds an illness. I caught sight of Georges with another young man. In the sunlight that flooded the courtyard, he was slim, elegant and transparently pale but the expression of his face betrayed great weariness. The fair-skinned face was no longer tanned by the heat of Peru. I looked at him for three or four minutes before he saw me. With an incredulous smile, racking his memory for my name, he came up to me, paralysed at the sight of someone emerging from a forgotten past, and held out his hand.

'How d'you do. . . .'

A brief silence and he added, uncertainly:

'Christine. . . .'

'How d'you do, Georges. . . . Didn't you go to Peru? What happened to the silver mine?'

He made an embarrassed little grimace.

'The mine? It's flooded.'

Suddenly all the details of Georges's good or evil fortunes seemed so close and familiar that I exclaimed:

'Oh! Poor Georges. . . .'

'It's not so serious as all that,' he replied and added almost at once: 'Can I come with you, wherever you're going? . . . And, by the way, how do you come to be in Paris? You had difficulties in Innsbruck. . . .'

We left the courtyard of the church. The street was already bustling, but I caught sight of a café. Seeing an Italian espresso coffee apparatus through the window, I thought, if I could get as far as one of the little tables, I should be saved.

'You do walk fast,' said Georges, smiling, and I crossed the street without looking right or left.

'I'd like to have a coffee, now this minute. . . .'

He took hold of my elbow to guide me and this gesture produced a curious reaction: the left half of my body, on his side, turned burning hot; the other half, the right, became cold, objective and full of suspicion. At last, seated at a tiny table and nibbling a *croissant*, I looked him in the eyes. His eyes frequently changed colour; the iris turned blue, grey or green according to the play of light. Then I drank my longed-for coffee with considerable difficulty; I would have liked to hide my ruined hands. . . .

'Yes, all alone.'

I heard my own voice: 'And you too?'

'Absolutely alone; my parents stayed in Hungary.'

'And now that you're not going to Peru after all, what are your plans?'

'I've put myself down for a course in International Law . . . and later on. . . .'

He took out a cigarette and I noticed the signet ring on his left hand.

He was aware of my glance at the ring and excused himself, saying:

'Oh, I don't always wear it, you know. I don't like it. . . . And what about you? What do you want to do in Paris?'

'Write.'

I was genuinely astonished by my own admission, as if I had begun to speak in a language hitherto unknown to me.

'What do you want to write?'

'Novels, lots of novels – and short stories.'

176

He drank the last mouthful of his coffee.

'Do you know any Paris publishers?'

'Me? Paris publishers? I don't know a soul in Paris and I'm working in Versailles. I'm a little girl's nurse. . . .'

After a long walk, we reached the banks of the Seine.

'I'll show you Paris,' he said.

But I shook my head.

'Not yet, later on. . . .'

How could I have told him about my resentments and my obscure troubles, about that feverish little rebellion that made me hostile and unjust towards Paris? How could I explain this life I had to lead, this working from morning to night? How could I tell him that it would have been better if he had gone off to Peru because I was already attached to him? My loneliness was too great not to fall in love at once; there was an empty, hungry place in my heart that I was preparing as carefully as a mistress of a house expecting a guest. . . .

'But I *shall* show you Paris all the same,' he said, with charming insistence.

I looked at the Seine; I pretended to be lost in my thoughts but nothing could have been falser; I was observing him and I was observing myself. How easy it all was for fate; two lonely young people meeting in Paris; the quay from which a fisherman was casting his line in the water; the pair of lovers kissing on the steps. They were sipping each other's lips – as if they were tasters and we were kings, and they were proving to us the wine was not poisoned. No, my friend, I don't want all that; it would be a love affair too scientifically prepared; the sky is too blue; the air is too charged with spring already ripening into summer! . . .

'You're not listening to me. . . . I was saying that Octave Aubry was right when . . .

. . . And, once again, for the last time, I made a final effort to detach myself. I went through all the things I had heard about love. And, besides, a fair person should never love another fair person.

I turned towards him to say goodbye and, suddenly, my throat went tight with emotion. He was handsome and anxious, tense and serious.

I replied:

'Yes. . . . Yes, we can see each other again next Sunday. . . .'

I had the feeling that this day would last for ever. There was no more Versailles, no more Monique, no more suburban train. There was nothing but a vague, shy love. . . .

Chapter Twenty-one

MY LIFE AT Versailles had the imperturbable rhythm of an hour-glass. The hours dribbled on from morning to night without a moment's rest. I did not like Madame Bruller's shrill, urgent orders so I hurried to anticipate them. It was an appalling rush; I had the entire house on my hands. In the morning, I got up first and prepared the breakfast; then I went up to wake Monique who was invariably sulky and invariably ready to invent ways of irritating me, with a cistern of tears behind her black eyes. Madame Bruller came down to the dining-room tottering with sleep and bowed under the weight of her dreams. Monsieur Bruller nervously fingered the razor-cuts on his cheek and examined his bloodstained handkerchief with the slow intentness of a schoolboy. While Madame Bruller was doing the shopping, I cleaned the house, while keeping an eye on Monique, who, thanks to the school holidays, spent her days in the garden. The despairing cries of Undine frequently made me descend with a broom in my hand. One day, Monique faced up to me.

'Leave me alone, it's *my* hen.'

'But I don't allow you to torture her,' I replied fiercely.

She almost hissed the threat at me:

'Mamma said she's going to boil the hen. She doesn't lay any more.'

It was only too true that Undine was tired and languid. For the past week, I had looked in vain for her egg. She clucked in a lost way and turned her head to the right, looking at me with a puzzled expression and displaying her red eyelid like a tiny shutter. But I had never suspected that her life was in peril.

During my animated conversation with Monique, she had escaped and vanished behind a bush.

I went upstairs again and resumed my perpetual motion. The bed with its stale warmth, the windows I flung open, the objects I gave life to in my imagination – I decided that each had a soul. And now the comb stuffed with Madame Bruller's black hairs would groan: 'How disgusting. . . .' and the down-at-heel slippers whimper: 'You'd think they were camels or elephants. . . .' Madame Bruller shivered in the well-aired house. 'What a draught!' 'Madame, we're in July.' 'But the child will get earache. . . .' I said not another word; I shut the windows, singing a tune in my own mind of which the words ran: 'It's all so stupid, I'll get away. . . .'

Madame took the only deckchair in the house and lay in the sun; her face anointed with grease and her arms hanging inert. I was almost certain that she had never given herself to her husband with such voluptuous sensuality.

I finished cooking the lunch about one o'clock, when Monsieur arrived. He ground the brakes of his car and *I* wanted to grind my teeth. I waited at table and, when I was able to sit down, I pecked at my food; I was too tired to feel hungry. I carried the coffee out into the garden; they had retired into the shade: 'You know it's so dangerous, a full sun on a full stomach!' I went in again to wash up and scraps of conversation floated in through the open kitchen window. Without their having told me so directly, I knew that the villa at the seaside had been rented from the first of August.

'A real rest . . . absolute peace and quiet. . . .'

Monsieur's voice promised marvels as he built up castles in Spain.

'You don't even think about the cooking. But, of course, Christine will be pleased – the air's so good there. . . .'

Tomorrow, I would tell them my decision. Today, I was still a slave, but tomorrow they would know that the bird was about to fly.

If I had had time to lie down for one minute, I should have

fallen asleep straight away. I pined for a long, dreamless sleep, a semblance of death. I trembled with fatigue and I started whenever I heard Madame's voice. After doing the washing-up, I got the *goûter* ready. After *goûter*, I took Monique for a walk. 'The poor little thing's been shut up all day.' She adored running off and disappearing into corners; I ran after her, panting. I had learnt to weep without shedding tears. I swallowed my tears; they burnt my throat and left a bitter taste on my palate. When I caught Monique, I gripped her hand firmly in mine. 'Ow, you're hurting me,' she cried. But I did not answer; I went on walking, with my knees shaking under me.

When we returned, I began to prepare the dinner. Madame Bruller came into the kitchen; she sat down on a chair and looked at me.

'We're soon going to the sea, Christine. You won't look so pale down there. . . . By the way, why are you so pale? I hope there's nothing the matter with you. I can't help worrying, because of the child.'

I peeled the old potatoes; they were bluish and withered and full of 'eyes'. Madame Bruller leant her elbows on the table and flung a sentence at me that was like a signal for the hounds to tear their quarry to pieces.

'Tomorrow, Sunday, I'm going to boil the hen. She's very fat, she'll make a good thick stew. My husband adores that.'

I went on peeling potatoes without looking at the executioner's face. On Sunday morning, I was going away for ever.

That night, after dinner, I had permission to have a bath. I locked myself into the bathroom and, as soon as I was naked, I looked at my back. It was thin and narrow and the salient shoulder blades looked like weights attached to my shoulders.

For two months I had been living like some monstrous hostess who adores having people round her and has invited an entire family to stay in her cottage. My guests were Monsieur and Madame Bruller and their daughter Monique. I had looked after them well, but it was over; I was leaving tomorrow morning.

With two months' salary in my pocket, I would rent a tiny room and I would look for some other work.

Someone knocked at the door.

'How much longer are you going to be?'

'Just coming, madame.'

In my bed I doubled myself up as I did every night. Monique made me get up again to give her a glass of water.

When they were all asleep I thought things over. I could not return to Kufstein. I wanted to stay in Paris; I *must* stay there. I would easily find another job. My body ached with weariness and sleep would not come. My thoughts were lit up by a terrifying lucidity, an intellectual aurora borealis. It was impossible to keep one single dark corner in my soul. What was the good of lying to others or to oneself? Georges would be waiting for me tomorrow at the Gare Saint-Lazare as usual. And our meeting tomorrow would be decisive.

The heat of that house was stifling me. I felt dazed, hovering between dream and reality. I threw off the blanket as I might have pushed away an old dog lying on my feet. The mildewed smell of my pillow was insidiously suffocating me. Motionless and lethargic, I felt the sweat trickling down my back and loneliness gnawed at me like a relentless pain.

With burning eyes, I waited for the dawn and, as soon as it began to be light, I got up and dressed. I sat down, fully dressed, on the edge of my bed and, about seven o'clock, I picked up the cardboard suitcase. It had served me as a wardrobe for two months. I left the house, shutting the door carefully behind me. I made my way to Undine's cage. She was lying on her straw; I woke her up. She fluffed up her battered feathers and wanted to protect her invisible eggs; she was broody. I chased her out of her cage but she did not understand and kept lying down every five steps with an indignant cluck. I whispered:

'You're a fool; she'll kill you if you stay here. . . .'

But Undine, in the grip of her obstinate maternal instinct, kept lying down in front of me; she wanted to hatch those invisible eggs. I grabbed hold of her and the sickly heat of her body burnt my arm. I left the wrought-iron gate wide open. In a little street near the station, I had often seen an old lady cleaning out her canary's cage at the window. She would certainly not roast *her* bird when it stopped singing. With Undine clutched under my arm, I walked fast and I deposited her in front of the old lady's closed door.

Half an hour later I took the train to Paris.

Chapter Twenty-two

IT WOULD HAVE been better if, from the very beginning, I had had the courage to admit that my marriage was a failure. But the first year of it left me no time for analysis. Now that I can see it in perspective and so judge it objectively, I can recreate in myself the rhythm of that past unhappiness – the first kiss and the first blow, the first false smile and the long, disturbing silences that often fell between us.

I can still see myself arriving at the Gare Saint-Lazare. He was waiting for me on the platform, with a bunch of flowers in his hand. He took my case, and we went to his quiet little hotel in Passy. I had clothed him with so many qualities that I was like a designer who had run wild and in a fever of enthusiasm, so overdressed a wax doll that, in the end, the doll had melted and she was left with empty hands. I never stopped interpreting his words and his gestures, and, with a monstrous egotism, I distorted everything. I wanted to live with a hero and I had made up my mind that the father of my children would be a world celebrity; for example, a barrister whose speeches would make a public sensation. I was completely taken aback when he told me one day that the law did not interest him in the slightest; however it was only for a moment that my obdurate will slackened.

'But what *would* you like to do?'

Before he answered, he lit a cigarette and, through the smoke, his face looked pure, almost childlike.

'I always wanted to be an engineer.'

'But that's marvellous,' I exclaimed. I could already see his hand pressing the button that would start up the machinery of a dam that would bring prosperity to an entire country.

'That's out,' he said in self-defence. 'Being an engineer was only a boy's dream. . . . I'd like to become an architect.'

And, already, I was admiring him as if he were Le Corbusier.

I ought to have been more indulgent and more sincere; I ought to have abandoned that atmosphere of dreamy optimism I myself had created.

So my loneliness persisted and, when I woke up beside him for the first time, I felt that everything had changed, except myself. I emerged from that night cruelly lucid and utterly stupefied. I could no longer understand Madame Bovary. Had she really gone to Rouen twice a week for *that*?

That morning, Georges took me to the Eiffel Tower. He wanted me to have a complete view of Paris. The lift was too expensive for our very meagre purse and Georges told me we were going up on foot by the staircase. I raised my head and looked up at the gigantic tower with utter despair. I was terribly thirsty and I felt a scorching pain at every step.

I did not want to disappoint him, we knew each other so little. He gazed enthusiastically at the tower, his eyes shining, and added:

'I only like sporting women. . . .'

'I'm very thirsty.'

Had Madame Bovary been thirsty too?

'You shall have a drink up there. On the third-storey platform, you shall have a nice bottle of Coca-Cola. . . . Come on, courage! . . .'

My high pointed heels tapped on the steps like the beak of a woodpecker searching for grubs. I held on to the iron rail and I had to keep up the same rhythm without ever slowing down for Georges followed on my heels without giving me a moment's respite. As the Champ-de-Mars became smaller and smaller, I forced myself not to look to right or left, but that enormous flayed animal which is the Eiffel Tower presented nothing to my eyes but its iron veins and muscles and arteries and, on either side, above and below, sheer emptiness. The sky that brooded over this folly vacillated; so did the tiled or slated roofs; the chimneys seemed to sway in the wind; I could no longer see the tower except as a loathsome giraffe, stretching its stiff, interminable neck up into the clouds and holding a bottle of Coca-Cola in its parched mouth! At last we arrived at a platform. . . . I have no idea whether it was the fourth or the fifth. I had the feeling that I had been turning round ever since I was born and that I should go on turning round in my coffin like a brainless top that someone starts spinning again with a flick of the hand every time it wants to totter to a stop. I did not know that I should go on revolving like that during the six years to come, that I should go on spinning on my own axis, always humming the same music, the same monotonous tune. . . .

On one of the platforms he took me towards the edge.

The tower itself began to tremble. I thought the wind was going to carry us away. Below, appallingly far away, in another world, was that the distant Earth or the nearby moon? I no longer knew. I saw the lines of motor cars flowing towards the great arteries, the tiny bridges over the miniature river and the houses that were no bigger than stooks of corn in a wheatfield.

I heard Georges's voice explaining to me:

'Over there you can see Notre Dame, the Panthéon, the Île Saint-Louis and the Palais de Chaillot. . . .'

A bitter resentment made me shut my eyes.

I did not want to see this inaccessible Paris, this Paris that was so perfectly clear and mapped-out and conceived for foreigners. Seized by a giddiness that made my stomach heave and clutching frantically on to Georges's arm, I imagined someone in one of those houses . . . those doll's houses manufactured for an enormous toyshop. I imagined a man alone in his room, reciting a poem to himself in a very low voice so as to keep himself company with his own words.

Fascinated, I turned to Georges and shouted in the wind:

'Do you like poems?'

'Not much,' he answered. . . . 'But, I say, do look at Paris! . . .

At last, we were able to descend and, from below, I gave the tower one last malevolent glance like a sick person who had just had a dangerous operation being shown the erring appendix in a jam jar.

We drank a bottle of Coca-Cola at the bottom; the bar at the top was closed. My weak legs trembled under the table. Georges, gay and happy, leant across and asked me a question:

'Are you tired, darling?'

I would have liked to burst into an energetic, sporting reply, full of tireless enthusiasm, but I was aware of a grain of pride in his voice, the glow of an accomplished feat that leaves a pleasant, intimate memory of satisfaction. His voice was tinged with an astonishing male arrogance. He was thinking of our night and my own mind was entirely occupied with those endless stairs.

'Yes, I'm very tired,' I admitted weakly, and I withdrew my right foot from my shoe without his noticing. I barricaded myself behind my eyelids whose long lashes aided and abetted me and I wedged my limp shoulders against the back of the uncomfortable little chair. It was an easy, kindly lie, a lie that had no apparent consequences. A lie that I launched like a ping-pong ball against the heights of that tower and which I knew would not rebound with a smart tap on my head. And, besides, I had to remember that Georges was my life-companion; I belonged to him, body and soul. I must not complicate the whole future by thinking too much. That night I went to sleep with burning feet and an aching body, but with a quiet mind.

Chapter Twenty-three

WE LOVED EACH other deeply through the medium of our common memories of Hungary. He described the bedroom he had had as a boy; it had had a flowered curtain and the light walls were always sunlit. I talked about our library, about my school on the hill of Rozsadomb, about my parents whom I now loved more than ever, about my uncle whose handwriting was the same as his. We had made plans for our entire life and he replied evasively to his parents' letters urging him to go off to Australia. The beginning of that autumn was dazzlingly warm and bright. Sometimes we strolled hand in hand through that old quarter of Passy. His parents, anxious about our future, would have liked us to have already left Europe as far behind as possible. Mine, especially my mother, kept insisting on a religious marriage.

Before taking up my new post as a governess which a Christian organisation had procured for me, I consulted the list of Paris publishers that Georges had copied out for me from a professional telephone directory at the post office. Through my compatriots, I had learnt that, at one of the big publishing houses, there was a Hungarian reader who advised for or against the manuscripts that were sent in.

I went to this address on a peaceful afternoon when Paris was still calm and somnolent. The office I was looking for was in a sunless cul-de-sac. I rang for a long time at the big, ancient door. The building had a deserted look. I stood waiting, with my heart thumping and my twelve short stories in a green folder. At last, footsteps. . . . A man opened the door.

'What do you want, mademoiselle?'

'Good afternoon. . . . Could I speak to the Hungarian reader?'

188

He looked at me without curiosity.

'You're Hungarian?'

'Yes. . . . Is he in?'

His eyes glanced from my face to the green folder.

'You've brought a manuscript?'

'Yes. Is he in, the reader?'

'The office is closed, mademoiselle, but you can come in for a minute. The Literary Director's secretary happens by chance to be in. . . . Go up to the first floor, it's the second door on the left.'

The ground floor to which he admitted me was bathed in darkness and I saw, heaped up on a vast counter, great piles of books. Everything smelt of mildew, like my pillow at Versailles; there was a smell of old yellowed papers, covered with fine dust, like the smell in our loft at home in Budapest. The commissionaire followed me, faithful and silent, like a big dog who is in the habit of accompanying his master to the cemetery. I turned towards him but I did not dare ask him whether they had any living authors too or whether this was only a waxwork museum, a monument to the frailty of human thought.

I knocked on the door he had indicated.

'Come in!' replied an astonished voice.

A woman with greying hair and a fleeting smile raised her head from behind a large desk and looked at me, her eyes full of question marks.

'Who are you, mademoiselle, and how did you manage to get in here?'

She was surprised but not hostile.

'Good afternoon, madame. It was the commissionaire who told me you were here. I've heard that you have a Hungarian reader here and I've brought a manuscript.'

I held the manuscript out to her over the desk but she did not touch it, as if she were unwilling to commit herself by any rash gesture.

'What is it?'

I tucked my file under my arm again.

'Some short stories . . . twelve short stories. . . .'

189

She was not in the least impressed by their number and told me to sit down.

During the first moment of silence, while she was studying me, I waited for the questions about my nationality, the exact date of my leaving Hungary; perhaps she would even want my fingerprints.

'We have no Hungarian reader, mademoiselle. There's some mistake. Who could have misinformed you like that?'

How could I explain about the courtyard of the church and the information we exchanged after Mass?

Already on my feet I asked her the direct question:

'You don't know where I could get my short stories read?'

She gave a kindly smile – exactly the smile one gives a baby who absolutely insists on walking but falls over at every step because its legs cannot support the weight of its body.

'You know, it's difficult with short stories. You can't sell short stories . . . at least, not unless you're an author like Maupassant . . . . What might interest us would be a short novel . . . packed with incident – modern – full of life. . . .'

I nearly screamed:

'You want a novel?'

And I saw the deliciously impertinent shade of Wanda appear before my eyes and sit down in the armchair beside the desk.

She was extremely affable.

'Why, certainly, mademoiselle. Write a novel and, when you've finished it, bring it to us. . . .'

I saw from her face that she was convinced she had got rid of me for ever. She did not know that, with the invisible Wanda, there were three of us in the office.

I said goodbye to her and, at the door, I turned my head towards her and added:

'I'll come back in three months with my novel. Will that suit you?'

Determined to be patient to the end of this scene which she obviously regarded as a frivolity one could allow oneself during the last days of the holidays, she replied:

'You mustn't hurry yourself too much; come whenever you're ready. . . .'

I went down by the back stairs. The man was placidly waiting for me below. I glanced discreetly at the books; they were not cut; they had grown old, still keeping their secrets like books closed for ever.

'Why are there so many books here?'

The commissionaire shrugged his shoulders and answered in one word:

'Stocktaking.'

I pressed him further.

'And after stocktaking they'll be sent to bookshops. So you *will* sell them after all, won't you?'

'*Sell* them?'

The sacrilegious word exploded like a tear-gas bomb. The man carefully blew his nose and, instead of answering me, sneezed several times.

He accompanied me to the door and, by way of farewell, he said:

'It's very hard to sell books. Very hard. . . .'

I found myself once more in the light and warmth of that late August day as if in another world. I was excited and happy at my first contact with literary life.

I passed a small terrace that encroached on part of the pavement and sat down on a little chair at a table no bigger than a plate. The tired waiter brought me a coffee with a faintly disdainful expression; all round me was an orgy of beers and pineapple juices. I contemplated the passers-by with a shy, profound happiness. I was trying to find the first words of my novel, the phrase that would arrest the readers' attention. I wanted to avoid landscapes, skyscapes and analyses; I would have liked to fling down some brutal, unexpected action on the paper. I sipped my coffee lazily and I was depressed at the thought of having to begin working for other people again. But nothing could stop the flow of ideas. Wanda was present to me; I could already see her on a road in a snowstorm, abandoned, with a child on her hands, near a frontier that she had to cross illicitly. If I had three months' freedom I could write my novel. . . . But what did it matter? I would write it just the same in someone else's house, during the night . . . or at dawn. . . .

In the métro, the vision of that cemetery of books returned to me, but I comforted myself: 'Even the most meagre thought must surely become nobler after such a long wait!'

When I saw Georges again and told him all about my afternoon I asked him outright:

'Do you think a writer can live by his books?'

'Why, of course,' he answered. 'Look at Margaret Mitchell, for example. . . .'

Chapter Twenty-four

THE FIRST MOMENT I saw the house at Garches, I forgot all about my distress at leaving Paris. Georges had remained behind at the little hotel hunting for work. Every day he cut out advertisements offering various jobs. I arrived at Garches one Monday, knowing I should not see him again until Sunday.

Under the spell of some indefinable charm I walked fearlessly up the path that led to the house through a garden whose fragile beauty was at the mercy of the first slightly harsher wind. Autumn was entrenching itself behind the full-blown roses; I only brushed them with my eyes, wanting to preserve the petals whose edges were already browned. The still supple stems carried the blossoms with the modest strength of young bodies unashamed of their ageing heads.

The big door opening on the white paved hall was open; I crossed the threshold timidly but, when I found myself in front of a glass that hung above an old chest-of-drawers, I saw that I was smiling. I carefully put down the cardboard suitcase on an Oriental carpet that had faded where the sun had faithfully shone for years on the same expanse of pattern, and I inhaled the smell of the house. Instinctively I looked round for the apples that must be lying somewhere on the top of a cupboard, already set out in orderly rows; for the smoke of a forgotten cigarette, left to burn itself out in an ash-tray. A scent hovered in the air, as if the billowing of a woman's dress had scattered it like dew before leaving the house.

'Mademoiselle?'

A round-faced woman, armoured in an apron that covered her from shoulders to ankles, came up to me.

'Are you Sibylle's nurse?'

'Good afternoon, madame. Yes, I'm the nurse. . . .'

I did not utter Sibylle's name; I did not want to mention her; I was afraid of breaking the spell too soon.

'I'm the cook. . . . I'll come and show you your room,' she said, holding out her hand.

Our hands had found an unexpected kinship in their rough contact. The first floor displayed great doors that gave on to the carpeted passage; the second of them presented me with 'the surprise'.

The cook showed me into a charming room with pink curtains and a pink counterpane; on a table, there was an ink-pot and some writing paper. In this house I would write often to my parents.

The cook leant back against the wall.

'Is there anything you need? The bathroom on this floor is next to Sibylle's bedroom, the third door on the right as you come out. . . . I'm going downstairs now. I must get dinner ready.'

I put my astonished suitcase down on a chair. 'Madame and the children, when will they be back?'

She gave a broad kindly smile.

'Madame went off with Monsieur and the children directly after breakfast. They'll be back just in time for dinner. Madame told me you'd be coming today. . . . Wouldn't you like something to eat? Have you had tea?'

'I'd very much like a glass of milk.'

The big light kitchen had two windows open on the garden. The cook put a slice of bread and butter and a glass of milk in front of me on the table and sat down opposite me.

'My name's Rose; you can call me Rose. . . . And what's your name, mademoiselle?'

'Christine.'

'Fancy, I've got a niece called Christine but she hasn't got fair hair. You, you're fair like Sibylle. Shall I cut you another slice?'

I was no longer in the least hungry, but I hoped she would tell me some more about this little girl, so I accepted.

194

'I think there are four children here, aren't there? And that the youngest is six.'

She folded her hands on the table and explained to me:

'Sibylle's only five and a half. . . . She's as pretty as a picture.'

I ventured on to more dangerous territory.

'Is she good?'

'Good? She's an angel. . . . I've told Madame ever so often that Sibylle didn't need a nurse. . . .'

With those words she had cruelly threatened my situation and my work. I put on a serious expression as if I had just arrived from a Swiss college with a highly trained nurse's diploma.

'You know, a child always needs so much special care. And, besides, there are her brother and sisters. . . .'

'Four,' replied Rose, as proudly as if she were their grandmother. 'Two boys and two girls. But you'll only have Sibylle. . . .'

Suddenly she broke off and I felt I could see what she was thinking behind her shiny wrinkled forehead.

'What country do you come from?'

'From Hungaria.'

The word Hungaria broke against the tiled walls and splintered in a thousand pieces on the floor. I was overwhelmed with an immense sadness; I clenched my teeth and fought desperately against my tears. Then, humiliated by their wet warmth, I let my head fall forwards on the table.

'There, there, I didn't mean to make you cry – forgive me, mademoiselle. . . .'

How could I explain to her that I was not annoyed, that the word Hungary had opened the floodgates? All those secret sorrows I had repressed had revolted. I was crying for the life I had dreamed of; I missed my parents; Georges was far away. And galled by weariness and by the eternal question: 'What country do you come from?' I would have liked to relapse into being a child again. Independence and loneliness were too hard.

I felt her heavy hand on my hair; I raised my head; she was crying too. She pulled her chair up close to mine.

'It won't go on for ever.'

I searched for my handkerchief.

'I don't want to go back there but I *would* like a home.'

With her clean starched apron and her white hair, she was like an old nurse for whom life and death no longer hold any secrets. If I could lay my head on that shoulder, how gladly I would recover the past – peace, the country, childhood!

She said, almost in my ear:

'You just see how happy you're going to be here. Madame's so nice and the children aren't naughty like other children.'

I wanted to protest that there were no naughty children but I was too exhausted to defend anything whatever.

I went up to my room again; I closed the door behind me, and sat down on my narrow bed. With a tired gesture I pulled off the coverlet and let myself drop, with my eyes closed and my head against the pillow.

The noise of a car made me start. Staggering from this brief violent sleep, I went over to the washbasin and washed my face in cold water. When I went down the hall was already full of people. I looked for a landmark and found it in Madame's face. I had seen her once in the office of the organisation which had recommended me but only for a few minutes. Here, she advanced towards me, her face radiant. . . .

'Good evening, Christine. . . . Have you been here long?'

'I arrived about four.'

The children were clinging round her in a little crowd; she introduced them one by one.

'This is Sibylle. . . .

The little girl, with her big periwinkle-blue eyes, held out her hand.

'Say how do you do,' insisted Madame.

I could hardly hear the faint voice.

'How do you do? . . .'

Madame added:

'Christine.'

And Sibylle repeated: 'Christine.'

196

Madame went on:

'And these are Bruno, Gabriel, Odette and Mireille.'

All those young faces were turned towards me. Their grave thoughtful looks scrutinised me. Madame hastily banished this tiny awkward silence.

'Children, this is Christine. I've told you quite enough about her for you to welcome her as nicely as possible. So make an effort to be a little more agreeable than usual.'

The front door opened. It was Monsieur.

'Ah!' he said. 'You're here. Good evening, mademoiselle; did you have a good journey?'

After a few minutes' chatting, Madame came upstairs with me and the children to show me their rooms and explain my work.

'You'll have nothing to do for Gabriel, Odette and Mireille. You'll look after Sibylle and, very occasionally, Bruno. . . . But we're late tonight; the children must have their baths.'

That evening passed in a pleasant whirl. I soaped Sibylle's frail body energetically; she had not yet asked me where I came from. She was submissive and I was suspicious. This goodness put me on my guard. Bruno was playing submarines in the bath and did not want to come out of the water.

At last, at eight o'clock, we were all sitting round the big table in the dining-room. I sat beside Sibylle and kept an eye on her to see that she ate enough. As I came in, I had seen a picture but, at the moment, it was behind me and it intrigued me greatly. I had been struck by its sober beauty and its muted light. Rose waited on us; I was embarrassed when she offered me the dish; I had cried on her shoulder and I ought not to let her wait on me. But she found this perfectly natural.

Madame had very beautiful hair with long plaits wound round her head like a crown. Monsieur had admiring glances for his wife, an absent-minded smile for us and a diet for himself.

The pleasantly slow rhythm of that dinner, the children's subdued chatter, the warm light of the table, the garden wrapped in the semi-darkness of that mild evening and the presence of that extraordinary picture I had noticed on entering the room, enhanced the personality of Madame. She kept the conversation going effortlessly; she had a word for each child, as if distributing sweets with scrupulous fairness; she made an intimate gesture towards her husband, laying her hand on his and, for a moment, they exchanged looks; she inquired after Rose's health and talked about a woman friend she had visited in the afternoon. Her regular, intelligent beauty was neither eclipsed nor emphasised by her crown of hair; she was one of those rare women who can carry the weight of long hair without being vinegarish or bad-tempered. She had a clear forehead. Her light grey eyes, with a speck of green in the iris, rested now and then on the silver dish of fruit that stood in the middle of the table. In those fleeting moments of absence, she was dreamy, almost defenceless, intimately engaged in some thought that was exclusively her own. But the voices of the children instantly brought her back to reality, and she returned to the conversation, sure of herself and of her secret.

When we left the table I found myself at last face to face with the picture. It represented a grave man with his profile shadowed by a large hat.

I ventured a supposition:

'School of Rembrandt?'

'It is a Rembrandt,' answered Monsieur, in a pleasant unemotional voice.

I took Sibylle by the hand, and, as I walked towards the staircase, I felt happy for the first time for a very long while.

'Christine. . . .'

Madame's voice made me turn my head towards her; we stopped with the child on one of the stairs.

'Yes, madame.'

'I'm so sorry but I must tell you I've had a letter from the nurse who's been with us for four years. She had to go off to Holland because her mother was ill. And, in today's letter, she writes that she will get one of her sisters to look after her mother so that she can come back to us. So I can't keep you longer than a month. But don't worry, my husband and I between us will find you something else. You do understand, don't you?'

'But, of course, I understand, madame.'

She raised her head and smiled at me.

'Don't be frightened, we'll arrange it all.'

I went on climbing the stairs with Sibylle. Her little hand became warm and friendly in my own. She spoke to me for the first time.

'It's a pity you've got to go. The other nurse is nice, but perhaps you can stay all the same. . . .'

In her little room, I took off her dressing-gown and put her to bed.

'Will you tell me a story? Bring one of my books, they're on the bookshelf.'

I told her a long story, and, after having tucked her well into her blankets, I went to my room.

The writing paper on the table had become useless. This month would go so fast. But what should I do afterwards?

The next day, when I took Sibylle and Bruno in to Madame, I saw that she was writing on a typewriter.

'I translate books,' she explained to me.

Almost instinctively I said to the children:

'Come along with me; your mother mustn't be disturbed.'

She gave me a look of astonishment.

'That's certainly the first time I've heard those words in this house!'

Seeing her typewriter, the papers scattered over the table, a pencil fallen on the carpet – all this in the shafts of autumn sunlight – gave me an irresistible longing to tell her that I imagined a life exactly like hers, with a work in hand and children coming in to greet me in the morning. But I virtuously kept silence and took Sibylle off for a walk.

It was an unforgettable month, saturated with joys and sorrows. I counted the days like a prisoner voluntarily locked up in her bliss of provisional peace. I wrote optimistic letters to my parents and I saw Georges every Sunday. He had found a chauffeur's job with one of those numerous White Russian princes who had survived the 1917 revolution. This prince lived alone in Paris in a sumptuous flat, looked after by a faithful cook. Georges who, in Hungary, had been given a little car as a birthday present by his parents, had had no qualms about accepting the job which made him the driver of an enormous luxury car, black and shining as an undertaker's in a funeral procession. It was a very famous car, of the kind built to order for millionaires, and on account of the classic shape of its body, no one suspected that it dated from 1927. From information supplied by the cook, Georges learnt that, long ago, the jovial prince with his blotchy, perpetually smiling face had married an immensely rich American and that they lived apart; she in America, with her title of Princess, and he with the money she sent him every month.

Our Sundays were filled with the stories we exchanged about the charms of Sibylle and the caprices of the prince. Georges drove him nearly every night to a nightclub near Pigalle and he studied his International Law by the light of the little lamp in the car. But this car deliberately stalled its engine at the moment the red light changed to green. Georges was harassed by impatient klaxons that suddenly hooted all round them and the prince would pull down the window that separated them so that the latter would be sure of hearing his oaths. 'We must have a life of our own. . . .' We were always repeating those magic words.

At the end of the third week, Madame sent me to see a family in their neighbourhood; she believed they were looking for a nurse for their child. I was invited in and carefully examined. My physical strength did not appear adequate to the work required. 'You are frail and the house is large,' they told me.

Madame was extremely upset; she would have liked to keep two nurses rather than send me out into a blank future. They never spoke of my lost country nor of my life as a refugee. They listened to everything I said in my strongly accented French; we talked about Balzac and Roger Martin du Gard. They were surprised that we had so much knowledge of French literature in Hungary but this surprise was never expressed; I was only aware of it in their eyes. During my long walks with Sibylle I learnt the

French I had not known before, the language of everyday life and children's favourite expressions. Sibylle corrected me with gay confidence. Once I asked her the question:

'Now, tell me, what *is* dreaming?'

She answered without hesitation:

'Thinking while you're asleep. . . .'

By making her define a word I had wanted to disarm her. I had hoped that I would be the one to explain it to her; I wanted to enjoy the cheap superiority of the grown-up who sets a problem with the certainty that the child cannot solve it. But this little fairy of five and a half got the better of me in intelligence and quickness of mind.

When I departed from Garches, leaving my provisional happiness for only too certain anxieties, Madame gave me an envelope with two months' wages in it instead of one. And her children, who had been born with white socks and had never had a grazed knee, kissed me, one by one, with that look typical of their age; a look full of curiosity, but passionless and detached. Sibylle said in a choked little voice:

'Will you come back to see me?'

'Yes, of course Christine will come back,' replied Madame.

Rose had given me a box of sweets; she greatly regretted that I had not had a chance to meet her niece who was also called Christine.

It was Monsieur who drove me back to Paris. He deposited me outside the little hotel.

'Au revoir, mademoiselle.'

'Au revoir, monsieur.'

Perhaps some day, I *shall* see them again?

Chapter Twenty-five

WITH MY TWO months' wages in my handbag, I decided to hire a typewriter and launch out on my great adventure – writing my first novel: *Wanda*. Now that I was back in Paris, Georges often dropped in to see me, and the little street was overcome by the sight of such a sumptuous car. But one day the engine stalled right in front of the door and Georges, surrounded by a mocking crowd, could not manage to start it up again.

The prince had worries; the money from America was in arrears and it was the cook who paid Georges. It was she who lent her master money so that he should not miss his evening's entertainment.

The little table in my room barely supported the weight of the huge typewriter. It was a double-bank Remington. The rickety keyboard groaned when I touched the keys, and, at the end of each line, the bell rang so violently that my neighbour, an Englishwoman, asked me several times to change my machine. I had to explain that this was impossible. I wrote in the midst of these shrill noises. I cooked on a board laid over the washbasin and the spirit-stove puffed and snorted like the first steam engine.

How does one write a novel? I had my characters, the quickening pace of an action whose end I could not foresee, the face of a woman and the atmosphere of Vienna. I paced up and down the tiny room and, one morning, I found my opening sentence: *The soldier brutally grabbed hold of Wanda* . . . I did not yet know which of the soldiers – I foresaw five of them – made this rough, decisive gesture, but, with those words, I was launched on my first chapter. I typed for seven or eight hours a day and, when I went out during the afternoon, I had an intoxicated sense of well-being and marvellous calm for which my own pages were responsible.

The weather changed and the rain imprisoned me in the little hotel bedroom. Georges came whenever he could get a free moment and we talked about our future. He explained to me that success was only a question of luck, backed up by an ingenious idea. It was about this time that he put an advertisement in an evening paper, whose text ran as follows: 'Young man requires capital of one million (possibly more) to launch publicity campaign for sensational invention. Immense profit for lender. I will negotiate loan in 24 hours. Address reply to this paper, Urgent.'

He would like me to have been more optimistic but, when he told me the principles of his invention, his enthusiasm filled me with alarm. He wanted to manufacture a refrigerator without ice. His plans were astounding and, in the end, he decided to set up the apparatus, piece by piece, in my room.

'But how will you get the electric current?' I asked timidly.

He was knocked off his perch and almost hostile when I recalled him to the brute facts of hotel life. I had wanted to change the bulb of my lamp for a stronger one and we had had a short-circuit. The proprietor was determined to keep his expenses down.

He went off in a bad temper, and, alone once more, I went over our conversation. It was only after he had gone that I realised the implication of certain words. 'There's only two years' difference between us. When you're thirty, I shall be a man of thirty-two. Just imagine the difference. A man of thirty is only beginning his life, whereas a woman. . . .' His silence had been eloquent. Nowadays I understood his silences better than his words.

That evening, my eyes were too tired to write. Under cover of darkness, hiding behind my burning eyelids, I thought I had still nine years of youth left.

Monsieur Szabo appeared in our life like a shooting star

promising the fulfilment of every secret hope. His name seemed to destine him to be a Hungarian like any other Hungarian, but he was totally different from any I had met hitherto. His round head, with its friendly, shining baldness, and his generous gestures – he would give a five hundred franc tip after drinking a fifty franc coffee – had made his reputation in an elegant tea shop not far from the Champs-Elysées. We knew that he had been a big business man in Hungary; before the war, according to the respectful gossips who hovered round him, he had sold wheat, by the truckload and sheep by the flock. He lived in a luxurious villa just outside Paris and never went anywhere without an old Pole who acted both as his chauffeur and as his indispensable interpreter. Monsieur Szabo did not know a single word of French and said his friendly 'good morning' to the smiling waitresses in Hungarian. He had left Hungary in the last days of the war and had apparently succeeded in getting an entire train full of merchandise through defeated Germany. Switzerland had accepted Monsieur Szabo and his train and, a few years later, he had arrived in Paris with the remains of his fortune and a severe Swiss wife who had given him four children in five years.

The red nape of his neck mounted guard over two small ears which nature had carefully stuck flat against his skull and his quick eyes darted from objects to people and rested on both with the same interest.

Georges was the first to have the idea to ask Monsieur Szabo to lend him some capital. But it was no longer a question of the refrigerator; we wanted to have the management of a little restaurant and to make a fortune thanks to homely, wholesome cooking.

I would have preferred to remain in my little room and go on writing, without thinking of the world about me, but the sum I possessed when I left Garches was diminishing very fast and I looked every day at the advertisements to find another place as nurse. Moreover, Georges wanted to leave the prince and the car in which he had to keep vigil every night outside the famous

Pigalle nightclub. Through an agency we had discovered a *bistro* whose present manageress wished to leave. The agent had explained to us that the restaurant was in a working-class district and that, on account of its situation, its future was assured with a minimum of work.

'I shall serve in the bar and you'll do the cooking,' Georges told me, his eyes shining with enthusiasm. 'I shall work till dawn but you'll go to bed as soon as possible because you'll buy the provisions in the big market, the Halles, and you'll have to get up very early.'

Monsieur Szabo listened to our projects with the faintly absent-minded attention of big business men who have to solve several problems at once. The Pole never left his side and, barricaded behind a trolley loaded with cakes which the waitress left constantly within his reach, he put questions to us. After long complicated conversations it was agreed that he should give us the sum necessary to start us off and that, for several years, he should have a percentage of the receipts.

He looked at, me very uneasily.

'Do you know how to cook for forty or fifty people?'

I assured him that I did but I was paralysed with terror.

It was also necessary to envisage a Frenchman who would act as a dummy and take the restaurant in his name. As refugees we could not get the necessary permits.

One day we were invited to Monsieur Szabo's home and we made the acquaintance of his wife. She was a tall, bony blonde with cold eyes and fat hips. She openly despised us and the languishing conversation in bad German made me sleepy and frightened. During luncheon I felt Madame Szabo's sharp gaze hovering over my head, brushing my hair and settling on my plate like an obstinate wasp that refuses to go away before it has stung you.

'Are your children well, madame?'

'Very, very well,' she answered, and she rolled her 'r's' so strongly that I suddenly imagined those noisy 'r's' were roller-skates that she attached to her tongue every time she spoke.

'They're at Basle, with my mother, for a fortnight. . . .'

Monsieur Szabo helped himself to another large slice of meat that had already gone cold in its sauce, for the servant had forgotten to remove the dish and left it on the table.

Madame Szabo exclaimed:

'Your stomach! . . . Don't make yourself ill – think of your children! . . .

She went on, with a violence unusual in big blonde women:

'You must be careful about that restaurant too. Losing money's a great deal easier than making it. Think of your children's future. . . .'

Her husband shrugged his shoulders, unmoved, and wiped his plate with a piece of bread.

'Don't be afraid, Hilda; it's not a bad enterprise and they've got courage. Besides, think of the three thousand typewriters I'm waiting for.'

Up till now, taking refuge in a feigned indifference, I had let the words go on swirling round me. I was as morally weary as I was physically and the presence of Georges now seemed an enigma rather than a solution. Did he really believe that I should be able to cope with that amount of work? He had promised me a little maid to do the washing-up and, later on, a waitress. He had so much confidence in my strength and thought I was so courageous that I had not dared to disillusion him. I wanted to be the woman of his dreams. The word 'typewriter' came as a pleasant surprise. Suddenly awakened I turned to Monsieur Szabo:

'Are you talking about typewriters?'

I looked at his lips, all shiny with grease and at an audacious little drop that was making its way towards his chin.

'I'm waiting for three thousand typewriters from the United States. I shall break the European market with this influx of cheap machines. After that, I shall order them by tens of thousands.'

'Could I buy one? I'd so much like to. . . .'

His broad smile made the drop run down on to his neck; I no longer saw it.

'Nothing easier,' he replied. 'You can have two if you like. . . .'

The maid brought in some fruit. Madame Szabo attacked an apple and Monsieur Szabo took a banana.

Georges shot a question across the table like a bullet.

'Shall we go and see the restaurant tomorrow?'

'About three o'clock? . . .' said Monsieur Szabo reflectively.

I broke in, excited by the thought of my future typewriter:

'It would be better to go in the evening. During the rush hours the agent says there are lots of people. . . .'

He agreed.

'Come and fetch me at the tea shop at six; we'll all go together in the car.'

Madame Szabo once more addressed her husband as if we were not present.

'Have you really got confidence in them?'

'Why, of course I have. They're fine, courageous young things. . . .'

'But it's our money that's in question,' she insisted. 'The children. . . .'

Oh, those children! I saw them as famished monsters who drank a glass of liquid silver for breakfast and ate bundles of crisp thousand-franc notes instead of rolls.

We left the overheated villa about four in the afternoon. The cold wind slipped under the collar of my old winter coat and ran all down my back. I carefully avoided the puddles for my shoes were no longer good for anything but dry, sunny weather. I shivered, and Georges, who was holding my arm, asked me:

'Is there anything wrong? Why are you depressed?'

His boyish face was full of frank curiosity. He was not laughing at me. He really wanted to know. But how could I explain our own situation to him? I loathed his man's hat, that hat that made him look so absurdly young. All the same he was twenty-three, nearly twenty-four. . . .

I did not answer till we were in the métro and the kindly underground warmth enveloped me.

'There's nothing the matter with me, absolutely nothing.'

207

He said, in a business-like way:

'You mustn't be ill, now that we're going to have our *bistro*.'

Without comment I silently fixed my eyes on the black walls of those extraordinary tunnels along which the métro was running at full speed. He took my motionless hand in his. Did we love each other? . . .

From the very first moment I had felt a profound antipathy towards Monsieur Szabo's interpreter and he reciprocated my hostility without disguising his feelings. He had the head of a worn-out old *roué* on a thin, wrinkled neck and his almost skeleton-like hand was always nervously brushing the revers of his coat that shone like the seat of an old pair of trousers. Leaning on his stick, with his hat laid on the table beside his empty cup, he would watch us like a bird of prey whose age has dimmed its keen sight so that it has to stoop lower and lower in order not to miss its victim. He spoke French and Hungarian well enough to translate Monsieur Szabo's sentences and, in our presence, he rushed the words out quicker than ever so as to show off his prowess as an interpreter.

Before we left the tea shop Monsieur Szabo dismissed him with a 'We'll meet later on, at the club', and, installed in our friend's car, we set off for the restaurant. Monsieur Szabo drove very badly, making his brakes screech at the red lights that lit up along our route, bright and burning as little braziers that could resist that icy rain.

'Got stage fright?' asked Georges under his breath, and I had the feeling that, with that question whispered in the hollow of my ear, he was laying the whole burden of the enterprise on me.

'Yes, I have got stage fright,' I answered aggressively like someone owning up to their fear with pride.

After minute researches on a very worn map, we found ourselves in a long and narrow street in Levallois. Monsieur Szabo advanced cautiously; an enormous lorry parked in the middle of the street blocked the view. Dark shapes, dripping with rain, were unloading the lorry, and by the light of the yellow street lamps we saw split carcasses of bleeding beef on their broad shoulders.

The butcher was standing in the doorway of his shop observing these blood-stained shadows going to and fro and, when he saw Monsieur Szabo lower the car window and lean out as a sign of protest against the obstruction, he shouted some unknown words at him.

'What's he saying?' asked Monsieur Szabo, turning round to Georges. Georges hastily replied:

'Oh, nothing important, he just wants you to go on being patient. . . .'

But this was untrue. Behind Monsieur Szabo's back I gave Georges an inquiring look but he put his finger to his lips.

At last we were able to proceed and to search for the number. I tried to catch sight of the restaurant through a misted pane. Just when Monsieur Szabo was about to lose patience, we at last found our *bistro*. From the street all we could see was a glass door with a check curtain and windows covered with the same stuff. By a miracle a van was just moving off and Monsieur Szabo occupied its place.

Monsieur Szabo went in first and we followed him, submissive and trembling. The restaurant was empty and, in the dimness of the back room, we could see chairs piled up on tables. The front part was dominated by a zinc bar counter and a kind of dresser with shelves. Standing fixed and motionless in the bright light of the bar itself, we felt as if we were imprisoned in a luminous circle drawn by a magician.

And suddenly there appeared out of a dark corner a woman of overwhelming beauty, the kind of beauty blondes call common and men respect out of prudence. Her masses of black hair, whose glossy curls shone with brilliantine, and her plump, voluptuous, friendly shoulders, created expressly for men to lay their heads on that marvellous cushion of living flesh, presented a startling spectacle to us and intoxicating one to Monsieur Szabo.

'You've come about the business?'

Her voice invested the prosaic question with something intimate, almost sensual.

Monsieur Szabo turned to me excited and enchanted:

'What does she say?'

The young woman came towards us and I saw the shape of her long thighs under the tight sheath of her skirt.

Monsieur Szabo forgot that the restaurant was empty. He installed himself at the bar and the woman poured him out a drink. I watched in silence and we learnt that she was Spanish, that she had run the restaurant for the last two years but, because of a serious quarrel with her husband, she wanted to go back to Barcelona.

Georges faithfully translated her precious words and Monsieur Szabo, lulled by strong drink, leant on the counter and never took his dazed, admiring eyes off the voluptuous proprietress. She was not in the least embarrassed by the fact that the restaurant was empty.

'I haven't bothered about it since my trouble,' she said, and her pointed breasts asserted themselves with shameless candour through her yellow jumper. With a mechanical gesture she wiped some dry glasses; when she shook her head she set the big rings in her ears dancing.

I saw a jukebox in a corner. I slipped a coin into the slit indicated by an arrow; I wanted to furnish this emptiness. Georges was standing close by me, alert and expectant.

'Are you coming?' he said. 'The woman speaks a little German and I've left Szabo with her. Now we can look over the restaurant. . . . Do you think Szabo will fork out?'

My answer was drowned in a burst of music and the waltz set everything spinning round me: the dust, the shadows, my own misery. It was too much for me: the 'Blue Danube' fixed on a scratched record; the curtains whose folds were solid with encrusted dirt; the tables heaped with chairs; Monsieur Szabo and his swimming eyes, avid with the hope of possessing that body, at least in his dreams; the smell of stale beer and the thick cloaks of dust on the bottles.

'Oh, *do* come along,' Georges insisted.

I went to see the sinister kitchen with its enormous saucepans suspended over a coal range.

'It's a bit old,' Georges admitted. 'But we'll get it all into condition again.'

Through an open trapdoor we descended into the cellar which was lit by one small electric bulb. The smell of mildew took us by the throat and enormous spider's webs were draped, motionless, over a cask that had entirely rotted away.

'You know what we'll do here, darling,' said Georges. 'We'll make a bar . . . a frightfully smart bar. . . . The French love cellars provided they're romantic or unusual. We'll repaint the walls and then we'll put up some artificial spider's webs. . . . Maybe we might hang up a skeleton, cleverly lighted, in a corner. . . . And, to please you, we'll stress the intellectual character of this bar . . . it'll be a literary nightclub. . . . Later on, of course, we'll have an orchestra. D'you agree, darling?'

I preserved a hostile silence and I was afraid even to smile. When we went upstairs again we found Monsieur Szabo completely tipsy.

'I'll give you the money for the business,' he mumbled thickly. 'Even more than you wanted. . . . Wonderful thing, youth. . . .'

The Spanish woman smiled and planted her black gaze on us. She yawned behind the bar and, as she stretched her arms, the tight jumper nearly split over her breasts.

'How glad I shall be to be back in Barcelona,' she sighed.

This did not surprise me. I, too, would much rather be in Barcelona than here.

When we left Monsieur Szabo outside his club he thanked us, almost with tears in his eyes, for our excursion. He also promised us the money we needed to sign the contract at the beginning of the following week. We accompanied him right to the door of the elegant building.

When he was in the lift Georges asked the porter:

'What's his club, that gentleman who's just gone upstairs?'

211

The porter replied with great disdain:

'It's a gaming club: baccarat and roulette. . . . But exclusively for members.'

I hastily stifled a wicked hope. 'If he lost his money, there'd be no more restaurant! . . .' I did not dare say a word. Georges was too worried.

After that we only saw Monsieur Szabo in the waiting-room of his club. He promised us the money from one day to the next and it was always about six o'clock that we arrived in this richly furnished little drawing-room which, for us, was furnished only with anxiety. I took not the slightest notice of another woman who was waiting for some man and I put my sopping shoes against the radiator.

A helpless, frantic Georges asked me the same question every time:

'Do you think he'll sign the cheque today?'

I shrugged my shoulders, disguising my lassitude as much as I could and, huddled in a soft, well-upholstered armchair, I said nothing.

When he arrived we stood motionless, almost hypnotised in his presence. Every day he would burst into the room with his hands outstretched, always with the same overwhelming enthusiasm.

'My dear young friends, how ashamed I am to keep you waiting like this, but I couldn't leave the table.'

His congested face, his eyes with their network of red veins, the thick finger he thrust between his collar and his swollen neck to assist his breathing, the overnight beard flourishing on his chin like the bluish imprint of some strange malady, inspired us with a kind of terror.

'The estate agent has given us just one week more,' Georges would explain and in the heavily furnished, never-aired room his voice sounded abnormally loud.

'But, with a week, we've got all eternity before us,' Monsieur Szabo would say joyfully, and he would add:

'I've got to get my luck back. My interpreter wins all the time, playing with *my* money; it doesn't make sense. . . .'

Already his gaze was turning towards the door.

'I must go back, dear children.'

One day, I intercepted that look and, staring at the contracted pupils, I searched for the light of reason, for the proof that he was still capable of sustained thought.

'Monsieur Szabo,' I said. 'Why don't you go back to the tea shop? All your business is waiting there for you to attend to it. . . . And the typewriters. . . . What's happened to them?'

He bit his lower lip and its thick flesh retained the sharp imprint of the tooth.

'They're in the customs at the moment, I can't pay the duty.'

I insisted cruelly, feeling as if I were hitting an unconscious man:

'And your children, Monsieur Szabo – are they all right?'

Tiny drops of sweat beaded his dilated pores. It was as if a strange dew had covered his face.

'I've sent my wife to her parents in Switzerland. The villa was too expensive but she'll come back as soon as I've bought a flat.'

The woman, who was listening to our conversation, lowered her heavy eyelids, as if she were hearing that phrase for the hundredth time. Suddenly, the unknown woman became an ally; I wanted to turn to her and say, in the most natural way:

'Are you waiting for a madman too, dear?'

The door opened and we saw two men standing there – the interpreter and a thin little man who rushed up to the woman mumbling:

'Everything's going splendidly, love.'

'Come home with me,' said the woman in a dull, unimpassioned voice.

The thin little man was overflowing with jovial good humour. . . .

'You go, love, and I'll be back soon.'

The woman raised clear eyes, shining with hatred, then she whispered with an impassiveness that made our flesh creep:

'Moron. . . .'

The little man came up very close to her and whispered something with his lips pressed against her ear.

The interpreter, still standing in the open doorway, shot a word of command at Monsieur Szabo.

'Hi, come back, you!'

'Is that how he speaks to you now?'

The remark came out entirely against my will.

Monsieur Szabo, already on his feet, held out his moist hand to us.

'He's a friend, a good old intimate friend. . . . And he understands gambling. It was he who introduced me here. . . .'

To show his impatience, the Pole drummed on the door:

'Hurry up, old chap. . . .'

He was animated by the excitement of his all too easy revenge. He took Monsieur Szabo by the arm, like an attendant in a lunatic asylum conducting his patient back into the insane ward after a visit from the outside world.

In the cold, harsh street, Georges turned to me.

'Do you think he's going to stop gambling? If he doesn't, he's a lost man. But, after all, that's how it always is in life. . . . Once a drunkard, always a drunkard. . . .'

A hitherto unknown rebelliousness made me bristle up at these bromides. I shook myself like a dog trying to get rid of its collar.

'How on earth should I know? What we've got to do during the next five days is find a job.'

'We might have been so happy with the *bistro*,' Georges went on, without even noticing my despairing fury.

It was one of his greatest qualities, this ability to dream. He went on his way in life with the terrifying serenity of a sleepwalker who walks over the roofs, unconsciously reassured because the people around him are awake and have sufficient tact not to waken him abruptly. . . .

I no longer understood anything about him. What had I to do with his body there beside my own and with his grey thoughts? I wrote enthusiastic letters to my parents; I was so used to my own lies about a pleasant life, full of work, but lit up with all sorts of possibilities that, when I had finished a letter, I was almost happy. I lulled myself with my own words and I kept on telling myself that it was marvellous to be in Paris, to be twenty-two and to have a great romantic love. But the truth was far otherwise. The meaning of my life, adorned by the elements I would have liked to believe genuine, was hidden in the pages of my novel. I knew already that I was born to write but I felt too, that, before my work was published, I ought to keep quiet about it. To be published! . . . I looked at the names of publishers in the windows of bookshops and I sometimes went inside without any possibility of being able to buy anything. I would shyly ask for some information and I would savour the smell of books and touch their covers. I had done a hundred pages of *Wanda*; she had achieved her third lover and, when I was very hungry while working, I stuffed her with foie gras and champagne. I wrote with blankets wrapped round my thighs and my old coat over my shoulders, but *she* was spoilt and her flat in Vienna was so warmly heated that she walked about barefoot on the thick carpets. At one time when I lay listless and depressed in Georges's arms, I had just made her swoon with pleasure at the end of a chapter. I envied Wanda. . . .

Chapter Twenty-six

MADAME SAULNER, OUR new employer, was tall, without being fat. She liked wholesome cooking, finished her meal with yoghurt, wore a well-disciplined smile on her face and starched collars round her neck. Her domestic world was made to her measure. A huge twelve-roomed flat; eight tall children of whom the six boys had their mother's round eyes; a kitchen perfectly equipped to deal with all these ferocious appetites. The table in the dining-room always presented the same problem when I had to clean it. Covered with a plastic cloth, this table was as big as a skating rink; I had to climb on a chair to wipe away the wine stains in the middle of it. The children might drink a glass of wine at each meal. It seemed it was good for their health whereas we, in the kitchen, were condemned to the water tap. Madame was very thrifty but she also had a highly developed sense of responsibility. She did not want to expose her staff to the temptation of becoming drunkards.

When we came to this luxury flat for the first time, in reply to a small advertisement, the concierge pounced out of her lodge; she was a cantankerous woman whose black frock, obviously given her by one of her tenants, lent her a sham air of distinction. She asked us suspiciously:

'Where are you going?'

'To see Madame Saulner. . . .'

Her look became evasive and she repeated, with avid curiosity:

'You're going to see Madame Saulner? . . . Is it about the advertisement or a personal call?'

'The advertisement. . . .'

Victorious, she indicated the back stairs, which ran straight up from the street, on the left of the main entrance.

So, very suitably, we arrived in Madame Saulner's flat by way of the kitchen. The cook showed us into the drawing-room.

'What do you think of her?' Georges asked me. He wanted to know my opinion before having one of his own.

I could not answer because Madame Saulner had just come in. Shaking hands with us so forcefully that she crushed my wedding ring painfully into my finger, she said:

'I engage you; your references are good.'

The cook brought in a tray with three cups, a tin of powdered coffee and a jug of hot water.

Madame Saulner poured us out some coffee, and, with a brusque gesture, held out the sugar bowl to me.

'Sugar? How much?'

It was as if she had said: 'Arsenic? How much?'

She added, gazing at me:

'Are you an intellectual too?'

That little 'too' was like a slap in the face, but I had no shoes and I wanted to keep my hired typewriter. I answered meekly:

'I don't know, madame.'

'Because *you*,' she went on, turning to Georges, 'you wanted to go on studying, didn't you?'

Georges was astonishingly firm.

'I *am* going on studying, madame.'

She shivered and a little grimace turned down the corners of her smile.

I don't know if that will do here; there's a great deal of work. . . .'

Georges replied obstinately:

'I shall find a little time, madame.'

She gave a short nervous laugh.

'You know your own mind. . . .'

She came back to me, like a dog with two bones who gnaws first one, then the other:

'When did you leave your own country?'

'In 1948, madame.'

'Your studies?'

'I took my School Leaving Certificate and University Entrance. I did eight years of Latin at school.'

'Ah, did you indeed? Well, well. . . .'

She was so surprised that she stopped chewing her bone for a moment or two.

'You could help my elder daughter, Patricia; she's not very keen on Latin. . . .'

Instinctively compelled into a duel that amused me, I told her:

'I also did six years at the Conservatoire. I nearly became a pianist. . . .'

Madame Saulner fell into a dangerous torpor; she repeated under her breath:

'Conservatoire . . . Patricia plays the piano too. You could take her teacher's place.'

Georges, who had not the faintest notion that an extraordinary battle had just begun, put in, with innocent candour:

'Christine is writing a book. She has a great deal of talent.'

The match was already very near the gunpowder. Madame Saulner exclaimed:

'I want a housemaid . . . a good housemaid! On Sunday afternoons, you can do whatever you like, even write. But during the week, I warn you, I will not stand for any deviation from your work. . . . Do you darn well, Christine?'

I did not like hearing my name on her lips. I would like to have invented another name and proffered it to her on my palm, as one shows a coin one has found behind a cupboard. I should like to have said I was called Catherine or Rose – why not Antigone?

'Are you daydreaming, Christine?'

It was her declaration of war: 'Are you daydreaming, Christine?'

We spent the month of November like shipwrecked people keeping their heads above the waves while they wait for a ship. But there was neither ship nor lifeboat for us. There was only Madame Saulner and her voice; her voice that galloped in front of her like a messenger; her voice that made me tremble; her sugary voice that was so sure of itself.

'What are you doing, Christine? Are you daydreaming?'

Georges had a green apron and I had a white apron. Hélène, the cook, never stirred out of her kitchen. It was Madame Saulner who did the shopping; she did not wish Hélène to grow rich too quickly in her service. We were up at seven and we went to bed at eleven after having washed up a mountain of dirty crockery. Georges was as pale as a ghost and I had no idea how I looked myself: I avoided looking glasses. The kind Hélène, who had already lost some years off her life in Madame's service, was a philosopher. She helped me as much as she could and supported me physically and morally; her affection was inexhaustible. She had no husband and no private life; her destiny was to be a slave but she had a marvellously warm heart. How should I ever have stood up to that life without her?

Georges pressed Monsieur's innumerable pairs of trousers. Monsieur was extremely insignificant. It was only his trousers that made me aware of his presence. During meals, I waited at table. I often thought of a housemaid we used to have in Budapest. She never smiled. Was she as unhappy as I was? Madame Saulner always kept me waiting when I presented the heavy tray to her.

She pretended not to know I was behind her; she hated me and felt the need to express her hatred whenever she had the chance. When she condescended to take the meat, she promptly put the dishes back on the tray.

'But it's cold. . . . You people in the kitchen, are you incapable of serving our food hot?'

I would return to the kitchen with the meat. Hélène, scarlet with indignation, would exclaim:

'But it was piping hot!'

And the business would begin all over again.

We began our luncheon when they rose from the table. Madame's impatient steps would echo along the passage and we would eat hurriedly, our muscles contracted.

219

One day she came raging into the kitchen:

'I find you waste a great deal of time over your meals. You take longer to eat than we do, the family!'

I did not want to look at her; I fixed my eyes on the rim of my plate, but I could feel my legs shaking. I braced my feet against the tiles; I wanted to stop shaking, but the trembling ran through my whole body and I, who had not prayed for a long time, said inwardly:

'Oh, God, make her go away, make her disappear; oh, God, make her be less unkind. . . .'

Madame Saulner invented apparently delicate tasks in order to entrust them to me. She had a real silk nightdress, pleated from neck to hem. She would wear it for one night and give it to me to iron the following morning. For a whole week I did this pointless ironing; she watched me with satisfaction out of the corner of her eye. During that period of ironing, I took certain notes for my novel *Wanda*, and I wrote key sentences on scraps of paper. 'Frigid women adore luxurious nightdresses. For them real silk is a kind of sexual satisfaction. Wanda's friend was as big and strong as a horse; at night, she wrapped her large body in fine lace and repelled her husband's advances with disgust.'

But, as my bedroom had no key, I had to hide my manuscript every day in my suitcase and push it under my bed.

In their drawing-room there was a bookcase. Wiping off the dust I looked at the titles. Henry Bordeaux was most in evidence, followed by Duvernois and Pierre Benoit. The Comtesse de Ségur took up an entire shelf; I could not bear her and I always left a layer of dust over the misfortunes of that perverse, detestable Sophie. I do not like this unconsummated marriage between the Russian soul and a French name. I had a keen desire to re-read Cholokhov, Gogol, and, above all, Tchehov, but I consoled myself with the thought that, even if my favourite books were presented to me on a silver platter, I would be unable to read them. At eleven o'clock at night, I fell into bed, dead with exhaustion.

Madame Saulner had a great weakness for Georges. She tried

to chat with him to prove that she too had a mind that was no stranger to social problems. Georges's nerves were infinitely more robust than my own and, with impeccable politeness, he did chat, if Madame was so inclined.

For the winter holidays, we went off to their country house which Georges and I had to clean from top to bottom in one morning. Hélène told us that, every time they came here, they invited a young Englishman, because it was very smart to have an English boy for the holidays!

How happy Madame was in that country house! She was always running up and down the stairs; she was so sorry we were not seeing her house with its spring flowers and she assured us, like a threat, that we should often be coming back here. In Paris we did have our Sundays from three o'clock on. Here, the situation was hopeless; there was no village anywhere near and we were entirely delivered over to Madame. Nevertheless she did send us out for an hour's walk on Sundays. 'Take advantage of the air, my friends; take good, deep breaths of it. . . .'

The Englishman arrived on the Monday. He was a youth of seventeen whose transparent skin was not ruined by adolescent pimples. He was tall, slim and fair-haired, and he did not speak a word of French. He reminded me of Dickens, of the unforgettable David Copperfield, and I offered him the tray at meals with the loving care of a faithful reader meeting her favourite hero at long last in the flesh. Out in the kitchen, from which I could see the garden, I followed him with my eyes, as I did the washing-up, and I thought of my uncle and aunt who always spoke English when they talked about literature and who quarrelled in Italian because my uncle had lived for many years in Fiume. Heavens, how far away they were! Not because they were dead, but because of the life I was living now.

Hélène laid her heavy hand on my shoulder:

'Something wrong, little one?'

'I'm so tired, Hélène.'

'You're not cut out for this work,' she said. 'You'll ruin your health if you keep on at it. . . . Couldn't you find something else?'

I answered lethargically:

'I don't know. I don't know anything any more. . . .'

Two days later when I went into the English boy's bedroom I smelt a peculiar smell. I opened the window, I swept the room and made his bed, but the smell obstinately persisted. I thought it was only my imagination. However, the next morning, I was aware of the same smell, only stronger, more diffused; in fact, definitely established.

At first I summoned Hélène; she sniffed with me and said, shrugging her shoulders:

'Madame was very unpleasant to the builders when they were rebuilding the house. Perhaps they've hidden something in the brickwork, as a revenge. A dead mouse. . . .'

'Do you think a sweet little mouse could produce such a stench?'

'I don't know, but a decaying corpse does stink, you know. . . .'

With much regret I had to take Madame into my confidence. She came while the young Englishman was out on an excursion.

She planted herself in the middle of the room, and, with quivering nostrils, tried to define the smell. Then, without a word to me, she literally flung herself on the English boy's possessions. She opened the wardrobe and emptied it in one sweep. She removed a suitcase from the top of a cupboard and, placing it at her feet, she opened it. With a shout of victory, she drew out a round box with a red label: a Camembert! We all laughed together, Madame, Hélène and myself. We laughed till the tears ran down our cheeks and, when we recovered our gravity, we had only to look at the box to burst out laughing again. Madame was almost likeable when she laughed. Perhaps I had been mistaken; perhaps I had been morbidly sensitive; in that wild, hysterical giggling I was ready to become her ally, to serve her smilingly, without resentment. That blessed laugh made it possible to envisage the beginning of a friendship. . . . But she recovered her breath and stammered out:

'Oh, all these foreigners. . . . It's fantastic, how stupid they are. . . .'

I turned to ice once more waiting for the allusion to my accent. My accent sometimes got on Madame's nerves. But she said not another word and went off with the cheese.

The next day, at luncheon, the English boy admitted that he had wanted to take a Camembert home to his family; he was completely bewildered by the general mirth.

I hardly ever had a chance to talk to Georges now. We were submerged under the work. He polished floors all day and the unleashed children ran all over the shining parquet with their snow-covered boots. Madame did not want me to darn the socks in the room where Georges was cleaning the silver.

'If you chatter you'll both work more slowly. Besides, you have the whole evening to yourselves. . . .'

Having said this, she vanished from the room.

Would she not, one day, also vanish from our lives?

Chapter Twenty-seven

AFTER THE WINTER holidays we returned to Paris. There was also a Christmas Day whose memory I want to blot out. I found my big typewriter covered with dust; I went on paying its hire with desperate tenacity and, whenever I could, I added a few words to my manuscript.

It was on the day after our return, when I was handing round the salad, that I was seized with an attack of dizziness. The back of Madame's neck became enormous, the table grew blurred and looked like a great sheet of ice melting in the sun. I put down the salad bowl and ran into the scullery where I collapsed in Hélène's arms.

'I'm ill, Hélène; I want to be sick. . . .'

She gave me a large glass of water and Georges appeared too, looking astonished.

'Are you ill?' he inquired incredulously.

'Go away,' I said. 'Get on with serving the salad. I've left the salad bowl in there.'

I leant against the wicker back of the chair I was sitting on; my legs had gone flabby and no longer seemed to belong to me. I listened to the wild, irregular beating of my heart. It was the first time I had seen Hélène's head so close; she was standing right beside me and her hand, though coarse and rough from the washing-up water, felt light on my forehead.

'Liver attack,' she said, but I did not answer. Sunk in a physical torpor, in a marvellous immobility, I felt as if I were floating. I shut my eyes and I would like to have hung a placard round my neck with the inscription: 'Please do not disturb'.

But Georges came back with the empty salad bowl and picked up the tray of cheese.

'She asked what was the matter with you,' he said, as he brushed by me. 'What am I to tell her?'

'*Nothing*,' I said, in English. It was one of the few words that had survived my studies, as if I had learnt English for eight years simply and solely for that word which I brought out now in the most off-hand way.

'Tell her: *nothing*.'

Georges went off with the cheeses and when Hélène learnt what the word meant she was disappointed. She had vaguely hoped it was a swear word.

After luncheon I washed up and I imagined I was a cabin-boy on a wave-tossed boat. About four o'clock I ran into Madame Saulner in the passage.

'But you're frightfully pale!' she exclaimed. 'What's the matter with you?'

I faithfully repeated Hélène's diagnosis.

'A liver attack, madame. . . .'

She was almost happy.

'You see how well you eat in my house; the cooking is too rich for you. . . . Restrain yourself in future. . . . One must learn to say 'no' when one's too fond of eating. . . . And now, go to your room for half an hour and lie down; your face looks quite alarming. . . .'

In my bedroom I was alone with myself and, lying on the bed with my eyes closed, I formulated for the first time that magic phrase: 'I think I am going to have a child. . . .'

I did not want my thought to be expressed aloud in the kitchen. I wanted at least a partial liberty for it. I was afraid that this atmosphere of slavery might contaminate the child like moral measles. . . . Suddenly Georges came in. He sat down on the edge of my bed and took my hand in his. I kept silence for some moments; I was not trying to be dramatic but my supposition was so much my own private affair that I hardly dared to share it.

I looked at Georges as if I had never seen him before. He wore his green apron like a schoolboy in disgrace. He did not try to break my silence; he had always liked the security of uncertainty.

'Take off your apron,' I told him. And as I raised my head the nausea returned.

'I must go downstairs again. . . .'

'Take off your apron. We've got to talk as if we were free people.'

He stared at me, and I said:

'I think we're going to have a child. . . .'

'No!' he said, at once proud and terrified. 'It's not possible!'

Then he added feverishly, 'Are you sure?'

It needed another pillow for me to be able to see his face properly without having to raise my neck which was contracted by the effort to fight down my nausea.

'Yes, I'm almost sure.'

He confronted me like a big boy owning up to his first lapse to his mother: 'What are you going to do now? . . .'

The question was followed by words that I absolutely refused to listen to. I flung myself against him and pressed my palm against his lips. I could feel his young, unconscious lips like a wound; I did not want him to go on speaking.

'Be quiet . . . oh, do be quiet! Or do for once say the words I want you to say. . . .'

He disengaged himself, hostile now.

'You always want me to say the words *you* want. Well, you've only got to dictate. . . . What ought I to say? What *do* you permit me to express?'

I turned my face to the wall and I was ashamed of my tears; I made them disappear into the pillow. It was strange how the tears Georges provoked always humiliated me, as if a stranger had made me cry.

'I love you,' he said, from far away. 'You *know* that I love you.'

His limpid voice became more intimate; once again it was tinged with a pride I would never understand; that voice wanted precise details; it wanted to know past and future dates.

But I did not answer; I retired into my unhappiness like a snail retiring into its shell.

Later, when he had gone away again, I sat up. I put my hands on my stomach. It was flat, almost hollow. I felt my narrow hips; under my uniform dress I was abnormally thin. I left the room. This floor was reserved for the maids. They worked late into the evening and now, at five in the afternoon, it was totally silent. My steps echoed as I walked towards the stairs; I continued my way on tiptoe. The spiral staircase seemed narrower than usual. I looked carefully at each step and held on to the banisters which, up till then, I had never used. I went down, turning endlessly round and round; I was no longer frightened. Another feeling had taken possession of me: I was responsible.

What a triumph for Madame Saulner, my leaving her! She did not even allude to our terms of agreement; the opportunity was too splendid! She showered her opinions on me:

'I quite understand, Christine. You're too delicate for this work. . . .'

But she promptly regretted the word delicate; it was too elegant for a servant. She hesitated for a moment, trying to find a more suitable adjective, then said disgustedly:

You're anæmic. . . . I wonder how you'll manage in the future. You haven't even a nationality and French people don't like foreign nursery governesses for their children.'

'I've heard the opposite, madame,' I said. 'There are English girls here. And Swiss girls and Dutch girls and Swedish girls. . . .'

She made a little movement to show her impatience; I could see, from her face, that it was going to be very difficult for her to explain her ideas to me.

'A governess who comes from a country everyone knows is quite a different thing. One can ask for references, one has a minimum of safety for one's children. . . . But you, a Hungarian . . . with your impossible Slavonic language. . . .'

I said mechanically as I always did on these occasions:

'Hungarian is not a Slavonic language, madame. . . . It's a language of the same origin as Finnish. . . .'

She did not like my audacity. She did not like being interrupted and, moreover, I embarrassed her too much with my references to Finland. In her mind all Nordic countries were indistinguishable and she had just had a mental image of Sweden. . . .

I saw that she was drawing towards the end of our conversation. She stumbled over her sentences; she spoke faster and faster like steam raising a saucepan lid higher and higher.

'And that extraordinary notion of yours . . . writing!'

Under her nervous little laugh I sensed a jealousy that she would never admit to herself.

'Writing . . . whatever next? Building castles in Spain, eh?'

She was as violent as if she had guessed my thoughts. She kept reverting to the word 'writing'. She savoured it, she wanted to annihilate me, but I remained completely calm. She was so far removed from reality. . . . She did not know of my current manuscript nor of a future one in which I should devote a few pages to her! And, above all, she had no suspicion that I was going to have a child. I could bear anything but I could not have endured her staring at my body; that look of hers that would have travelled down from my breasts to my stomach and stopped at my hips. I could not have borne her playing guessing-games with my life: when, how, why? Passion or carelessness?

I listened to her and I was grateful for that very violence. She fidgeted and twisted about in her chair; she fought so hard to have the satisfaction of seeing me in tears that I was almost sorry for her. What an empty life hers was in which the world was divided into two camps, one filled only with the triumph of the conquerors and the other with the obedience of the conquered.

Finally, she stood up, taller than ever and, with a gesture like that of poor, mad Nero, indicating the blazing ruins of Rome, she pointed to the bookcase.

'You may choose a book as a remembrance. . . .'

She had gone over the borderline and upset the balance of power. Suddenly I was the one who dominated. Thanks to her I was able to reply in a calm voice:

'I do not want any remembrance, madame. I should like to forget you, madame.'

Chapter Twenty-eight

WE HAD NOT been able to make many social contacts. Nevertheless the miracle happened. One of our few friends lent us the little maid's room that served her as a refuge. She was a newly fledged mother-in-law and, instead of persecuting her family, she believed herself persecuted by it. I knew her son, a charming, extremely amusing man, and her patient, submissive daughter-in-law. I have never noticed the slightest sign of their being hostile towards her, but, according to my friend, her life was nothing but suffering.

'I'll lend you my room,' she said. 'But on one condition. As soon as I need it you'll leave within twenty-four hours. Because, you know, I'm on very good terms with them at the moment, but it's only the lull before the storm. And, if my pride is hurt, I retire here at once and wait till they come and implore me to return. The fact is they can't live without me, but it's only my going away that makes them realise how much they need me there.'

I consented wholeheartedly to my friend's conditions. Each day was a gift. I would have preferred to know that I had to go on some definite date rather than stay on in this complete uncertainty. I had acquired the habit of breathing deeply; I retained the air in my lungs so as to overcome my incessant desire to vomit. My charming friend did not know I was pregnant and she advanced along the passage with the confidence of those who are blessed with insensitive nostrils. Whereas I. . . .

This room was on the ground floor of one of those enormous buildings in Passy that stand along the banks of the grey indifferent Seine. By some odd caprice of the architect it contained a few maids' rooms. The elegant front of the house looked out on a busy square; the severe and useful part was hidden in a little street dominated by doors bearing inscriptions: 'Service. Service staircase. Tradesmen'. I followed my friend who had entered by one of these back doors; we brushed past some solemn, well-closed dustbins and she drew my attention to the conspicuously placed minute-switch at the right of the entrance. It was dark here, even in daytime, and I was assailed by various odours. I put my handkerchief to my mouth.

She turned to me.

'Have you got a cold?'

I nodded, without speaking.

We went into the dark room that looked out on a tiny square courtyard surrounded by forbidding walls.

'In summer I get a lot of sun here,' she affirmed, with as much conviction as if she had wanted to sell me her room. She gently touched the window, saying:

'You see, dear . . . in summer the window is always wide open and I put my plants out of doors. I'm never gloomy here.' She opened the window to its full extent and I hastened to lean out of it. It was impossible to glimpse the smallest patch of sky, whether grey or blue.

'And besides,' she went on, 'it's quiet. I can cry as much as I like here; nobody persecutes me. . . .'

There was a divan with a blue cover, a little table, two chairs and a cupboard. And my friend stood there in the middle of it enraptured, with her grey hair all over the place and her little hat still tipsy from the summer sun that lingered in its yellow felt. The scene was slightly ridiculous; I so longed to be alone and never again to have to utter the words 'thank you'. Moreover, I would have liked to know where to find the W.C. and water to wash with.

She guessed my thoughts.

'The water, yes, the water. There isn't running water in the room but you've got the tap at the end of another passage that I'll show you . . . and the toilet's down there too. . . .'

Suddenly, I felt very ill and I sat down on the edge of the divan. She settled down happily on a chair and removed her coat, in preparation for a long, intimate conversation. But, suddenly carried away by an idea, she stood up again and hunted for something in the cupboard. She found a spirit-stove. I began to be frightened of the smell.

'Before we have a chat, I'll make you a nice cup of coffee.'

She took a bottle from its hiding-place in one of the dark corners and poured a little alcohol into the container.

My stomach turned over in one heave, and, with my handkerchief to my mouth, I plunged into the dark passage in quest of the sinister ill-lit lavatory.

I returned, emptied of all my strength and shivering, with the bitter taste of bile on my tongue.

The little blue flame was flickering under a battered saucepan. My friend looked at me in surprise.

'You did rush off in a hurry! Did you find it?'

Warmed by the coffee, I huddled against a cushion and listened to her without hearing what she said. But, making an effort to come back to reality, I said:

'Georges will be coming soon. . . .'

She turned livid.

'Oh, no. . . . I don't want a man to come into my room!'

I protested feebly:

'A husband's different.'

She lowered her voice to explain:

'The neighbours on the right and left don't know that you'll be living here; they're used to seeing me about. . . . I don't want them to get wrong ideas about me; they mustn't hear a man's voice in my room. . . . My reputation. . . .'

She added generously:

'But he can help you with carrying the suitcase and the typewriter.'

She had managed to find the key word to my existence.

She went on without noticing my thrill of gratitude:

'Because your novel may be good . . . I liked the parts you read to me; you've got talent. . . . And, besides, it's an interesting subject. . . .'

I trembled with delight as I listened to her. It was the first time in my life that someone had taken my work seriously. To hear those magic words 'your novel'; to see her look of conviction! No, she was not laughing at me.

I got up, went over to her and hugged her. She pushed me away, saying:

'Mind my hat!'

But I loved her definitely and for life; I loved her just as she was. I no longer envied her her age and I was no longer unhappy about being young. Perhaps, I told myself, the world lay open before me? She had spoken about my novel . . . my novel. . . .

She went away very late, but I was able to endure that evening. My loneliness was alleviated by hope.

After she had gone I sat alone waiting for Georges. He arrived about nine o'clock, by special permission of Madame Saulner. The cardboard suitcase took its place on a chair like a well-trained old dog that always returns from its wanderings.

'You'll be all right here,' said Georges, looking round the room with as much interest as if he were in a museum.

'Yes. . . .'

Perseveringly I waited for a touch of gentleness. I would like to have seen him at my feet burning with enthusiasm. But, instead of comforting me, he asked the definite question:

'Are you sure?'

'Yes, I'm sure. I've been sick three times. . . .'

'It's incredible,' he said, but I saw no sign of wonder at the situation on his face.

'Is your bed comfortable?'

'I don't know. I shall be sleeping in it tonight for the first time.'

'True,' he said, and added thoughtfully: 'You won't be frightened, all alone?'

I wanted to cry with rage. Why did he talk about fear? I had been terrified ever since my friend's departure but, not for anything, would I admit it.

'What's she up to?'

'She' was Madame Saulner.

Georges replied discreetly, as if he were a relative of hers:

'Nothing special, much as usual. . . .'

'And Hélène?'

'In a bad temper. She had to do the washing-up all by herself. I was ironing trousers. . . .'

I was overwhelmed with a sudden tenderness; an acid tenderness. This boy who spoke five languages, who had been destined for a regular career in the Diplomatic Service – Secretary at thirty; Councillor at fifty – had to iron somebody's trousers!

I exclaimed:

'It's appalling this slavery. You really do deserve something better. What idiotic work!'

But he remarked philosophically:

'There's no such thing as an idiotic job. . . .'

We talked for a little while longer, then he went away. I was left alone, in bed, with the little bedside lamp and *Eugénie Grandet* which I was re-reading in French.

Soon, I switched off the lamp, and decided to go to sleep at last. Then, in the pitch-black room, I heard a strange noise, like the twittering of very lively birds. Sometimes I also heard a bang, as if someone had flung themselves against the door. I got up, icy with terror, and examined the door; it was well and truly shut. Now I knew where the noise came from; the birds were twittering outside in the passage. Now and then, after the click of the minute-switch, the birds would be silent. I imagined a thousand frightening possibilities. I no longer dared to move; beads of sweat ran down my neck. I had the feeling that a strange face was looking in at me through the window; it had a flattened nose. Was it Doctor Jekyll or Mr. Hyde? Which of the two was the monster?

I went to sleep with great difficulty, and, the next morning, when I went out into the passage, I saw a little woman in a blue apron who was just closing the door. She gave me an inquiring look and I replied with a 'Good morning, madame.'

'Are you living in that room?' she asked.

'Yes, for a few days. Madame, could you tell me what that noise was all last night, like birds?'

She smiled and said:

'Rats, mademoiselle. We have a lot of them. . . .'

Chapter Twenty-nine

THAT VERY MORNING I decided to leave the ground floor and its rats with as little delay as possible and I undertook one of the most difficult tasks imaginable, that of finding a maid's room. All about me the world had changed its familiar face; I hesitated longer before venturing on to a studded crossing and I had to force myself to eat in spite of the profound repulsion I felt for every kind of food. I also wanted to finish my book. I looked on the birth of the child as the frontier of a new life that I must cross with a manuscript in my hand. I was ready to love Georges with a new love fed by this miracle I carried in my body. I wanted to forget all the great and small miseries he had caused me. I looked on love as a sublime duty towards the unknown, towards my child. We had agreed that Georges should stay on with Madame Saulner and that I should find an easier job. We had not so much as adumbrated the word 'flat'; that wish would have been quite crazy. But we did talk incessantly about a little room where I could cook without being pursued by an angry hotel proprietor and where, most important of all, I should have a corner for the cradle. I looked at advertisements and my one idea of happiness was to find a few lines that ran: 'Wanted, a young couple. Husband to act as secretary; wife to be employed in typewriting.'

In that dark little room in Passy I worked fervidly, but the song of the rats had a very demoralising effect on me. I always came in about five o'clock, when it was still light. I pressed the button of the minute-switch and walked down the passage, my heels clattering on the concrete. One Sunday night – I had been living for a week in this handsome building – Georges and I arrived at the entrance. It was ten o'clock – we had been to a little cinema in the neighbourhood – and I wanted to show him the pages I had written during the week. But the minute-switch was no longer working. Despairingly I pressed the little button but with no result. The passage lay before us, drowned in total darkness, as menacing as one of those marshes that swallow up their victim before he has gone three steps.

'I'll never dare to go as far as the room,' I whispered, as if I were afraid of being overheard by the rats.

Georges had an ingenious idea.

'If we had a newspaper we could make a torch. . . .'

But where could we find a newspaper? All the kiosks in the neighbourhood shut at eight o'clock. We waited for some other inhabitant of the ground floor to come along, so as to reinforce our caravan a little. But, on a Sunday night, they were all away. We took the métro again and, in the end, we found a newspaper seller at the Gare Saint-Lazare. An hour later we were back again and Georges lit his torch. Sick with disgust we finally reached the door of my room.

The next day I went off in search of another room. I had decided to ask the concierges in the big expensive blocks of flats, the ones where the lucky tenants were entitled to two or three maids' rooms to a single flat. That foggy morning in February was saturated with the smell of petrol. I walked to the Trocadéro and, on my way, I counted at least six stations where the men, with their big tubes and their meters, were pouring petrol into the avid interiors of cars. I passed them with a handkerchief pressed against my nose, holding my breath, but, though I did not smell the reek, I imagined it and my nausea returned violently.

I crossed the Place du Trocadéro and entered a large block of flats. I was suddenly greatly impressed by the white marble paving of the vestibule and I knocked softly on the glazed door, covered with a yellow silk curtain that was gathered like an eighteenth-century lady's petticoat. A strident voice that contrasted with the sumptuous setting called out:

'What is it?'

How could I answer in one word through a curtained pane?

'I wanted some information, madame. . . .'

The voice moved about behind the curtain; I could hear it grumbling. Incomprehensible words burst out in a little flood and broke, like waves, inside the lodge.

At last, with a sharp click, a woman opened the door and I saw that she was in process of drying herself. She held a towel in front of her, with which she was both covering herself and dabbing the hollow of her left armpit with her right hand.

I mumbled:

'Madame, is there, by any chance, an unoccupied maid's room in this building?'

Her face expressed such utter incredulity and her shock was so great that she stammered as she replied:

'Wh – what – what . . . a *maid's* room?'

She nearly fainted.

'And you come and disturb me for a crazy thing like that? It's a disgrace, mademoiselle!'

She banged the door and the shivering panes tinkled with alarm in their yellow petticoats. I heard one last tart observation:

'These Englishwomen, they're all cracked. . . .'

I could not help smiling as I mentally compared my temporary permit that had to be reauthorised every three months with an English passport that must certainly have a crown on its cover. At least I hoped there was a crown!

Nevertheless I had the courage to go on because someone had thought I was English. The second block was just as big but the lodge was plainly visible through the uncurtained pane. It was like a little stage scene. A round polished table stood in the middle of the room surrounded by three chairs. There was an open newspaper and on the opposite wall an enlarged photograph of a smiling young man in uniform. I knocked and a man appeared from an inner room. He stared at me through the glass door and slowly opened it.

'Mademoiselle?'

He had just been drinking his coffee and I recoiled as I smelt his breath.

'Good morning, monsieur ... I came to ask for some information. Might there perhaps be a maid's room to let in this building? ... I am a student and ...'

He shook his head; the door was already closed. He vanished into his kitchen still shaking his head. ... Perhaps he was dumb?

Going into the third block I ran full-tilt into a severe-looking woman who was preparing to go out shopping with a string bag. I could not see the porter's lodge so I seized the occasion to ask the woman:

'Madame, you don't happen to know where I can find the concierge?'

She replied suspiciously:

'What do you want? *I'm* the concierge.'

I was delighted. At last a concierge outside her cage! She would definitely be more amiable, more on a level with human beings. I adopted a polite sophisticated tone:

'I don't want to keep you, madame; I see you're just going out. ... You don't, by any chance, happen to know of an unoccupied maid's room in this block of flats?'

Her answer was brief.

'No. Not one.'

She opened the large elegant front door and waited for me to pass out in front of her. I hurried away, feeling her gaze planted in the middle of my back.

By midday I was already full of bitterness. As I walked along the street I stared now and then at the huge blocks with all their windows and thought that, in Paris, you had to be born in a flat to get one. But my poor child whom I was expecting would have been only too glad to be born in a properly heated flat! ... For the moment it was hopeless. By way of lunch I drank a glass of soda water and ate two rolls. Afterwards I resumed my search. I saw a great many concierges from then on until evening. Nervous concierges, resigned concierges, astonished concierges, angry concierges. Once a woman said to me in a modest little street near the Étoile:

'What a quaint little thing you are, to be sure! Ever so comical . . . . Wanting a maid's room . . . as if it was as easy as anything!'

Discouraged and mortally tired I returned to the Place du Trocadéro, and, suddenly, I found myself in front of an extremely elegant cemetery. Impelled by a melancholy curiosity, I went in. A conscientious keeper warned me:

'We close in half an hour, mademoiselle. . . .'

I nodded; it seemed perfectly reasonable to me to close a cemetery. My nostrils were full of the stale smell of the wintry fog; it was difficult to breathe.

I sat down in front of a well kept-up mausoleum. I had no thought in my mind; I felt neither morbid nor indifferent. I was drained completely dry by that cruel unproductive day.

I got up slowly, left the cemetery and walked along a quiet little street. 'I'll try just once more,' I thought, as, clenching my teeth, I noticed a large building. I knocked at the door of the lighted-up lodge; no one answered; I timidly went in. A smiling woman appeared in the doorway of another room, next to the one I was in.

'What do you want, mademoiselle?'

I told her in a dull voice, not at all eager and none too polite, that I was looking for a room.

'Take a seat,' she said, and she dusted the chair with her hand.

I thought I must be hearing wrong.

'Take a seat,' she repeated, then added:

'There's an empty room on the eighth floor, a very pretty room with velvet curtains and a silk counterpane. And a big wardrobe all decorated with carving. It's well heated because we've got central heating through the building, it's just been installed. . . . And then, besides, there's a lovely view, with a real window looking out on the Eiffel Tower. . . .'

Taken aback by my silence, she looked at me hard.

'Would that suit you?'

'Yes . . . oh, yes!'

240

I heard my voice from very far away.

She became more friendly.

'Go up quietly to the first floor; the owners live just opposite the lift. They're ever so nice, especially Madame. But so's Monsieur – I've nothing against him. . . .'

'I think it's too late today,' I said. 'Quarter-past seven. . . .'

She made a face.

'The room's been empty for two days; you'd do better to arrange things straight away. You know, it's very hard to find such a pretty room in Paris. . . .'

I went up to the first floor and I rang the bell. A housekeeper with a gentle, slightly tired face opened the door to me.

'I'd like to speak to Madame.'

After a moment's hesitation she showed me into a drawing-room that was furnished both richly and with taste. It was lit by soft, discreet lights concealed behind silk lampshades.

My lucidity returned in this drawing-room bathed in ivory-tinted, artificial light. Here, all the objects had their own life; nothing was brand new and nothing was shabby. It was a drawing-room where the family had coffee after luncheon, where one straightened a crooked picture with a mechanical little gesture, where a fourteen-year-old adolescent retired now and then to dream. . . .

'Mademoiselle?'

'Madame. . . .'

She had the beauty of a piece of Sèvres porcelain. Tall, slender, dressed in grey, with a jabot of filmy white lace, she advanced towards me. The sly tenacious workings of time, that goes by so fast, were hidden in the velvety half-light and veiled by the kindly lamps. She held out her hand, with its long delicate fingers and her hesitant smile did not destroy the harmony of her face; on the contrary, that smile made her other-worldly beauty friendly, accessible and human.

'Mademoiselle, do sit down. . . . What is it that you want?'

I was embarrassed by a very distant smell of roast meat that had found its way into the drawing-room through a kitchen door that had been left ajar for a moment. Instinctively I wanted to define that smell, as one searches impatiently for the name of a tune one knows. In a soft voice I began to explain the object of my visit. My words, almost whispered, made little circles in the stillness of the drawing-room, like pebbles thrown into a calm lake.

She must have heard much talk of human misery. I felt myself transformed in her eyes into a living illustration of a theory she must have studied extremely conscientiously. I was the refugee intellectual whom one sees, at first sight, comes from an excellent family. My accent became almost an added charm. The unusual hour of my unexpected visit was pardoned the moment she had reminded herself that misery is entitled to present itself at any time of the day. She questioned me with a great deal of tact. I told her about my departure from Hungary, about my parents in Kufstein, and about my plans, but I did not dare mention the child and I am almost sure I forgot Georges.

Sitting in a patch of pink light, with her sitting opposite me, I did not want to look to right or left. But I was aware of the presence of others. A furtive glance showed me a tall boy with black hair, leaning against the drawing-room door, and the anxious face of the housekeeper hovering mysteriously in another room. She was worried about her dinner.

Suddenly the master of the house made a precipitate entrance. A polite man, whom nothing surprised, he kissed my hand, supposing I was a guest of his wife's, a friend whom he had not met before. But when she explained my 'case' to him, he agreed with her at once.

'If that will help you, you can have the room. . . .'

She had not added the word I most dreaded: *provisionally.*

They promised to let me have the key next day, and, as I left, I had the feeling that my poor little winter coat was growing too tight and that this extraordinary piece of good fortune was making me sprout wings.

When I was already in bed listening to the farewell song of the rats who were gaily frisking about in the passage, I remembered something that a furious concierge had said to me: 'These women students, what a lot of giddy gadabouts they are!'

I went to sleep, thinking over the day's events and waiting impatiently for the moment when I could tell Georges the great news about the room.

The room on the eighth floor was ravishing and I took possession of it on a sunny day in February. Georges was not in the least amazed by my success and said to me:

'When you want something, you always manage to get it.'

This absolute confidence in my strength filled me with apprehension about Georges himself. I was more and more haunted by the idea that I ought to change him. I was waiting impatiently for him to grow up. He had rigid and definite opinions about life. He spoke with great contempt of politics, which had been his family's profession for several generations. Literature bored him, and when I mentioned Baudelaire, he talked about petrol engines and steam engines. I had vaguely heard it said that totally different temperaments understand each other very well because of some mysterious law of attraction; I also had faith in the fact that we were both young. I really and truly wanted to be interested in his affairs, but I had a frantic desire to yawn when he attempted to explain the function of valves or how ball-bearings worked. During the long Sunday afternoons when I lay on the divan, he sat beside me with sheets of paper scribbled over with tiny figures. He added and multiplied at astonishing speed and I had to make a tremendous effort not to close my weary eyelids.

'Is it quite clear to you now?' he would ask, and I would reply, suppressing an impertinent yawn:

'Yes, it's more or less clear. . . .'

I was afraid of taking away his courage if I admitted that he was boring me to tears, but, one day, when he had explained that our future life depended on the success of one of his inventions, a toy aeroplane, I could not help being anxious.

'It would be much better for you to go all out to try and get a student's grant and go to the University. You'd be an excellent engineer. I've got to work in any case, and in a few years, you'd have a splendid future before you. . . .'

'Do you think so?' he said dreamily. 'Do you really think so?'

'I'm absolutely sure of it. . . .'

He was so childlike that I suddenly had the feeling that I was Colette's Lea; I was fifty, and he, sitting there beside me, was Chéri.

'I say, darling. . . .'

Hearing him say that word 'chérie' made me start.

He put his hand on my shoulder.

'Don't be so jumpy. . . .'

'What were you going to say?'

He gave a great stretch, like someone wanting to deliver themselves of a thought.

'I shall go on with my studies in the United States. . . . I shall be an engineer in an atomic centre.'

His delicate high-bred face had an expression that worried me. I realised that I had two children; this adolescent dreamer and the one I was carrying.

I heaved a sigh.

He leant over me.

'What are you thinking about?'

He was so rarely concerned about my thoughts that it was an occasion for telling the truth. But I could not see so much as a shadow of uneasiness in those eyes full of frank curiosity, and I did not want to upset him.

'I'm not thinking of anything. . . .'

He smiled radiantly.

'Then I can go on, can I?'

I said, 'Yes.'

Whereupon he began to explain all over again just how many months it would take, if his invention got going, for us to become millionaires. . . .

Chapter Thirty

When my novel was finished I returned to the publishers and the secretary had to make an effort to recognise me. She was completely taken aback by the manuscript I laid on her table and said:

'I'll send you to another publishing firm. . . . I know their Hungarian reader personally.'

The publishers to whom she sent me received me kindly and the secretary to whom I spoke assured me that I should shortly receive a letter from her.

I took the métro about six o'clock. The carriage was full and I stood beside a seat on which there were three women. Suddenly one of them stood up.

'Take my seat, madame.'

I did not dare protest; I sat down, surprised and embarrassed. I turned my head towards the window and saw the dim reflection of my tired face. Suddenly I knew why she had given up her seat to me. Instinctively, I shifted my right hand towards my stomach and I realised that my winter coat was not buttoned up. Before leaving I had left it open; it was beginning to get too tight for me and I could not move the buttons; they were already on the edge. So people could see that I was expecting a baby. . . . It must be four months old, my child.

As I stepped out of the train I had already made up my mind to go off as soon as possible, to see my parents again; I wanted to feel my mother's warmth. And they knew nothing yet! . . .

Having been unable to obtain a visa for Austria, we decided to get as far as Munich. We hoped that, on the spot, we would be able to obtain a twenty-four-hour permit so that I could introduce Georges to my parents. We believed with blind confidence that, after this journey, Georges would find some job that was worthy of him and that would assure our future and that of the child. I was not in the least frightened of the tiring journey; I knew that we should have a long night sitting up in the train, but I was sustained by my longing for this meeting. Now that I was expecting my child, I loved my parents more than ever. I wanted the time to go more quickly: I counted the days and the hours.

Nevertheless, it is extremely difficult to travel when one does not possess the most natural thing in the world: a nationality. It is most difficult of all for a mother-to-be who might give birth anywhere – in the train, in an aeroplane or in the sacred portals of an embassy, and, by that fact, become the stateless mother of a newly born Frenchman, German or American!

The customs officer stared long and carefully at our travel permit and everyone in the compartment awaited the outcome with lively interest. I got the impression that, in whichever country I arrived, I should be the extra mouth that would finally let famine loose, the superfluous body that would provoke a housing crisis.

At last he gave us back the apparently inoffensive little book whose scrupulously filled-up pages concealed one of the victims of this day and age, suffering from the worst of contemporary diseases, that of being an émigré.

The night was very hard to bear. My aching body, heavy with the still invisible weight of the miracle inside it, wanted to lie down, but all the seats were occupied. Tormented by a persistent nausea, I left the compartment several times, stumbling over the stiff legs of sleepers in the dim blue light. Out in the corridor, I shivered, but at least I could breathe. Near the door of the lavatory a young soldier lay fast asleep, lying doubled-up, with his head on his knapsack. Like a child. . . .

Suddenly I felt an infinite tenderness for the human beings all round me. It seemed to me that no one could ever be wicked any more and that the entire world was a vast cradle waiting for my child. I wanted to kneel down by that soldier and wake him up with the great news, the marvellous news that my child was going to be born into happiness.

As I pressed my burning face against the damp pane I saw the scenes of my past life unroll before me. But nothing seemed harsh or wounding any more. And, suddenly, I realised that my lips were uttering those magic words, those wise, sweet words that have come down through the ages:

'When God sends a child, He also sends His help.'

When we arrived in Munich we learnt that, if we wanted to see my parents, we should have to cross the Austrian frontier illicitly. Austria was still occupied by the four great Powers, and it was they who would have to give us our visas after long months of waiting. I did not want to wait.

Georges and I decided that we would have our marriage regularised religiously and, afterwards, cost what it might, we would try and rejoin my parents.

The idea of a religious marriage filled me with profound alarm. But having been brought up in the strictness of a fervently Catholic family, I wanted to be faithful to tradition.

In Munich we stayed with friends, poor like ourselves, but full of kindness and hospitality. Soon after our arrival I found myself, at eight o'clock in the morning, standing beside a grave and solemn Georges in a little church in Munich. Standing in front of the altar and thinking of the toothless old women muttering their prayers, I had the impression that my back was as broad as a house. Were they going to discover that this early-morning bride was no longer able to button up her coat? Oh, if I only had a really voluminous coat, how well I could have hidden both myself and the child! But, dressed as I was forced to dress, I was exposed to the stares of all and sundry.

We heard Mass on our knees. I was cold, but, on the prie-dieu, I could not clutch my coat tighter round my body. Yet I did not want the child to catch cold; I was thinking of it and of nothing else.

Lulled by a kind of torpor, as I said my neglected prayers

again, it was to my child that I vowed eternal fidelity. . . . As we came out of church I was seized with an irresistible desire to tell the truth; I wanted to tell Georges, that, when I had pronounced the words of the marriage vow, I had been thinking only of my child. But, when he turned to me and I saw his tender, defenceless face, I kept silent.

With my left hand in his and my right hand clutching my coat, we went off to have breakfast.

The old priest with his gentle, impersonal smile had given us the address of a friend of his who was a parish priest in a little town near the Austrian frontier.

At dawn we took a little local train that deposited us in the rain-drenched village. We crossed the main street and took a little beaten-earth track that ran up the side of the mountain. The village was solidly enclosed in this tiny valley which was probably starved of sun, even in July. We were guided by the plan the priest had drawn on a half-sheet of paper, so that we should not have to inquire our way of the villagers.

I turned to Georges:

'Can you see anything remotely resembling a road in the mountains?'

He looked about him like the captain of a ship and shook his head.

'I've no idea how the priest will make us cross the frontier. . . .'

Our coats were becoming heavier and heavier with rain and we stopped in front of a well-kept little house, stuck against the steep rise. Georges pulled the string of the little bell fixed beside the door. The sound was stifled almost at once by the rain that came down in torrents. Looking up at the mountain that rose up just behind the house, I saw a foaming river pouring down from the heights and rushing furiously towards the valley.

The door opened abruptly but the grey-haired woman who stood in the doorway had nothing hostile about her; she merely seemed extremely surprised at our intrusion.

'Could we speak to His Reverence?' Georges asked, and his impeccable German dissipated the housekeeper's uneasiness.

Without taking off our coats we went into a dining-room where a table was laid for breakfast and a fat earthenware coffee pot gave out a friendly welcoming smell.

'Sit down,' said the housekeeper. 'The Father has just finished saying his Mass. He'll be back in a few minutes to have his breakfast.'

'I'm terribly hungry,' I muttered in Georges's ear, and the big country loaf and the fresh butter looked more and more appetising every second.

The priest arrived and welcomed us very kindly, especially when he heard that we had been sent to him by his best friend. Without inquiring the reason for our visit, he rang the little bronze bell that stood by his plate. When the housekeeper appeared, he asked her to bring two more cups and said we must have some coffee with him.

It was a long time since I had eaten with such appetite. As we ate, we explained our project to him.

The priest promptly became very uneasy.

'The frontier is near,' he said, 'but I don't at all like risking a business like this. Go back to Munich and wait quietly for your visa.'

I was seized with a vast despair. I turned to him so as to catch his faded blue eye.

'Father, I'm expecting a child; I must see my parents before it is born.'

He stared at me with astounded eyes.

'You want to cross the frontier on foot when you're expecting a child?'

I absolutely had to persuade him.

'I implore you. Truly, truly, I can still walk very well. The priest in Munich told us it was only ten kilometres. We'll walk slowly but I *must* see my parents again. I shan't have a moment's peace if I can't see them again. . . .'

And I added, as a reference, as a final recommendation:

'I did thirty-five kilometres with my parents when we had to cross the Austro-Hungarian frontier. It's true I wasn't expecting a child, but it was quite an ordeal, all the same. . . .'

The priest's delicate face, further refined by the nobility of age, softened again.

'What hardship! Poor, cruelly tried generation. . . .'

I was profoundly struck by those words that came back to me from the past like an exact echo – a distant echo, but clear and sorrowful. Monsieur Radnai in the cellar. . . . During that infernal siege. . . . When he looked at me his eyes were misty with a strange tenderness; he was one of those persecuted men who are terrified by the world's savagery but who no longer think of themselves but of the young who would have liked to live. . . . 'Poor generation,' he used to say during the bombardment. . . . I was fifteen, and, at the time, those words had filled me with an extraordinary pride; an immeasurable pride that had annihilated fear. It was as if he had dubbed me knight . . . knight of that capricious fate that made grass grow between the outspread fingers of the corpses that peopled the lunar streets of Budapest. . . .

'Christine . . . Christine. . . .'

Georges's insistent voice brought me back to reality.

'Are you feeling ill?' the priest inquired anxiously.

'Oh, no, thank you. I was only thinking. . . .'

Georges whispered a well-worn schoolboy joke to me in Hungarian. He had an inexhaustible repertory of them.

'You always turn pale when you think, it's the tremendous unaccustomed effort. . . .'

The priest stood up.

'My children, the important thing is that you shouldn't be seen climbing the mountains.'

He threw me an anxious glance; he had frightened himself by uttering that word 'mountain'. I straightened my back, and, with a great sigh, I pulled in my stomach to show him how slim and athletic I was, ready to face up to this insignificant little stroll.

In the hall he picked up his black overcoat and his umbrella and called out:

'Madame Hilda!'

She appeared.

'I'll be back in an hour.'

As we went out we walked round to the back of the house, then through the garden. After a few minutes' walk through the deluge, we passed through the iron gate that marked the end of his domain, and found ourselves on the steep mountain slope strewn with pine-needles and rotting leaves.

We walked in Indian file. His black umbrella bobbed among the trees like a mushroom swelled to giant size by the wet. The water squelched softly in my shoes and I held on to Georges's hand: he was walking between me and the priest.

Suddenly the curtain of rain thinned and I had the sensation that the inhabitants of the village were looking out of their windows and watching us attentively. We were so alarmingly visible: big black ants climbing awkwardly up in the wake of a black umbrella.

When we were on the crest of the mountain it stopped raining. At the bottom of the descent before us stretched a vast meadow; farther away, covered with mist, we could dimly see a farm. We could even make out some cows, tiny as drops of water.

'Don't be frightened when you get to the farm,' the priest told us. 'The people who live there are good-hearted. . . . Near the house you'll find a road that will lead you into a little forest. You'll also see a chapel where I say Mass every other Sunday, and, after that chapel, you'll come to the main road, a concrete road. That's already Austria. Follow it and you'll find a village where you can get a train that takes you to Kufstein.'

He went off hurriedly without waiting for us to thank him, and soon he had disappeared behind the trees.

Thus, we found ourselves alone, on the edge of an unknown world, committed to cross an invisible frontier that separated two countries.

'Come along,' said Georges, and we plunged into the tall,

soaking grass that froze my legs. But why should the cold do me any harm on the road that was leading me to my parents?

I was transported by the uplifting idea of accomplishing a great feat. I looked ahead of my feet. I did not want to stumble unnecessarily. I was thinking of my child whose first journey this was.

Exhausted and mortally weary, we arrived on the outskirts of the farm. The cows had resumed their normal size; they stared at us with mild complacency as we walked into the farm kitchen.

When the farmer's wife heard that we had been sent by the parish priest, she put two bowls of milk, still warm from the cow, on the table and two big hunks of bread. She would not accept the money Georges offered her and her tall daughter, with her plaits wound round her head, accompanied us as far as the little chapel. When we were on the main road, in Austria at last, I began to shake all over.

'Just a little more courage, and we'll be at the station,' Georges told me.

But I could only see a village as far away as the farm had been when we had seen it from the summit.

I walked like an automaton and the sun no longer traced more than a faint yellow streak on the fields. Georges looked at his watch.

'It's half-past four,' he said.

We had left the village about half-past eight.

I would like to have talked to Georges, to have expressed the thoughts that haunted me, but he profoundly loathed my touching on our feelings towards each other. He would almost have preferred a bombardment to an analysis. All the same I would have liked to tell him that, in spite of his closed, hermetically sealed mind, we had never felt ourselves so much at one as during that crazy walk.

'Georges?'

I had spoken his name aloud in spite of myself.

'Are you very tired?' he replied.

'Yes, but that doesn't matter in the least. . . . I'd like to tell you that. . . .'

I silently implored him: 'Help me . . . we have a unique, marvellous chance to find each other. . . .'

But he noticed nothing whatever. . . .

By the time we reached the station, I was no longer walking, I was just dragging myself along.

The compartment was empty; I was able to lie down on one of the seats.

I shut my eyes and thought that our marriage was a true marriage, not like the ones I had seen contracted at the French Legation in Budapest in 1945 . . . so as to be able to leave the country with a passport! . . . But I did not want to remind myself of all those old stories. One day, perhaps, I may tell them. . . .

Georges woke me up at Kufstein.

I found the little station just as I had left it, with all my hopes, a year ago. It was dark when we arrived at the hut where my parents lived. There was a light in their window. I made a sign to Georges and we looked in at my parents sitting quietly at a table. The room had changed its appearance. I saw books everywhere; my father was reading and my mother was mending a shirt. Although I was exhausted I still lingered outside; I was afraid to disturb their apparent peace, even with a joy.

When we knocked at the door my mother opened it. For some minutes she stood there, quite stunned at the sight of us.

How lovely that evening was! I was happy and I found once again a security that I had so terribly lacked. My parents were very sweet to Georges. They embraced him as if he were a son who had returned from a distant journey. When my parents learnt that I was expecting a baby and that we had crossed the frontier illicitly, they could find no words to say.

Mamma put me to bed and heaped me up with pillows. I had my dinner in bed. I wanted to laugh and cry with happiness. How I loved my parents! And, thanks to them, I was going to be a little girl again, even if only for two days. . . .

Our arrival caused a sensation in the camp, and, at the end of the second day, the Commandant sent a man to warn us that he wanted to see our papers the following morning. A submarine that has long been lying motionless in the depths of the sea does not welcome divers who come from another world. And we had returned from another world. We were obliged to leave the next morning at dawn and to go back the way we came. My father accompanied us through the fields as far as the frontier. It was a heartrending goodbye. That day I made a vow to myself that I would do everything I could to have them with me for life.

Before taking the train from Munich back to Paris, I followed my mother's advice and went to see a doctor. When he had examined me, he said:

'You are very narrow in the hips, madame. . . . It's extremely likely you may have complications. . . . You must take great care of yourself. . . . You must have a good doctor. . . .

We took the train back to Paris that very night.

Chapter Thirty-one

IN PARIS WE went back to the little room that was our one and only refuge and Georges did the impossible to find some work. He presented himself everywhere that the advertisements announced someone wanted a capable young man. During the first days after our return, I waited for him, lying on the divan with a book bought for a few francs from a second-hand bookstall. I read from morning till night, but I had only to raise my head to be seized with a nausea that obliged me to run the whole length of the corridor to reach the lavatory. I was hungry, with an impetuous, arrogant hunger that was difficult to appease. But we had so very little money that I did not dare so much as venture into those elegant shops that surrounded the block of flats. I went down with Georges into the busy Rue de Passy and there, for fifty francs, we bought oil, a salad, a few potatoes and, very occasionally, a little rib of pork. But, during the long afternoons, I would imagine tables exquisitely laid, with flowers scattered on an embroidered cloth and candles shedding soft golden light on the heavy silver. And, on this elegant table, I served all sorts of Lucullan menus. Before our departure to Germany we had still been able to buy quarter-bottles of soda water that marvellously subdued my nausea but, since our return, this had become too great a luxury.

When, by exceptional luck, I felt a little better, I used to go and sit at the window during Georges's absence and look at the roofs of Paris. The spring was still too young and twilight fell fast and early, but there were moments when the roofs were flooded with pink light and when the Eiffel Tower looked like a child's drawing done with a heavy, blunt pencil. How far away Paris seemed from that window! I was tortured by the idea that I was going to die when my child was born. In the four months of life that remained to me, I wanted to write another novel. But I lacked the physical strength; my back was too painful and I was hungry all the time. Georges arrived towards evening. I was full of cares and anxieties but what could I have told that boy who came in pale and exhausted, not knowing where to turn next? I was convinced that my future life, if I survived, would be merely a dreary vegetating, with ideas cut off at the root and resentments one could not even express.

When the child kicked me during the night I seemed to feel its sharp, impertinent little toe; in the darkness, I kept saying ardently to myself: 'I want you to be strong; I want you to be *very* strong. . . .'

I shall never be able to define my behaviour towards Georges. At what precise moment did I begin to keep silent? I was probably the egoist who does not like being unhappy or the vain woman who will never admit defeat. I wanted, with a morbid obstinacy, to preserve the appearances of happiness. and, when I looked at Georges asleep – he slept on a mattress on the floor beside my bed – I felt responsible for him. I had now got into the habit of tidying up after him, as if I had replaced the nurse of his childhood, and, to comfort myself, I had to have recourse to well-worn phrases such as: 'Men will always be children.'

But, when I looked at the Eiffel Tower, I never stopped thinking of our expedition, already long ago now, and that monster of iron lacework filled me with horror and admiration.

Our hopes of a peaceful future rested on a very slender foundation. One of our Hungarian friends was attempting the apparently impossible so that we could settle in Belgium. I felt a dull lump of misery inside me at the thought of our being forced to leave France in order to be able to live and I knew that the real France, the kind, welcoming France had not yet shown us her face. I sometimes wanted to cry out: 'France, I'm here, I love you! I was brought up admiring you; I want to write French books; I want you to be my other native country. Great France, marvellous France, why don't you want to know that I am here?'

The roofs and the grey smoke that wreathed up into the impassive sky did not answer me.

In the old days, I had never thought that one could suffer from hunger and look covetously at a grocer's shop window. Not far from us, there was a dairy, and the good woman, who always wore a white overall, one day hung up a bunch of bananas in her window. At first the bananas were almost green and the bunch intact, but what contemptuous, almost cruel arrogance in their exorbitant price! Each day they grew yellower and yellower. Sometimes, when I hurried very fast past her shop, I saw the dairy-woman cut off four or five of them with an enormous knife. I would have really loved to eat one.

Georges came home one night with excellent news. He had found a job. A Hungarian carpenter, long settled in France, wanted his French wife to learn Hungarian. So he had engaged Georges to give his wife an hour's lesson every day at two hundred francs a time. The only snag was that they lived near the Invalides and we lived in the neighbourhood of Passy. The daily métro ticket would have taken a cruel slice off his fees. Georges decided to go on foot. The next day I went with him for the first lesson. We had constantly been told that, if a pregnant woman walks a great deal, the birth will be easy.

While Georges was giving his lesson I sat meekly in the workshop on a stool. I breathed deeply so as to be able to endure the smell of glue that assailed me like little waves breaking against a rock.

The carpenter, ankle-deep in wood-shavings, said to me from time to time:

'All right, madame?' Then he bent lovingly over his plane. He spoke to me in laconic little sentences, without waiting for my reply, and I found this one-sided conversation profoundly restful. 'Because that's how life is, madame,' he said. 'Love. After love comes the child, and worries and little bits of happiness, too. You've got a young husband, he'll make his way. But it's not funny, being far from one's own country. . . . Me, I've been here

257

twenty years. I fought in the war with them. I've got French nationality; my wife's French; my children are French. They don't know a word of Hungarian. What d'you expect? They speak their mother's language, it's only natural. . . . You see, I haven't got the time. . . . I'm from Szeged. . . . Ah, so you know Szeged? Beautiful city . . . so's Budapest. . . . My mother died two years ago. . . . She never understood how one could live with anyone who wasn't Hungarian. . . . She was a very brave woman, my mother – eight children . . . and two miscarriages. . . . I'm not saying this to frighten you, but it's not easy, giving birth. . . .'

Here I was overwhelmed by a feeling of peaceful eternity, a third-class eternity, simple and kindly. It was warm: there were murmurs from the neighbouring room; an occasional customer would come in, more to chat than to order some work. But the carpenter did not interrupt his own task and I watched him with admiration. This was a man who had a bedroom, a table, plates and all the food he needed. Here, I had an unbearable desire to have a tiny lodging, a wardrobe with at least two dresses in it and a big, warm, loose coat. Where was my child going to be born? What bed would I be in . . . and what country?

After the lesson the cabinet maker's wife gave us some really hot coffee and that friendly drink gave me an incredible sensation of well-being. They thought that Georges gave lessons all day; they never suspected that the two of us and the child subsisted on their daily two hundred francs. But, afterwards, about seven o'clock, we had to go out and walk back uphill to Place du Trocadéro. On those return journeys, the city seemed vast and the streets endless. Hanging on Georges's arm, I walked conscientiously, with small, even steps; I did not want to jolt my child.

'You'll give birth to it just like dropping a letter in the letterbox. . . .'

I did not like comparisons of this kind; without my knowing why, they humiliated me a little. But, I replied, with false gaiety:

'Yes, of course. . . .'

All the same, in the depths of myself, I was preparing myself

258

for a tragedy. Involuntarily, I lived through a thousand imaginary death-beds. I saw Georges a widower, with a new wife who would have a pony-tail and flat heels. He often told me he would like me to wear my hair like that and he regarded my high heels with ill-disguised hostility. I have never been able to understand his crazy passion for youth: he was so young himself .... For him, anyone over thirty was already middle-aged and, if it were a woman, it was better not to mention her. ... A woman of thirty! ... That was something ridiculous! ... He had told me once that I still had seven years left in which to wear bright-coloured dresses because, after thirty, one had to be careful. Without expressing the thought, I felt in my bones that I should leave him before that fatal birthday. But I knew, too, that I should make a superhuman effort not to die in giving birth. I wanted to bring up my child myself.

Georges went off to sleep quickly at night and I imagined touching or grotesque scenes that made me smile or cry in the dark. I saw Georges at my funeral in a top hat and a morning coat and I shivered when I thought of him saying to my child: 'Oh, your Mamma was very nice; she was fond of writing; one day, I can't imagine why, she cut off her long fair hair.' And I also saw my photograph covered with dust. ... After visions of this sort, I sat up in the narrow little bed and I clasped my hands over my stomach so that the child should not feel my useless emotion. I loved my child with a wild passion and, when I was very hungry during the night, I consoled myself by thinking of the wisdom of nature; I knew that the child was nourishing itself on my blood and my heart. I was aware of its presence with a feverish joy, full of excitement and apprehension. The absolute poverty in which we lived filled me with a blind trust in God. I awaited his miracle with the steadfastness of those who are no longer anxious for themselves but who want to create a new world for their children.

Once, when I was going to the carpenter's with Georges, I was seized with a violent attack of nausea. The world swam dizzily round me, and, leaning against the wall of a house, with my handkerchief clutched against my mouth, I told Georges I could not stay sitting up on a chair for an hour; I simply must lie down. He could not come back with me; the lost lesson would have meant our having to go without food. I allowed myself the luxury of a métro ticket and returned home alone. The journey seemed interminable; I kept my handkerchief against my face the whole time. Opposite me a man who was reading his paper gave me a glance from time to time that said very plainly that sick women ought to remain at home.

I ran, stumbling, all the way from the métro station to the block of flats. I was trembling as I passed through the glass door and I barely said thank you to the smiling concierge, all set for a chat, for the letter she handed me and which I put in my worn little handbag. I crossed the courtyard to go up the back way, but the lift was stuck somewhere higher up and I had to climb all the stairs to the eighth floor. When I reached it at last, I fumbled in my handbag for my key; alas, Georges had it in his pocket. The little door looked to me as high and inexorable as Mont Blanc. Seized with an uncontrollable giddiness and nausea, I had to go to the lavatory. There, I sat down on the tiled floor and burst into tears. Later, I went back to my door; my next door neighbour, hitherto invisible, was standing in her doorway.

'Are you ill, madame?'

'Yes, I am ill . . . and I can't get in; I've forgotten the key.'

'Come into my place,' she said.

She took me over to her window and opened it.

'You see, there's a concrete ledge,' she said. 'And, below that, there's a little zinc platform. You could climb along to the window of your room, if it's open. . . .'

Shaking all over, I answered that it might be open.

With the help of the neighbour, I climbed on to a chair and found myself outside on the ledge. She had hold of my hand.

'Don't be frightened and, whatever you do, don't look down!'

I clutched her hand tight but eventually I had to let go of it and, all alone, I did the four steps that separated me from our window, that was luckily half-open.

260

'Yes, I can get in,' I called out and, two seconds later, I was in our room.

Opening the front door, I said thank you to my neighbour out in the passage. And then, I collapsed on the divan without an ounce of strength left in me. The eight storeys, the walk along the ledge, my violent sickness and my utter exhaustion sent me to sleep almost at once. As I drifted into unconsciousness, I heard someone, very far away, muttering the cruel words: 'It is not so easy to live.' But the person was myself.

Chapter Thirty-two

THE LETTER I received that day was from the Hungarian reader. He had read the manuscript of *Wanda* and wanted to talk to me about it. I rang his telephone number and a man's voice, a pleasant, friendly voice, answered me. He invited me to come and see him. Later on, in the afternoon, I realised that he had been a successful author in Budapest and that one of his plays had been acted all over the world. I remembered that my parents had often spoken of him; Mamma had once described him as a young man with black hair who had been married successively to the three greatest actresses in Hungary.

We made an appointment for the following morning and there was no possibility of making myself even a tiny bit pretty. My heavy, clumsy shape was even more apparent in my ridiculous coat; I had no lipstick and I had had to do my hair in a little bun, which I hated, to disguise its length.

The block of flats where he lived was a luxurious one; red carpet on the stairs; a lift; a well-polished bell beside the imposing door of the flat. I rang: a maid opened the door.

'Madame?'

'I want to speak to Monsieur Gindy.'

'You have an appointment?'

'Yes.'

'Wait a moment, if you please.'

She disappeared, and I was extremely impressed. So one could live in exile and not be poor!

The maid reappeared with a more reassuring face and showed me into a large, luxuriously furnished room where a white-haired gentleman, with a face furrowed with wrinkles, rose from his armchair to greet me.

'Mademoiselle,' he said, in Hungarian, and he added, in an almost frightened way: 'But you're appallingly young! . . . Do sit down.'

I took a chair and looked at him with undisguised curiosity.

He was tall and elegant and he wore a silk dressing-gown. The remains of breakfast on a silver tray looked like a sumptuous still-life in the background. Clumsily, I tried to say that I had imagined him younger, when his face was suddenly lit up by a smile. And that gay, unaffected, boyish smile effectively restored his youth.

He took a cigarette and I reached mechanically for my handkerchief; I could not endure the smell of tobacco.

'And *I* was expecting to see a *femme fatale* this morning!' he said. 'The author of *Wanda*, with her numerous lovers! And I see a thin little girl, indecently young.'

He had not noticed that I was pregnant. This brilliant man, accustomed to extraordinary women who queened it on the stage, had never had a child.

'How old are you?'

'Twenty-two. . . . Have you read my novel?'

'But of course I've read it . . . and I think it's very good.'

The room seemed to be revolving round me and I heard his voice:

'Are you ill?'

'No, I'm happy. You know, I was so longing to hear you say that.'

'I've told the publisher he ought to get it translated,' Monsieur Gindy went on.

I interrupted him excitedly:

'I'm going to write another one soon.'

He made a gesture with his big, white, ringless hand to calm me.

'Not so fast: the problem of publishing is a very difficult one . . . . Don't forget there's always a publishing crisis on when a young author turns up. . . . But I have confidence in you,' he added, with a charming smile.

And suddenly, seized with a man's curiosity, he leant towards me and asked me, in an intimate voice that demanded a sincere answer:

'What gave you the idea of writing that story.'

I explained volubly, completely forgetting the smoke of his cigarette:

'Monsieur Gindy, I once saw a woman who was like my heroine, but I've invented innumerable things. . . .'

We talked for half an hour, and, for me, it was like the beginning of a new life. A well-known man, an established writer believed in me! Before I left, he gave me one of his books that had appeared in French, and wrote an inscription in it:

'To a young colleague, with every friendly wish from Gindy.'

By the word 'colleague', he had consecrated me a writer.

During the following weeks I saw him several times and our friendship developed smoothly and naturally. I told him how much I admired his not being poor like all the other Hungarians I knew. He was suddenly taken aback.

'Goodness, don't think this place is my own. I rent one of the rooms in the flat and they bring me my breakfast; they know I never get up before ten. They're charming people, but don't imagine that life's easy for me.'

His uneasy glance came to rest on an extraordinary picture.

The picture showed, from the back, a slender, naked young woman with translucent flesh, her profile turned towards a mysterious landscape. Over her left shoulder, hiding the soft curve of one breast, floated a tiny muslin scarf. The picture was exquisitely evocative; it was the living presence of a woman, of the eternal woman. . . .

'Even if I were starving, I wouldn't sell it,' Monsieur Gindy frequently said. And, when he said it, the childish shoulders of the frail beauty seemed to become the very symbol of love.

He did not often speak of his famous wives. He had lived so

264

close to them, for so many years, that he had not found them as extraordinary as all that.

I told him that I was married and, once, I took Georges to see him. I was still waiting for a definite answer from the publisher.

'I'm going to write my next books in French,' I told Monsieur Gindy. He replied:

'You're still very young; no doubt you'll really manage to do it. . . .'

He never knew that we were wrestling with troubles of the most menacing kind.

One day I saw that his picture had disappeared. That day he was mortally pale and I did not dare ask a superfluous question. When I left, he said:

'Poor little future French writer. . . . And you're expecting a child. . . .'

We held hands longer than usual at parting. But he was looking at the empty space where his picture had hung on the wall.

Good luck arrived in the form of a brief letter posted in Belgium. Our faithful friend had not forgotten us. He wrote, sending us the money for the journey, and saying that his Belgian friends had been touched by our plight, and that we were invited to stay in a château. A job was already in sight for Georges and a layette had been prepared for the child.

It did not take long to pack the cardboard suitcase! I returned the key of our room and I warmly thanked the people who had given it to us. On the day of our departure, I learnt that an ambulance had just removed the concierge to a lunatic asylum.

'Apparently she's mad,' said the people on our floor.

It wrung my heart. I did not know whether the kind concierge's madness lay in loving human beings who rebuff every friendly feeling or whether she had gone mad on account of those very human beings around her. But I shall always remember her face and those words she uttered: 'There's a very pretty room, mademoiselle. . . . It's empty. . . .'

In the train, I said to Georges:

'My child is going to be born in security.'

He stifled a little laugh, as if I had made some schoolboy joke.

'You always say "*my* child". . . .'

I turned scarlet and, the first time I crossed a frontier legally, I crossed it with my teeth clenched.

Chapter Thirty-three

EVER SINCE THE morning I had been lying motionless on that bed. The walls were light blue, and, in the right-hand corner, there was a china statue of the Virgin. On the bedside table lay the book I had been reading last night: it was the last volume of *Les Thibault* that I wanted to reread in French. That morning I had been gripped by a new, deep pain I had never known before. Georges had already gone to his office; it was his second day at work. They told me he would come and see me between one and two. Beside me, on the left, was a little empty white bed. It was the bed of my child who was soon going to be born. When a wave of pain broke over me, I gripped the white-painted iron bars. That little empty bed helped me enormously. From time to time, a silent nun entered and walked up to my bedside. I tried not to see her face; I looked up at the white ceiling; I did not want to be disturbed in my suffering.

I was thirsty and, during the rare moments of respite, I moistened my lips with iced water. Georges's pale face appeared; he wanted to talk to me, but I turned my face towards the little bed and did not answer. I wanted to be alone with my child. This birth was a personal affair between the two of us. We were accomplices in the act of creation. No one and nothing must come near its little bed.

Twilight fell. The doctors' incessant bustling to and fro annoyed me. They were there all the time, asking me pointless questions and being surprised that I did not scream. The extravagant pain kept attacking me, cutting me in two; often it left me without any breath. But, through this crazy suffering, the child would belong to me and me alone. A nun told me that

Georges was outside in the corridor. The number of doctors increased; at certain moments there were five of them round my bed. When they wiped the sweat off my face, I asked for some information. I wanted to know the exact time. Eleven o'clock at night.

Suddenly there was more bustle than ever in my room. Two nurses pushed in a trolley and laid me on it as if on a stretcher. We trundled very fast along the corridor. Everywhere, outside the doors, I saw vases of flowers. It was hot, and deft hands were pushing me towards an unknown destination. The operating theatre was full of blinding light and, in the multiple mirrors of the projectors, I could see myself lying prone. A young doctor bent over me and the very moment I felt the needle in my arm, I fell into unconsciousness.

Suddenly, I heard a voice repeating over and over again: 'Where's my child? . . . Where's my child? . . .'

The face of a nurse, enlarged out of all proportion, was right in front of my eyes. She was not saying anything. Who, then, was asking: 'Where is my child?'

'You're going to see her soon,' she answered at last. So it really was I who was speaking.

I thought that grey light must be the morning.

With a tremendous effort I turned my head and saw Georges sleeping peacefully in an armchair. I called to him. He did not hear.

A nurse came in with a swaddled bundle in her arms. She held the bundle out to me. My child was asleep. Her skin was pink and transparent.

'It's a lovely little girl, madame,' the nurse told me.

I did not hear anything more.

I was obliged to wake up from that lethargic sleep because the doctor was slapping my face. Everybody wanted me to wake up but I had an irresistible desire to abandon myself to sleep once more.

My body was one mass of pain. And I thought of all the pains that were awaiting me.

I told the nurse in a hoarse voice that I would like to feed my child.

'Madame, one never has any milk after a Cæsarean, especially when it was such a serious one.'

She knew nothing about life, that nurse. She thought I was going to be satisfied with a rule or a principle. I wanted to feed my child so I *must* have some milk.

My daughter was beside me in her little bed. She was asleep, and I had not the strength to hold out my hand to her. But I looked at her; my life was anchored in her pink, peaceful face.

Later on I thought about flowers. I must have flowers in my room like the others; I did not want the nurses to say that. . . .

'Georges?'

'Yes?'

He came up close to me.

'Would you bring me some flowers?'

'Yes, I'll bring you some flowers. . . .'

Holding the door ajar, he said:

'What kind of flowers do you want?'

I was too weak to know which month we were in. I tried to think, but I could not.

I repeated obstinately:

'Bring me some flowers. . . .'

I wanted to be alone with my child. In the little room, there were only the two of us now; she and I. Suddenly she began to cry. It was the first time. And it was to me she was crying. My beloved daughter. . . .

Georges came back with the flowers. I stared at him as if he were a stranger. I did not understand what he was doing in this room. That night had separated me from him.

During the days that followed, I was in pain. Pain was my entire occupation. I could neither eat nor drink, and an absent-minded nurse, a novice in discretion, told me that I had nearly died.

But, on the fifth day, I had some milk and the round head of my child at my breast filled me with tranquillity. I looked gravely at her avid little lips. The nurses said it was incredible. I myself found it perfectly natural. I wanted to feed my child; I wanted to make her drink my life. . . .

It was the miraculous fulfilment.

It was happiness.

All the happiness there could be? . . .

Afterword

WHEN I LEFT my parents' house I believed that I had saved myself from a life of inactivity and that the future belonged to me. I wanted finally to earn some money and be independent. Although I didn't believe for one second in so-called love stories, I met up with Georges again in Paris; I think we stayed together so as not to be alone. Both of us were looking for jobs appropriate for 'displaced' people of doubtful origins. This desire to support myself by getting a job had shocked my parents: 'You'd do better to apply for a study grant and enrol at the Sorbonne,' my mother said. 'You never even had patience with your dolls, how will you tolerate unruly children?'

As I explored French people in their natural environment and analysed another social class, I was able to turn the slightest detail, even shocking, to my intellectual advantage. I was confronted at last with the real France, a long way from Giraudoux and Anouilh, in which no one was sophisticated and where bathrooms and kitchens were disgusting. The joy of entering into the linguistic world of slang and picking up numerous phrases gave me great satisfaction. The tedious part of my jobs (for my employer I was an unidentified object, somebody from the central European aristocracy barely capable of washing windows) came when I had to read to children. I tried to invent innocent, fictitious short stories, but soon, overcome by profound boredom, I took mental refuge in my own.

I was saved by the incredible energy I had inherited from my mother. My official relationship with Georges, who was working as a valet, continued. I typed out stories on my old Remington in my maid's room, sustained by a diet of baguettes, sandwiches and apples.

When the landlady of the maid's room discovered I was pregnant she swiftly kicked Georges and me out. Thanks to the help of a friendly concierge, I found us somewhere to stay on the squalid ground floor of a very chic building. To reach our pitiable, miniature room, we had to walk down a corridor that was poorly lit by two flickering light bulbs. I started to suffer from the lack of air. 'What consoles me,' I said to Georges, 'is that there are so many birds here, although I've never seen any trees.'

'They aren't birds,' the owner of the neighbouring room told me the next day, 'they're rats. The rats feel right at home in this mouldy corridor, so they sing with joy.'

Having so many rats about limited my willingness to go out. I also wanted to continue working on a book, which I wrote whilst suffering from morning sickness. I had to finish the text before the child was born. But how could I bring a child into a world full of rats?

The Belgians saved us from our misery. We owe them our lives. I didn't waste any time there in asking the radio station for a job. An attractive director sent me to interview Mr. Spaak, the Foreign Minister, who was curious to meet an eyewitness of Soviet oppression. The same director encouraged me to send *I am fifteen and I do not want to die* to a well-known French daily, the *Parisien Libéré,* which was looking for submissions for the Grand Prix Vérité award. He felt that a document with historic content would have a certain literary quality. Unable to believe what I was doing, I sent *I am fifteen,* which I had quickly re-typed on my Remington, and won the prize. At midday on the 17th December 1954 I was told to present myself at a Paris restaurant. I went from being a complete unknown the day before to finding myself face to face with the most illustrious representatives of the French press. On that day I also met the founder of *Parisien Libéré;* we fell in love instantly. Two months later, driven by his insistent demands and my mad love for him,

I moved into Claude Bellanger's house in Paris. How could I have imagined then (although even if I had known I wouldn't have been interested) that his liberal paper would weigh down so heavily on my career?

Ten years of suffering tempered with large doses of happiness followed. From its first publication in 1955 *I am fifteen* enjoyed popular acclaim the world over. Under pressure from my editor and the public, I was persuaded to write my next book. I thus had to do some intellectual acrobatics and transport myself back to a past that took place before the Prix Vérité. Aided by my memory that plays even the tiniest details back to me like a silent film, I started to write about my life after my first departure from Kufstein.

A conclusion to my life? I had and I have the joy of being loved. The love of my parents remains unforgettable; my husband's passion has always served as a bridge that's carried me over the bad times; the love of our son François prolongs my existence and makes me want to live; I was born to write, and I hope to die on a finished page. I have experienced dramas, catastrophes and periods of no man's land. I have found beaches of happiness here and there along the way. Scarcely tarnished by the years, I dare to say without wishing to boast or incite jealousy, I have always been happy, especially with a pencil in my hand. Writing.